Separatist Violence in South Asia

Since decolonization began in the late 1940s, a series of often lengthy and destructive separatist insurgencies have imposed severe financial, economic and human costs upon the states of South Asia. Whereas previous analyses of these conflicts have typically focused upon the parent state or separatist group as the relevant unit of analysis, this book adopts a broader framework, arguing that separatism cannot be understood in isolation from the concept of state sovereignty.

This book explores the motives, tactics, successes and failures of South Asia's separatist movements by deconstructing sovereignty into its constituent components and offers an explanation for why separatism, but not political violence, has recently declined in the region. Taking a comparative explanatory viewpoint, it offers a comprehensive review of relevant explanatory theories dominant in the scholarly literature on separatism and an examination of their application to the South Asian states of India, Pakistan, Sri Lanka and Bangladesh.

As a thought-provoking discussion of statehood and sovereignty, this book will be of interest to students of political theory, comparative politics, international relations and South Asian politics.

Matthew J. Webb is Associate Professor of Politics and International Relations at the Petroleum Institute, Abu Dhabi, United Arab Emirates. His previous publications include *Kashmir's Right to Secede: A Critical Examination of Contemporary Theories of Secession* (2012) and *The Political Economy of Conflict in South Asia* (2015).

Routledge Studies in South Asian Politics

1 **Nepal and the Geo-Strategic Rivalry between China and India**
   Sanjay Upadhya

2 **Security Community in South Asia**
   Muhammad Shoaib Pervez

3 **Refugees and Borders in South Asia**
   The Great Exodus of 1971
   Antara Datta

4 **India's Human Security**
   Lost Debates, Forgotten People, Intractable Challenges
   Edited by Jason Miklian and Ashild Kolas

5 **Poverty and Governance in South Asia**
   Syeda Parnini

6 **US–Pakistan Relations**
   Pakistan's Strategic Choices in the 1990s
   Nasra Talat Farooq

7 **Public Policy and Governance in Bangladesh**
   Forty Years of Experience
   Nizam Ahmed

8 **Separatist Violence in South Asia**
   A comparative study
   Matthew J. Webb

9 **Pakistan's Democratic Transition**
   Change and Persistence
   Edited by Ishtiaq Ahmad and Adnan Rafiq

Separatist Violence in South Asia
A comparative study

Matthew J. Webb

LONDON AND NEW YORK

First published 2017 by Routledge

2 Park Square, Milton Park, Abingdon, Oxfordshire OX14 4RN
711 Third Avenue, New York, NY 10017

Routledge is an imprint of the Taylor & Francis Group, an informa business

First issued in paperback 2018

Copyright © 2016 Matthew J. Webb

The right of Matthew J. Webb to be identified as author of this work has been asserted by him in accordance with sections 77 and 78 of the Copyright, Designs and Patents Act 1988.

All rights reserved. No part of this book may be reprinted or reproduced or utilised in any form or by any electronic, mechanical, or other means, now known or hereafter invented, including photocopying and recording, or in any information storage or retrieval system, without permission in writing from the publishers.

Notice:
Product or corporate names may be trademarks or registered trademarks, and are used only for identification and explanation without intent to infringe.

British Library Cataloguing in Publication Data
A catalogue record for this book is available from the British Library

Library of Congress Cataloging in Publication Data
A catalog record for this book has been requested

ISBN: 978-1-138-92654-7 (hbk)
ISBN: 978-1-138-58377-1 (pbk)

Typeset in Times New Roman
by Wearset Ltd, Boldon, Tyne and Wear

For Sayuri, Jamie and Mia

Contents

Acknowledgments   ix

1 **Introduction**   1
Introduction 1
Explaining separatism 7
Grievance versus greed 12
Ethno-nationalist explanations 16
Understanding the causes of separatism in a South Asian context 18
Conclusion 20

2 **Genesis of conflict**   24
Introduction 24
The states of South Asia and their pre-modern antecedents 29
Mobilization against the parent state 38
Economic under-development 42
Ethnic dilution and population demographics 47
Education, political consciousness and external interference 51
Repression and human rights abuses 55
Conclusion 61

3 **Conduct of conflict**   63
Introduction 63
Return to the state of nature 65
The use of legislative power to coerce and co-opt 73
External assistance 78
Internal discord and fratricide 83
Conclusion 87

4 Redemption 89
Introduction 89
Clear state victories: Sri Lanka and Punjab 90
Ongoing conflict: Balochistan, India's northeast, Kashmir and
    Bangladesh's CHT region 95
Conclusion 106

5 Conclusion 108
Introduction 108
Sovereignty as a contingent and contested property 109
Is separatism a spent force in South Asia? 116
Conclusion 122

Bibliography 125
Index 139

Acknowledgments

This book was made possible by a research grant from the Petroleum Institute, Abu Dhabi, to whom I would like to express my gratitude. Others who deserve a mention include Wisam Sabeel, who acted as a research assistant in the early stages of the project, and Brian Bielenberg, Hamad Karki and Mark Hayman for their encouragement and support.

1 Introduction

Introduction

This is a book about separatism and, more specifically, the rise of violent separatism in the South Asian states of Pakistan, India, Bangladesh and Sri Lanka. Home to approximately one fifth of the world's population, these states have faced significant challenges in overcoming the legacy of colonial rule to unite diverse populations under a single national banner since gaining independence. Included within these difficulties have been separatist movements that, rejecting state-sponsored projects of nation building, have violently articulated an alternative construction of political community to challenge the state's territorial integrity and ideological foundations. Although only one of these movements – that which resulted in the creation of Bangladesh in 1971 – has been successful, the number and cumulative cost of separatist movements measured in lives lost, infrastructure destroyed, redirected government spending to less productive sectors, and foregone investment has been an enormous burden that these developing states could ill afford.

Understanding the reasons behind the advent of separatism, and the apparent failure of South Asian states to reconcile territorially concentrated sub-national communities to state-sponsored narratives of national identity, is important to the successful reintegration of these communities within the state's institutional fabric. Only by identifying the reasons why these groups failed to 'buy into' the rhetoric of national unity is it possible to construct a consensus around their inclusion. Moreover, understanding how processes of state formation can alienate some communities – prompting them to seek alternative jurisdictions of state sovereignty – is necessary if South Asian states are to avoid similar problems in their contemporary programs of economic growth and reform. The dramatic increase in population and disposable income of South Asia's middle and entrepreneurial classes holds out the promise of a reinvigorated national unity founded upon new economic opportunities that, if not properly managed, could also alienate marginal communities excluded from the benefits of economic development. However, the question of why some groups desire to separate from their parent state is far from a straightforward one. There are some communities whose grievances and marginalization on the state's ideological and economic periphery make them ideal candidates for independent statehood, but who do not rebel. In contrast, other groups that apparently have few good reasons to secede (and even less prospect of being successful) decide to do so. These concerns raise the question of to what degree separatism is attributable to political processes, calculations of rational self-interest and other factors amenable to scientific analysis, or emotive and atavistic factors 'hardwired' into groups. Are there identifiable factors that make mobilization behind a separatist agenda probable or feasible?

In order to address these questions, this book adopts a comparative approach in which the major separatist movements in South Asia since decolonization are contrasted with one another in order to identify trends, dis/similarities and other factors pertinent to the origins and trajectory of conflict. In addition to sharing a common objective, separatist groups in South Asia have frequently been contemporaneous with one another and possessed other common characteristics, including a collective identity defined in opposition to that of the state's nation-building project; sentiments of economic and political grievance that sustain perceptions of difference and neglect; and the contextualization of these claims within the regional rivalries and superpower politics of South Asia. In addition, the factors associated with separatism in the scholarly literature – sentiments of injustice, calculations of self-interest and the development of a separate national identity – have all been true of South Asian separatist groups as their ideology, membership and tactics changed over time. This similarity provides sufficient construct equivalence to allow meaningful comparison between the cases included within the book, while also acknowledging pertinent differences that help to explain the diverse trajectories that each of these conflicts has taken.

This initial chapter introduces the project, defines 'separatism,' explains why a rational explanation for separatism is important, and details the mainstream explanatory theories that dominate the scholarly literature on separatism. The chapter argues that none of these theories is mutually exclusive of any other, and that separatism occurs as a consequence of a range of features that dynamically interact with one another and transform over time as various factions within a movement struggle for dominance and react to changes in the strategic environment. Indeed, it is important to recognize that, just like separatist movements, neither the state nor relevant third parties (such as foreign diasporas) are unitary actors. Consequently, a satisfactory explanatory theory must incorporate the dynamism, ambiguity, contradictions and instability that characterize the different parties to a separatist dispute. This theme is continued in Chapter 2, which examines the origins of separatism in India (Punjab, Kashmir, the northeast), Bangladesh (Chittagong Hill Tract), Sri Lanka (Tamil minority) and Pakistan (Balochistan). Particular emphasis is placed upon processes of state formation and how the liberal values and discourses of the equality of rights, universal human values, the supremacy of law and state sovereignty in South Asia's nascent post-colonial states clashed with social and political reality, in which *de facto* sovereignty was frequently exercised by extra-state actors and local despotisms through networks of patronage and power. The effect of this dissonance on the state's nation-building project is discussed in combination with other factors pertinent to the mobilization of a population behind a separatist agenda (e.g., effective leadership and external support from third parties) and how state policies have contributed to the development of separatism. More importantly, this chapter also examines the notion of state sovereignty and how its conceptualization as an absolute, exclusive and fundamental feature of the political landscape has dis-/incentivized separatism. Many prior studies have adopted a protagonist-centric approach by first selecting either the state or sub-group as the relevant unit of analysis, and then proceeding to isolate pertinent features around which an explanatory narrative is constructed. In contrast, this book adopts a broader perspective by shifting the conceptual focus from the protagonist to the institutional architecture and artifices that structure a group's pursuit of independence from its parent state. Put simply, because separatism does not occur in an institutional vacuum, it is first necessary to say something about what it is that groups aspire to in their pursuit of a separatist agenda, before moving to the secondary questions of why they hold this aspiration and the tactics used in its pursuit. More particularly, the book argues that many of the demands and strategies employed by separatists and the state from which they seek autonomy, although often apparently futile or contradictory, are explicable in terms of sovereignty's constituent claims.

Chapter 3 continues with a discussion of how separatist movements in South Asia have developed over time and the strategies used by these groups and their parent states. Of particular concern is the dynamic interplay between separatists and state as each attempts to gain a strategic advantage through a process of 'controlled disorder.' Common tactics employed by the state to this end include the indiscriminate use of military force, outsourcing of security functions to vigilantes, draconian security legislation, and infliction of economic harm upon inhabitants of the affected region though diminished investment and heightened unemployment. Similarly, separatists frequently target essential infrastructure and engage in high-profile, mass casualty attacks to demonstrate government impotence, cripple the local economy and put pressure on the state to concede to their demands. However, this is a high-risk strategy, as indiscriminate and large-scale violence can alienate essential public support. In this manner, factors pertaining to self-interest (strategic advantage derived from the use of violence and infliction of harm) intersect with grievance (perceptions of injustice engendered in consequence of a rival party's use of violence or infliction of harm) and the politics of identity to undermine the state's legal-rational legitimacy and claims to be the true representative of a region's inhabitants.

In Chapter 4, the focus shifts to the ending of conflict. Of the disputes considered in this book, two (Punjab and Sri Lanka) have concluded with state victory, one (Bangladesh) ended with a victory for the separatists, while the others continue at varying levels of intensity. The chapter addresses the reasons for the failure of separatists to achieve their goals and the factors that have restricted the state from re-establishing normalcy despite its clear military advantage. The chapter also contrasts the construal of state sovereignty as a binary and exclusive feature with the reality of its exercise by a range of un/official local actors within the context of efforts to address local grievances through power-sharing arrangements. Policies such as the linguistic reorganization of Indian states in the 1950s and the subsequent creation of new states have proven a double-edged sword, creating new divisions as they addressed long-standing grievances.

This theme is continued in the fifth, and final, chapter, which addresses the future of separatism in South Asia, given the rising death toll in the region as a consequence of sub-state political conflict but the decline in separatist-related violence. Of particular note here are sovereignty's multi-layered and diffuse characteristics, which, in conjunction with economic and political reforms, have reduced the 'pull' factors that incentivize sub-national groups to pursue a separatist agenda. Consequently, the book argues, there remains a dissonance between the concept of sovereignty as a binary, exclusive and state-centric property, on the one hand, and the reality of its exercise as a multi-layered, constantly emergent property possessed by a range of non-/state actors, on the other. Moreover, many of the 'push' factors associated with violent separatism in South Asia – economic discrimination, human rights abuses and poverty – remain a problem. Indeed, the states of South Asia continue to struggle to maintain a position of neutrality, instead championing ideological values and engaging in discriminatory practices, such as election rigging and distorted economic development, that reward mainstream communities at the expense of those on the nation's periphery. However, the decline of the state as the dominant social and economic actor in many spheres means that anti-government activism and violence generally take the form of civil disobedience, criminality and revolution rather than separatism.

Before proceeding to discuss the factors correlated with separatism, it is first necessary to discuss what separatism is. For the purposes of this book, separatism may be defined as the advocacy of a state of cultural, ethnic, tribal, religious, racial or political separation from the parent state and its majority population. Consequently, separatism may take a variety of forms, consisting in a range of positions along a continuum of independence (Wood 1981; Pavković and Cabestan 2013) from the state's authority, including: (a) claims for special rights, permissions, privileges, benefits or exemptions concerning the group's cultural rites and traditional practices; (b) preferential access to resources controlled by the state; and (c) a measure of political autonomy and self-rule up to (and including) independent statehood. Examples of these concentrically expanding rights include the right of Sikhs to wear traditional daggers (*Kirpan*) in public and to be exempted from motorcycle helmet laws, granting official status to indigenous languages and subsidizing their teaching in public schools such as the formal standing given to Maori in New Zealand, and the semi-autonomous territories of Nunavut and Nunatsiavut in Canada. At the extreme end of this continuum lies independent statehood – the complete political separation of a territory and its inhabitants from the state's sovereignty – which is the outcome of secession (Wood 1981). Thus, while secessionists are by definition also separatists, the inverse is not necessarily true; many separatist groups pursue an agenda that stops short of independent statehood. However, despite this conceptual distinction, a clear division between separatism and secessionism is unsustainable. Many secessionist groups start as separatist, pursuing lesser forms of autonomy than independent statehood, and become secessionist as these demands are rebuffed – often violently – by the parent state. Similarly, many secessionist groups may be prepared to settle for a lesser degree of autonomy than independent statehood, and employ the demand to secede as a bargaining tool to achieve separatist goals. Indeed, most political movements that aim to radically reduce the state's authority over their affairs contain both separatist and secessionist elements that vie for positions of leadership and influence within the group.

The concern of this book is with groups who have for the most part pursued secessionist objectives. Defining secession as an extreme point on a continuum of political independence has the advantage of side-stepping a dispute in the scholarly literature concerning whether secession occurs only where a former sovereign does not consent to the new state's creation (Crawford 2006) or, *pace* Radan (2008), includes cases of decolonization, the dissolution of federations and the partition of states. However, there remains the difficulty that, despite the feasibility of a conceptual distinction between separatism and secessionism, a practical distinction is not plausible, as most secessionist movements contain separatist elements and *vice versa*. Thus, while the main concern of the book is with secession and the descriptive and explanatory features of the groups that pursue it, because a practical distinction between secession and separatism is untenable, it is necessary to clarify the terminology used throughout the book. Accordingly, the term 'secession' shall refer to an act of political division whereby a group and the territory it occupies are removed from the sovereignty of the parent state to that of a neighboring or newly created state. In contrast, 'separatist' is a descriptive term used to denote groups, tactics, policies and other phenomena that have secession as their ostensible aim (but which may also include elements prepared to settle for lesser forms of autonomy from the parent state). Finally, 'separatism' is the advocacy or practice of removing a portion of the state's territory and its inhabitants, substantively or entirely, from the sovereignty of the state.

Separatism is perhaps the most contentious of political acts. To states that resist their demands, separatists are invidious malcontents whose agenda constitutes a frontal assault on the unity and integrity of the state – the most fundamental component of peace and order in the international arena. With few exceptions, separatist demands provoke a determined and often violent response from the parent state; the majority of separatist disputes descend into violence or civil war, and even in the case of secessions that do occur relatively peacefully (e.g., Singapore's departure from Malaysia or the bifurcation of Czechoslovakia), the aftermath of separation is often a legacy of mistrust, bitterness and rivalry. It is, therefore, unsurprising that many theorists have drawn an analogy between separatism and divorce, since both are emotionally charged events that can profoundly affect the self-identity and long-term economic prospects of the disputing parties and those around them.

In contrast, for its proponents, separatism holds out the promise of security, justice, peace and even collective self-actualization through the resolution of what may have become an inter-generational struggle that is a constituent component of a group's identity. Whereas the state may portray separatism as a destabilizing act of self-aggrandizement, minority groups view it as anything from a reluctantly pursued (but instrumentally effective) means to cultural and economic security, to a 'birthright' enshrined in a dialectical process of struggle in which independent statehood (or irredentism) is the putative, inevitable outcome. However, irrespective of its motives and justifications, underlying each instance of separatism is a claim of distinctiveness on the part of the separatist group vis-à-vis the population of the remainder state. Consequently, a significant element of any separatist dispute is a battle over the group's identity, its various constituent components and the degree to which these distinguish the group from the parent state as a political community. This struggle is often replicated within the group itself as various elites and factions attempt to take control of events to determine their outcome and the group's political future, often redefining what it means to be a member of the group in the process. Thus, whereas for some to be a Kashmiri is to ideologically wed oneself to India's founding ideology of secularism, for others it is to commit to lay down one's life for the concept of *Jihad* and the violent pursuit of Kashmir's separation from India to facilitate the creation of a pan-Islamic state in South Asia.

Moreover, separatism has been an established, increasingly common and bloody feature of the international system of states. For the past two centuries, state-breaking has been the primary method of state-making – more than half of the members of the United Nations originated in breakaway states emerging from the wreckage of colonial empires, the collapse of multinational federations or the dissipation of existing states (Armitage 2010). Contrary to popular perception, separatism is not limited to less developed states, but also occurs in economically advanced, Western nations, e.g., the Scots and Welsh in Great Britain, the Basque and Catalans in Spain, the Northern League in Italy, and the Québécois in Canada (Doyle 2010). Separatism is also a source of destructive conflict, with most incidences of secession – successful and unsuccessful – resulting in significant loss of life. For example, the bloodiest conflict between the Napoleonic Wars and World War One in the Western world was the American Civil War, which cost the lives of more than 600,000 individuals (Doyle 2010). Between 1816 and 2001, there were 484 separate wars, of which 296 were civil wars and 109 were fought with the goal of creating a new state rather than taking control of an existing one. Consequently, it can be said that separatist conflicts have accounted for more than a fifth of all wars in the past two centuries and a substantial minority of the civil wars during the same period (Armitage 2010).

Because of their often prolonged and brutal nature, separatist conflicts can also have profound consequences beyond the relevant sub-region and parent state. In addition to permanently altering the sub-region's and the parent state's borders, economy and demographics, separatism may affect the wider region through the disruption of treaties, trade agreements and the regional balance of power. Sri Lanka's prolonged conflict against Tamil separatists led to the redirection of significant resources to defeat the rebels, with pronounced economic, social and political consequences as large numbers of Sri Lankan youth were mobilized to join an expanding military, which came to occupy a position of political prominence, influencing Sri Lanka's relationship with neighboring states and the international community due to increased military spending and allegations of human rights abuses. 'Mobilization' in this sense refers to the process by which individuals collectively organize around a common identity or shared interests in order to achieve mutual goals, and should not be confused with 'radicalization,' which refers to a willingness to use violence in pursuit of these goals. Moreover, once a group's members are mobilized behind the goal of secession, the consequent dispute is not merely a political disagreement over the territorial sovereignty of a geographical area; it is a struggle over what it means to be a member, not only of the group but also of the parent state, with potentially destabilizing effects for the wider region.

In this chapter, I explore some of these themes within the wider context of the causes of separatism and the violence that often accompanies it. The following section outlines the importance of, and some of the difficulties with, the study of separatism's causes. This is followed by a comprehensive survey of the scholarly literature on separatism that further clarifies key terms and highlights the competing claims of different explanations and methodologies in the study of the causes of separatist violence and their various limitations. The remainder of the chapter revisits the concept of causality in the social sciences and how certain factors can be said to 'cause' separatist violence. Specifically, I argue that a separatist conflict may have multiple causes that interact with one another in a dynamic and unstable environment, in which the influence of existing causal factors is constantly changing and new causes emerge to replace waning influences. The implications of this instability for identifying the causes of separatist violence are discussed, as well as the question of how competing explanatory accounts might be satisfactorily assessed and rival claims adjudicated. The chapter concludes by situating this discussion within the context of South Asia and outlining the comparative methodology that is adopted in the remainder of the book.

Explaining separatism

While there is nothing inherent in separatism that requires the use of violence in its pursuit, most states fiercely resist attempts by sub-groups to secede or attain a significant measure of political autonomy. Frequently, this prompts an equally violent and uncompromising response from separatists, for whom the state's tactics only serve as a validation of their demands, sometimes transforming a separatist agenda for greater autonomy into a secessionist movement dedicated to achieving independent statehood. The consequence of this mutually reinforcing obduracy is an escalating war of attrition as each side attempts to demonstrate its ability to 'out wait' the other while placing itself in a superior position to extract concessions in future negotiations. Of the many attempted and successful secessions in recent history, only a small minority have not resulted in significant violence, destruction of property or loss of life, e.g., the Québécois in Canada, the departure of Norway from Sweden in 1905, the expulsion of Singapore from Malaysia in 1965, the separation of the Czech Republic and Slovakia in 1993 (Young 1994) and the departure of Montenegro from the Union of Serbia and Montenegro in 2006.

The violent and destructive nature of separatist conflict raises two important issues pertaining to its analysis. The first of these concerns the importance and potential value of accurately understanding the pre-conditions for, and the driving factors behind, separatist conflict. Because separatist disputes generally entail considerable property destruction and loss of life, understanding their dynamics holds out the promise of reducing the negative outcomes they produce. In order to persuade minorities to abandon or moderate demands for political autonomy and disown violence, or for the state to devolve some degree of political autonomy to a sub-group while regulating its use of force within bounds that respect fundamental human rights, an understanding of what motivates separatism is required. Moreover, if separatist demands could be anticipated through an accurate understanding of the motivations of separatists and the preconditions for widespread violence, then future conflicts might be avoided and existing conflicts shortened or reduced in severity.

In contrast, the second issue concerns the amenability of separatist violence to rational analysis, given the almost certain resistance of states to separatist demands, and the fact that most attempted secessions (even if successful) are preceded by destructive and lengthy conflict. In other words, the value and importance of an explanation for separatist violence are belied by the behaviors of separatists, which frequently defy explanation from the standpoint of rational self-interest. This is because, if a rational action is one that is directed toward the realization of a state of affairs that advances the interests of the agent/s performing it, then separatist violence is often highly irrational. How can we rationally explain the decision of individual combatants to engage in acts of violence in the knowledge that not only are the prospects of success very low, but the chances of being maimed or killed are extraordinarily high? Aside from the fact that the group's economic and security needs might be better satisfied by remaining a constituent region of the parent state, there seems little sense in risking one's life (or many of the things that make it worth living) for an unlikely benefit that one may not live to enjoy. Additionally, the tactics adopted by many separatist groups often seem to defy explanation as an instrumentally effective means of furthering the group's collective interests or stated goal of independence. For example, the destruction of essential infrastructure and persecution of local populations that the group claims to represent are common occurrences in many separatist conflicts, despite the fact that these actions undermine the group's ability to establish an economically viable state and alienate potential supporters and benefactors, thereby diminishing the group's long-term prospects of success.

Given its apparent irrationality, it is tempting to conclude that separatism relates to emotive or atavistic sentiments that are tribal or inherited (rather than reflective or goal-directed) in nature. Accordingly, we might abandon the search for a rational explanation for separatism to explicate the tactical choices of elites and the behavior of individual participants. If, however, we discard the possibility of a rational explanation, then this will make a negotiated settlement premised upon principled dialogue, compromise, shared interests and common understandings much harder to obtain. To attempt to end a dispute through negotiation is to presume that the various parties to it can identify, articulate and prioritize their interests in order to arrive at a workable compromise that furthers each side's welfare at least as much as continuing the conflict would. Accordingly, a negotiated settlement requires a degree of rationality amongst the belligerents, who must agree a common framework in order to critically evaluate and adjudicate rival claims, which neither assumes the im/permissibility of separatism nor leaves any participant worse off than before the settlement. In contrast, if the reasons underlying the decisions and behaviors of separatists are not amenable to rational analysis – but are instead 'hardwired' into the group's members or attributable to emotive, irrational or naturalistic factors – then there can be no practical purpose for a negotiated settlement, since the various parties to it cannot be relied upon to abide by its terms. To emphasize, where a group's desire for secession and willingness to use violence in its pursuit are innate or beyond the purview of a rational cost/benefit calculation, then even a settlement that maximizes the group's interests may be insufficient to secure peace. Therefore, the corollary of failing to affirm the premise of rationality is to endorse the proposition that the only viable way of ending separatist conflict is for one side to achieve a military victory that renders all other parties unable to continue hostilities; i.e., an enduring peace is only possible once a clear victor has emerged.

Subsequent to affirming the premise of rationality, we may construct an explanatory theory of separatism that identifies necessary or sufficient factors for mobilization behind a separatist agenda to occur. Both the collective and aspirational dimensions of the definition are important; separatism requires a degree of mobilization behind an attempt at political independence from the host state that may, or may not, be successful. The target phenomenon of the theory is, therefore, groups that demonstrate a stability of membership, organization and purpose that prompts public debate and government response. Armchair revolutionaries, radical intellectuals, disaffected youth and other malcontents may have a role to play, but do not make a separatist movement. Consequently, the theory supposes a minimum standard of concerted, collective action, centered on the shared objective of withdrawal from the parent state's territorial sovereignty, that eliminates public speculation, isolated incidences of civil disobedience, fly-by-night associations, and other spurious or tenuously germane phenomena. In addition, a compelling explanatory theory of separatism should include successful and failed attempts at independence. While most separatist movements end in failure, this has not dissuaded groups from 'trying their hand,' with the result that at any point in time since decolonization began after World War Two, the number of active separatist movements has greatly exceeded the number of newly created states. Moreover, not only is public mobilization behind a separatist agenda almost always a prerequisite to seceding (Singapore's expulsion from Malaysia in 1965 being a notable exception), but also many of the more bloody and intractable separatist conflicts have ended in failure for the seceding group. Consequently, an explanatory theory that focused only upon the creation of new states or granting of significant political autonomy (rather than the prior question of why groups adopt a separatist agenda) would not only have comparatively light work to do, but would also miss most incidences of separatist conflict.

Accordingly, I define an explanatory theory of separatism as one that posits empirically verifiable sufficient and necessary conditions for the target phenomena of separatism that allow both: (a) the explanation of separatism across multiple and varied instances, including different geographical, historical, political, socio-economic and cultural contexts; and (b) the prediction of future instances of separatism. Thus, the scope of the theory is broad, as it attempts to identify a comprehensive theoretical framework that is universally valid and explains separatism across less/developed states, un-/democratic regimes, individualist and collectivist cultures, non-/Western societies and so forth. This is in contrast to existing explanations of separatism, the scope and utility of which are limited to individual or related incidences.

By definition, it is clear that a necessary condition for separatism to occur is the presence of a population in a bounded territory that is sufficiently numerous and distinct from the population in the remainder state to be mobilized. While the focal point of this mobilization is an injustice (real or perceived) for which political independence is held to be the putative remedy, the wrongdoing for which remedy is sought varies significantly between groups, as do the means of mobilization. In an attempt to sift amongst the milieu of grievances, injustices and other possible triggers of separatism and gain a more nuanced understanding of its causes, a number of quantitative studies have focused on direct observation of correlations between a variety of factors and civil conflict. One disadvantage of these studies is that they frequently group different types of conflict together, rendering findings specific to separatism problematic. Another difficulty is that the correlations uncovered are frequently contradictory and fail to illustrate causal pathways. A rare area of agreement concerns the importance of geography to the instigation and continuation of separatism and rebellion more generally (Ayres and Saideman 2000; Toft 2003; Saideman *et al.* 2005; Walter 2006; Jenne *et al.* 2007). For example, Fearon and Laitin (2003) found that a country that is half mountainous is twice as likely to encounter civil war (including separatist wars) as a country that is not mountainous at all. Possible explanations for this correlation include the demographic and military effects of mountainous terrain that inhibit population movement, trade and the exchange of ideas to facilitate development of distinct ethno-political identities. In addition, mountainous terrain may also reduce the disadvantage faced by smaller, armed groups against numerically more powerful, but less mobile, government forces, increasing a group's prospects of military success and making rebellion a more rational course of action.

Other factors that have exhibited a significant correlation with separatist conflicts include foreign governments or diasporas willing to supply weapons, money or training; land that supports the production of high-value, low-weight goods, such as coca, opium, diamonds and other contraband, that can be used to finance an insurgency; and weaker state apparatuses with less socially intrusive and elaborate bureaucratic systems (Fearon and Laitin 2003). As in the example of mountainous terrain, these correlations are generally explicable by reference to the positive effect that they exert on the group's likelihood of success and reducing the opportunity costs of conflict; e.g., recruiting young men to the life of an insurgent may be easier when the economic alternatives are worse (Fearon and Laitin 2003). However, because some of a group's strategic assets will be fluid, the willingness of the leaders of a separatist group to engage in violence may ebb and flow with the group's bargaining strength vis-à-vis the central government as the group's resource base, international support and other advantages alter over time (Jenne *et al.* 2007). For example, Tamil separatist violence in Sri Lanka gained momentum only after the rebels gained significant strategic advantages against the government (Rotberg 1999) and then receded when these advantages were rolled back and the government secured external assistance to defeat the separatists.

In contrast, other studies have focused upon a group's relationship with its parent state and the controversial topic of whether giving in to separatist demands (either wholly or partially) prompts similar or more vehement demands from the group to which concessions are made (or other groups). Whereas proponents of negotiated compromise see accommodation as a useful means of delegitimating separatist demands by relieving pressure from peripheral groups on the central government (McGarry and O'Leary 1993; Kaufman 1996; Gurr 2000; Brancati 2009), others claim that it sends a message of government weakness that exacerbates conflict by leading separatists to upgrade their demands and other, would-be separatists to 'try their hand' (Treisman 1997; Hale 2008; Roeder 2009). In support of the former claim, some authors (e.g., Saideman and Lanoue 2005) argue that a negotiated compromise that involves a degree of devolution or decentralization of state power may be an effective means of neutralizing demands for separate statehood while accommodating the values of the separatist movement within established political frameworks. Mitra (1995), for example, cites the linguistic organization of Indian states in the 1950s that effectively neutralized Tamil separatism, replacing the campaign for independent statehood with intra-Tamil disputes over 'who gets what' within the new political arrangement. Similarly, Sorens (2010) found that moving from no autonomy to extensive autonomy reduced the likelihood that a minority would be the victim of official political and economic discrimination – frequent justifications given by separatists in support of their demands – by more than four-fold. In contrast, other studies (e.g., Nordlinger and Huntington 1972; Treisman 1997; Snyder 1999; Walter 2006; Jenne *et al.* 2007) have found that greater levels of regional autonomy encourage separatism by empowering groups to make more credible separatist threats.

There is also a danger that giving in to one group's demands through devolution of power may facilitate splits within it, leading to new demands for autonomy at a sub-level that, if not adequately tended to, may produce another separatist movement (Riker 1964; Weingast 1995; Brancati 2006). Interestingly, this is what happened in the linguistic reorganization of Indian states cited by Mitra, when the creation of a new Telugu-speaking state of Andhra Pradesh carved out of the larger Indian state of Madras in 1953 resulted in new cleavages within the Telugu population (Kukathas 1995) and subsequent demands by speakers of a dialect of Telegu (Telangana) for the creation of a new state out of Andhra Pradesh. Thus, rather than settling the issue of identity politics centered around the variable of language, the creation of a new Telegu-speaking state simply altered political and social dynamics in a manner that encouraged and facilitated the emergence of previously latent sub-identities. Other writers have suggested that any relationship between autonomy and separatism is indeterminate (Horowitz 1985; Saideman *et al.* 2002; Sorens 2005) or significant only where autonomy has been lost (Cuffe and Siroky 2013).

Finally, other quantitative studies have focused upon the internal characteristics of a group necessary for sustaining separatism. For example, a recent study found that internally divided movements were more likely to get concessions from their host states in a 'divide and conquer' strategy: to maximize the effect of commitment problems that arise from internal divisions, to flush out strategic separatists (factions within the group that use the threat to secede as a bargaining tool) and to strengthen factions with more moderate positions in the movement. Moreover, whereas concessions to unitary movements were less likely to fail through violence or renegotiation of new concessions, those to divided movements saw the outbreak of or return to violence and the need to renegotiate new concessions more quickly (Cunningham 2011). States, it is alleged, may also use concessions strategically to reveal information about the preferences and resolve of a separatist movement in a 'divide and conquer' strategy, e.g., resources that accrue to moderate factions through concessions can bolster these while strengthening the state's hand in dealing with more recalcitrant factions that refuse to countenance an outcome less than full political independence (Cunningham 2011). These findings are explained by reference to the strategic interplay between the state and separatists as each attempts to accurately assess the intentions of the other. However, the relationship between concessions and the unity of a group may be bi-directional, or reflective, resulting in endogeneity problems, e.g., concessions might create new factions that emerge to resist accommodation, such as the Woman's Hill Federation that formed in opposition to the 1997 accord between the Chittagong Hill Peoples and the Bangladesh government (Cunningham 2011).

Grievance versus greed

An approach popular in much of the scholarly literature has been to group factors associated with separatism into two, often opposing, categories that emphasize 'grievance' or 'greed' as primary motivations. Grievance theories regard secession as 'justice-seeking' in consequence of an explosive mix of human rights violations, economic problems or cultural differences (e.g., Hechter 1975; Gellner 1983; Horowitz 1985; Hechter 1992; Hooghe 1992; Treisman 1997; Stepanov 2000; Saxton 2005). In contrast, greed theories emphasize 'loot-seeking' (Collier and Hoeffler 1998) behavior and are premised on the claim that individuals join separatist movements depending on the expected utility of their actions, understood as a function of opportunities forgone by engaging in violence and the availability of lootable income (De Soysa 2002). Consequently, it is claimed, groups pursue a separatist agenda when their members calculate that doing so is an instrumentally effective means of maximizing their self-interest. Hence, whereas grievance theories employ a socio-psychological understanding according to which *less* developed groups are more likely to secede in an effort to increase their social status, greed theories emphasize a 'rational actor' approach in which *more* (potentially) developed, higher-income regions are inclined to secede because of their comparatively better ability to provide public goods.

Note, however, that while the two models are often portrayed as being in opposition to one another, they are not mutually exclusive and may be causally linked (Korf 2005). For example, the decision to redress a grievance may be influenced by selfish calculations of rational self-interest; it may be more attractive to individuals to join a separatist group when there is low income and growth, and the opportunity costs of rebellion are lower, than when there are better economic alternatives (Collier and Hoeffler 2002; Collier 2005; Humphreys and Weinstein 2008; Hoeffler 2011). Moreover, perceptions of grievance responsible for initiating a conflict may be exacerbated by the economic gains of conflict entrepreneurs and war profiteers (Korf 2005) to fuel a conflict further. Alternatively, a group's bid for independent statehood motivated by considerations of economic self-interest may precipitate state-sponsored repression so severe that the movement is transformed into one that seeks justice, rather than loot. Others (e.g., Collier *et al.* 2009) see greed and grievance as referring only to the motivation for conflict, which, they argue, is irrelevant to the broader question of feasibility and the hypothesis that where rebellion is feasible it will occur. Moreover, while groups may claim to be fighting for reasons of injustice, often their actions speak otherwise, raising questions about the *real* reasons for the conflict. We need, therefore, to maintain a distinction between a group's ability to sustain a separatist campaign, its reasons for doing so and the justifications given to imbue its actions with moral legitimacy. For example, in the northeastern Indian state of Manipur, 26 'separatist' groups are active in drug trafficking and extortion to finance their campaign of violence (Vadlamannati 2011), raising questions as to whether these groups are criminal enterprises or, as they claim, advocates for the region's aggrieved inhabitants campaigning for their political emancipation.

A number of quantitative studies have sought to test and expand on both theses with varying degrees of success, often producing ambiguous and inconclusive results. Beginning with the grievance model, some studies have identified a strong and significant correlation between low levels of per capita income and the onset of civil war (Fearon and Laitin 2003). For example, a study of India's northeast found that for every one unit increase in relative poverty, there was a 52 percent increase in the probability of armed conflict within the next year (Vadlamannati 2011). Injustice may also reinforce other causal drivers of conflict (e.g., inequality and claims of injustice may be part of a broader causal mix in which regional inequality in more ethnically distinct settings spurs demands for greater sovereignty). Similarly, Regan and Norton (2005) find that grievance-based issues are at the core of the process that leads to civil conflict, but that greed becomes salient when the rebel leadership confronts the difficult task of motivating followers as defections rise. In contrast, other studies (e.g., Ayres and Saideman 2000; Fearon and Laitin 2003; Jenne *et al.* 2007) have found that political discrimination is *negatively* correlated with separatism and civil war. Note, however, that this does not disprove the grievance thesis, as discrimination may merely rob minorities of the strategic resources necessary to mount a separatist campaign, but not the desire to do so. Even groups that suffer high levels of discrimination must first solve their collective action problems in order to mount an effective challenge to the state's territorial integrity (Sorens 2010), and while the poorest might have the most to gain from rebelling, they frequently lack the necessary means to do so (MacCulloch and Pezzini 2007).

These findings suggest that, while economic inequality that frustrates the upward mobility of minorities may be a root cause of separatism, a range of additional factors exist that mediate its effect. For example, not all kinds of discrimination may be equally effective in prompting rebellion and separatism; some authors have noted that vertical inequality (between individuals) may be less significant than structural horizontal inequality (between groups) (Stewart 2005; Ostby 2008). There may also be a self-fulfilling element to bids for political independence by a minority to secure its long-term interests or protect its members from discrimination, as the majority may be least able to commit to protecting a minority when the state's political institutions are in flux (Jenne *et al.* 2007). For example, the political insecurity produced by a threat to secede may undermine the government's ability to secure the political support and consensus necessary to achieving reforms that would convince the minority to abandon their desire for independent statehood (Jenne *et al.* 2007). Others have suggested that, if correct, the grievance model presumes a degree of popular irrationality; the suffering produced by separatist conflict will usually accrue disproportionately to the members of those groups in whose name redemption is sought, with the result that rebellion is far more likely to deliver devastation than justice (Alter 1989).

Most importantly, it is evident that economic grievance cannot explain all instances of separatism; e.g., Scotland, Quebec, Catalonia and Punjab are not the poorest regions of their respective states (Emizet and Hesli 1995; Hagendoorn *et al.* 2008). Accordingly, in contrast to the grievance thesis, the greed thesis argues that the threat to secede is a strategic tool for local elites to preserve wealth and power; e.g., in the Russian Federation, high economic productivity and strong exporting power have been the best predictors of separatist activism amongst leaders of ethnic republics (Treisman 1997; Hale 2000; Hagendoorn et al. 2008). This is intuitively plausible, given that the richest sub-regions have the most to lose should they be exploited by other groups that control the state (Rogowski 1985). Supporting this conclusion are a range of quantitative studies that have identified links between declarations of sovereignty by sub-regions and high levels of wealth, extractable natural resources, donations from diasporas, regional autonomy, pools of young men as potential recruits and low degrees of assimilation (Huntington 1993; Collier and Hoeffler 2000; Hale 2000; De Soysa 2002; Collier and Hoeffler 2005; Lujala et al. 2005).

The greed model has also been employed to explain the micro-foundations of separatism, i.e., why certain factors motivate individuals to join or otherwise support a separatist movement. Many of these explanations borrow heavily from economic analyses of human behavior, including agency, game and rational choice theories, in which rebellion and secession are understood as public goods (i.e., consumption is non-rival and non-excludable) because the entire population of a region will be part of the new political order created by secession irrespective of whether they supported it or not (Hoeffler 2011). Proponents of the rational agent model of group conflict explain individual participation in separatist movements by arguing that individual and group self-interest may be coextensive; e.g., individuals may reason that cooperating with a separatist group is rational if doing so opens up positions of influence to them or otherwise assists them to achieve their aims (e.g., Hardin 1995). In contrast, other theorists have rejected these claims, pointing to the problem of free-riding that bedevils many public goods and has historically crippled peasant and working-class mobilization (Lichbach 1990).

One difficulty with using greed to explain separatism concerns why rational individuals would assume the considerable risks of joining a separatist group before it is reasonably clear that the group is likely to achieve its aims. According to rational agent theory, an individual's willingness to join a separatist movement will depend upon the benefits and costs of participation – i.e., the chances of the group being successful and the availability of lootable resources – which are, in turn, a function of the number of individuals who join the movement (Hoeffler 2011). The result is a complex interplay between a group's ability to attract and retain members and its prospects of success; i.e., because the group's long-term success in achieving its aims will usually require that it attract more members, it must either ensure a proportionality between the size of its membership and economic rewards, or appeal to considerations of the public good to maximize recruitment (Hoeffler 2011). Individual self-interest might be an effective recruiting tool for separatists – in a recent survey, 40 percent of respondents said that they had joined a rebel group because they had been unemployed, compared with 13 percent who said they had done so because they believed in the group's cause (The World Bank 2011). However, its utility may be limited to the early stages of a rebellion, when the group is small and the spoils are shared amongst fewer participants. Moreover, if the composition of a group shifts too much in favor of those motivated by private gain, then ideological aims may give way to loot-seeking (Weinstein 2005), which alienates popular support and reduces the group's chances of success, with a concomitant negative effect on the group's ability to attract and retain members. On the other hand, Mason (1996) postulates that as a separatist movement becomes more successful, and its territorial sovereignty offers a safe haven from state punishment, the need to pay selective benefits to group members to prevent their defection diminishes; now that they are shielded from state repression, participants in the movement may be mobilized more by ideology than by individual self-interest.

As in the case of grievance-based explanations, there is limited and often inconclusive statistical evidence to support the claim that groups attempt to secede as a consequence of rational self-interest. For example, Jenne *et al.* (2007) found that residing in a wealthy country makes a group *less* likely to advance extreme claims or engage in violence. They explain this finding by proposing the inverse of the greed thesis; i.e., minorities that reside in relatively wealthy countries have more to lose from radicalizing against the state. In addition, while separatist leaders may attempt to gather potential supporters with promises of post-secession access to greater resources, the parent state may outbid the group due to its greater odds of prevailing in an armed struggle; e.g., the Biafran separatists' offer to external actors of access to Biafran oil in return for assistance in their struggle was ineffective because the Nigerian government was able to make the same offer (Saideman *et al.* 2005). In addition, significant resources or natural endowments may influence the tactics of a separatist group in a manner that makes the group *less* likely to successfully realize its ambitions. For example, Weinstein (2007) argues that groups that are better resourced may be less rigorous in recruitment, training and discipline compared with resource-poor groups that must rely on 'true believers' and more coherent organizational structures. This lack of discipline may increase group members' propensity toward criminality and human rights abuses, alienating critical support amongst locals and the international community, with a concomitantly negative effect upon the group's prospects of success.

Ethno-nationalist explanations

Cutting across the 'greed versus grievance' debate is an emphasis upon ethno-nationalism as an explanatory factor in a group's desire to secede. Numerous authors (e.g., Khan 1970; Nielsen 1998) emphasize a distinctive ethno-nationalist identity as a necessary feature of separatist groups and their efforts to mobilize members around a common cause. In addition to capturing a common descriptive feature of these groups, ethno-nationalist explanations also have the added advantage of avoiding the grievance versus greed conundrum; a group with a distinctive identity may secede as a remedial (or preventative) measure in response to state-perpetrated injustices, in an attempt to secure a greater share of resources for its members, or for a combination of these reasons. Finally, the predominance of ethno-nationalism as a defining feature of separatist movements may be explained by an ability to overcome the collective action problems that plague rebel movements (Murshed 2002). For example, Vadlamannati (2011) observes that if the grievance theory is correct – and deprivation and institutional decay are the main drivers of rebellion (Arambam 2001; Rajagopalan 2008) – then it is clear that not all regions with these conditions experience violent conflict. The key additional variables, he claims, are ethnicity and group identity, which overcome collective action problems by mobilizing individuals behind a shared cause.

Despite these apparent strengths, an emphasis upon ethno-nationalist identity as a cause of separatism is not without its difficulties. First, there is the problem that, because identity is not logically prior to the demand to secede, any causality may be bi-directional. Instead of a distinct ethno-nationalist identity preceding and causing separatism, it may be the other way around; i.e., a successfully articulated separatist agenda engenders a collective self-awareness and identity, which then incorporates ethno-nationalist elements as a convenient tool to bind the group members together. A second problem concerns the role of political processes in the development of a shared identity and the degree to which these may be manipulated by elites for their own, selfish purposes (Racine 2013). Culture, ethnicity and group identity may be salient to understanding the causes of separatism only to the degree that they are capable of being activated as a source of group mobilization by elites or so-called 'ethnic entrepreneurs' (Gurr and Harff 1994). Third, there is the difficulty in moving from a descriptive to an explanatory account of separatism. While a distinctive ethno-nationalist identity may be a defining feature of most separatist movements, it does not follow that this identity is the reason why these groups attempt to secede (Racine 2013). Indeed, for every ethno-nationalist minority that attempts to secede, there are many others that do not, indicating that, at the very least, there are factors additional to ethno-nationalist identity that influence the dynamics of separatism. Fourth, there is the problem of endogeneity; i.e., instead of ethno-nationalist enmity causing separatism, maybe it is the other way around and inter-group hatred is a by-product of the attempt to secede (Fearon and Laitin 2000).

Finally, as in the 'grievance versus greed' debate, the empirical evidence regarding the centrality of ethno-nationalist factors in the explanation of separatism – and the attendant claim that plural societies are more conflict-prone due to antagonisms between their constituent communities – is often inconclusive and contradictory. Fearon and Laitin, for example, find no correlation between ethnic/religious diversity and civil war, concluding that "[t]he estimates for the effect of ethnic and religious-fractionalization are substantively and statistically insignificant" (Fearon and Laitin 2003). This finding is echoed by Hagendoorn et al. (2008) and Hale (2000), who point out that in almost every case where a state has imploded along ethnic lines, there are examples of ethnically distinct regions that sought to preserve the union; e.g., whereas Lithuania sought to leave the USSR, neighboring Belarus supported continued integration, and while Slovenia and Croatia exited the Yugoslav Federation, Montenegro remained with the Serbs (Hale 2000; Azam 2001). In contrast, other studies (e.g., Hegre and Sambanis

2006; Walter 2006; Wimmer *et al.* 2009) have found a mixed or weak relationship between ethnic diversity and conflict that is mediated by a range of intermediary variables. For example, Walter (2006) found that the propensity of an ethnic group to challenge its parent state for greater territorial autonomy was positively correlated with the group's grievances against the state, in conjunction with many other features such as the loss of previous autonomy, the group's degree of territorial concentration and government instability. The presence of these intermediary variables and the ability of the group's leadership to use them to mobilize public support behind a separatist cause may explain why for every disadvantaged ethnic group that has attempted to secede there are other, similarly disadvantaged ethnic groups that did not, such as Brazil's Amazonian Indians, Botswana's San Bushmen and the Baluchis in Iran (Walter 2006).

Understanding the causes of separatism in a South Asian context

Most readers will be struck by the complex and contradictory nature of the preceding discussion. Each intuitively plausible explanatory account has an equally credible alternative that can call upon a range of empirical evidence to support its hypotheses and contradict those of rival explanations. For every ethnically distinct, aggrieved or economically well-off group that attempts to secede, there is a counter-example of one that does not. Before outlining the implications of this finding, it is worth pausing for a moment to consider the dimensions of complexity that characterize separatism. In the remainder of this chapter, I shall argue that the cumulative effects of these complications render untenable a universal explanation of separatism capable of empirically verifiable explanation and prediction from one set of circumstances to another across different geographical, historical, political, socio-economic and cultural contexts. This, however, does not mean that we must resort to case-by-case reasoning, or that meaningful conclusions cannot be drawn about the origins of separatism that are true from one set of circumstances to another. Comparisons between similar instances of separatism with a view toward uncovering shared features, dissimilarities and junctures may shed light upon factors that make separatism more probable in spite of the variety and complexity that characterize it.

One dimension highlighted by the contradictory findings of many of the statistical studies cited earlier is that mobilization behind a separatist agenda can have multiple antecedents. This is evident in the non-mutually exclusive character of the various causes of separatism. At a micro level, members of a separatist group may have numerous and different motivations for supporting independence from the parent state. At a collective level, this means that whether or not a minority group's political consciousness congeals around a separatist agenda will depend upon a range of factors, including: the values, beliefs and decisions of the group and the state's leadership; the economic and human resources available to mobilize the group's members and sustain a lengthy and perhaps violent campaign of resistance; the likelihood of international intervention and availability of foreign support in the form of diasporas living abroad; the geography and local economy of the region inhabited by the group and its suitability for sustaining an insurgency; and a host of other factors. The absence or inadequacy of just one of these additional variables may render the pursuit of a separatist agenda unfeasible in some groups, but not others.

Moreover, not only is there is no requirement that all the members of a separatist group are there for the same reason(s), but these reasons may change over time as the dynamics of the conflict alter and members reassess the group's likelihood of success and the extent of their commitment. For example, what begins as a peaceful protest for increased autonomy may later develop into a more violent and costly struggle motivated less by nationalistic factors or calculations of rational self-interest, and more by sentiments of revenge, as violence engenders its own logic of participation. This observation has three important implications for the explanation of separatism. First, it is necessary to factor in a temporal element that maps how the factors driving a struggle change over time. The influences that were responsible for the original outbreak of separatist fervor may not be the same as those later driving members of the group. As the original activists are killed, captured or leave the movement, they are often replaced by new, younger members and leaders with different tactics and motivations for continuing the conflict. Other developments that may precipitate a change in the drivers of a separatist movement include the depletion of resources required to sustain hostilities; the introduction of new technologies that alter the military balance of power or address the economic disadvantage or sentiment of injustice amongst a group's members that previously fueled their desire to secede; the criminalization or radicalization of a movement; and changes in the broader strategic environment, such as new alliances or foreign intervention. The result is frequently an inverse relationship between the length of a conflict and its amenability to resolution. As time passes and a conflict's dynamics change, its complexity and intractability increase, as solutions that might earlier have proven effective fail to address emerging grievances.

Second, it is necessary to distinguish between separatism and violent conflict. Not all separatist movements are violent. Many begin as peaceful campaigns for lesser forms of autonomy than independent statehood, and only later adopt a separatist agenda and violent tactics. Nonetheless, the introduction of violence to a dispute invariably alters its dynamics by creating its own motivations, with the result that the factors that sustain a contemporary conflict frequently differ from those that first engendered it (Widmalm 2002; Korf 2005). For example, the separatist-inspired uprising in Indian-administered Kashmir began as an indigenous, urban, middle-class and largely secular movement in 1989, but by the mid-1990s had been transformed into a foreign-sponsored, more rural and Islamist campaign. The common explanations given for the outbreak of the 1989 rebellion against Indian authority – election rigging, central government interference, institutional decay and Pakistani interference (Swami, 2007, 2008) – may still be pertinent to understanding Kashmiris' lingering discontent with Indian rule. However, ending the conflict will now also require assuaging a popular sense of injustice that is the result of more than 20 years of armed struggle and the memories of friends and family members who have been tortured, murdered, raped or simply disappeared in consequence of the nefarious actions of both the state and separatist elements.

Third, and finally, it is important to recognize that these multiple, changing factors do not exist in isolation from one another, but interact in a vibrant and evolving process. A change in one variable may produce changes in others, which then exert an influence upon the original and other variables in a constantly developing process. This feature has important implications for understanding the drivers of separatism, as causal levers may be multiple, bi-directional and simultaneous, making it exceptionally difficult to isolate contributing influences and separate their effects from one another. For example, many separatist movements in South Asia have been associated with a dominant individual (e.g., the Liberation Tigers of Tamil Eelam's (LTTE) Velupillai Prabhakaran or the Sikh separatist leader Jarnail Singh Bhindrinwale). In both cases, the killing of these leaders was associated with the decline of their respective movements and a return to normalcy. In other instances, however (e.g., Kashmir, Balochistan and India's northeast), there has been no dominant figure, and leadership of the movement has been dissipated amongst various factions that are sometimes allied with, and at other times violently oppose, each other. Whether or not a dominant individual emerges, the consequences that this has for the trajectory of the conflict and the effects of the leader's removal will depend upon a range of intermediary social, economic and political factors that differ between conflicts. This is because the causal factors driving separatism are multiple, variable and inter-connected, consisting of a complex web of relationships and inter-dependencies, with numerous possibilities each leading to different outcomes. This intricacy renders both the prediction of a single event's consequences and the identification of universal causal laws highly problematic. Depending upon which features characterize a group and how these inter-react with one another and change over time, separatist movements may be violent or peaceful, protracted or short-lived, successful or unsuccessful.

Conclusion

The most plausible interpretation of these findings is one of 'multiple conjunctural causation,' in which factors combine to be jointly sufficient to cause secessionism in some groups but insufficient in others. This explains why some groups that appear to be prime candidates for independent statehood do not pursue a separatist agenda, while in other groups apparently dormant separatist tendencies are suddenly reasserted. It would also clarify why separatist movements that share many similarities nonetheless follow very different trajectories. It is a view that is gaining considerable traction amongst scholars who, abandoning the search for a 'master narrative' centered around greed, grievance or other factors, have come to reject an overly deductive approach that, for the sake of explanatory simplicity or conceptual coherence, sacrifices descriptive accuracy.

For example, citing Spencer's (1990) observation that villagers in Sri Lanka's civil war used the dynamics of the broader struggle to act out local issues – with the result that people did not become enemies because they were in different parties but ended up in different parties because they were enemies – Kalyvas (2003) cautions against epistemic preference for the universal over the particular, and the easily classified over contradictory evidence. Rather, he claims, "[c]ivil wars are not binary conflicts, but complex and ambiguous processes that foster the 'joint' action of local and supra-local actors, civilians, and armies, whose alliance results in violence that aggregates yet still reflects their diverse goals" (Kalyvas 2003).

Kalyvas's observations highlight the point made earlier that none of the common explanations for separatism are mutually exclusive at a micro (individual) or collective (group) level; the decision to support a separatist movement or engage in violence in support of its aims may be motivated by personal gain, a desire to settle old scores, local factors (which are distinct from the causes of the war or the stated goals of the belligerents), or a combination of these and other factors. The corollary of this finding is the abandonment of the search for a universally valid framework capable of explaining and predicting separatism across the myriad of contexts in which it appears. Rather, the objective now becomes one of developing increasingly refined notions of probabilistic causation, whereby separatism need not follow from necessary or conjuncturally sufficient factors, but the probability of its doing so increases as the presence and interaction of these develop. Analogously, just as we know the conditions for obtaining a royal flush in a poker game and the factors that make it more likely, we can never be sure whether or not a player will obtain such a hand (Pavković and Radan 2007).

According to this understanding, a comparative approach that systematically analyzes a small number of cases of separatism might yield useful conclusions regarding the origins and trajectory of separatist movements by highlighting suggestive similarities and differences. However, the cases selected for comparison and the analytical framework adopted to analyze them must meet certain requirements if the study is to yield valid or meaningful results. To explain, one persistent problem with comparative research is case selection. On the one hand, it is necessary to avoid bias, whereby the selection of cases is 'theory-confirming,' 'theory-denying' or favors specific findings. On the other hand, however, cases must also be sufficiently similar to ensure construct equivalence (i.e., the concepts being measured hold the same meaning and value in the different groups being researched). This is particularly pertinent to cross-cultural/national studies, where the comparison of insufficiently similar cases will fail to produce meaningful results. Similarly, if the number of cases is too large, then the findings may be superficial, whereas too few cases may be inadequate to yield substantive conclusions about the variables being studied. Because of separatism's multifaceted, dynamic and fluid nature, the selection of variables is also important. A myopic focus upon too few variables will fail to capture the multiplicity of factors that separate (often deceptively similar) separatist movements and the dynamic relationships that exist between them. In contrast, the inclusion of too many variables may obscure distinct effects and causal connections. Finally, it is also important to incorporate a temporal element to accommodate changes to a movement's membership, tactics and objectives that may significantly influence the trajectory of a conflict and its amenability to resolution (Stephens 2008).

Where these requirements are met, a comparative approach may permit insight into the various causal pathways upon which separatism proceeds through the identification of similarities, trends, outliers and other pertinent factors. Similarly, by affording a relative context in which important features may be viewed from a broader perspective, the comparison of a series of cases permits greater understanding of the interface between causal factors and the junctures at which these exercise more or less influence over events. Most separatist movements follow distinctive phases, from popular mobilization behind a separatist agenda, to the response of the parent state and third parties (such as neighboring states and diaspora), to a period of radicalization, consolidation, stalemate or decline. By expanding the analytical horizon from one instance of conflict to a limited range of similar conflicts, a comparative approach allows a richer understanding of the factors that influence separatist movements in a manner not possible through single case studies, while also avoiding the tendency to overlook pertinent socio-political, cultural and economic differences that characterizes large-scale analyses and generalizable explanations.

This book achieves the desideratum of a sufficient number of similar case studies for meaningful comparison by focusing exclusively on large-scale, violent separatist movements in South Asia in the post-colonial states of Pakistan, India, Sri Lanka and Bangladesh. The number of cases included is limited by type, scale and region. Movements such as India's Naxalites and Nepal's Maoists, while sharing many of the same tactics as separatist groups, are excluded because their political goals are revolutionary rather than separatist. Similarly, small-scale, largely non-violent movements and those that have agitated for lesser degrees of autonomy than independent statehood are not included (e.g., Nepal's Madhesi and Bhutan's Assamese populations). Thus, the focus of the book is on groups characterized by large-scale mobilization against the parent state, which has similarly responded at a significant level using the legal, political, economic and/or military means available to it. The problem of construct equivalence is addressed through the similarities exhibited by the groups and states included within the study. Each of these four states is a former colonial possession of Great Britain that has had to contend with a legacy of colonial (mis-)governance, economic under-development, considerable cultural heterogeneity and superpower rivalry in its nation-building project. Partly because of these similarities, all four states also share a history of significant military involvement in politics, which has been frequently justified by the need to maintain the state's integrity in the face of separatist and regional challenges.

In order to capture the multidimensional, dynamic and variable characteristics of separatism, subsequent chapters are not arranged by parent state or separatist movement but, instead, temporally into three distinct stages of mobilization, conduct and conclusion. Within each chapter, the themes of self-interest, grievance and identity introduced earlier are – in conjunction with additional factors including leadership, third party assistance, tactics and other features – analyzed at each stage of a group's history. This enables comparisons to be drawn, not merely between different factors, groups and states, but also temporally across each movement's stage of development, from inception to victory, stalemate or defeat. The result is a more nuanced – and, therefore, descriptively accurate – account that permits precise conclusions to be drawn about the specifics of separatism in a South Asian context.

Accordingly, the subsequent chapter begins by outlining the antecedents of separatist mobilization in each target group. Particular attention is paid to prior institutions of governance and how these provided both a constituent element of the group's identity and a source of organization around which separatists could mobilize public sentiment. Other factors also highlighted include outside assistance, political leadership, the reaction of the parent state, perceptions of discriminatory treatment, demographic imbalances and the interaction of these factors. This discussion is continued in the subsequent chapter, which deals with the intermediary phases of each conflict as the separatist movement and the parent state adjust their tactics to achieve strategic dominance. Not only do the tactics of the state influence those of a separatist movement and *vice versa*, but changes to a movement's membership, resource base, popularity and other factors exert their own influence on the trajectory of conflict as they inter-react and prompt responses from the state and third party actors. Consequently, the factors responsible for the initial demand to secede may be significantly different from those that sustain a conflict, as violence creates its own motivations and the different parties to a conflict reconfigure their strategies.

2 Genesis of conflict

Introduction

The purpose of this chapter is to examine the dynamics that influence mobilization behind the cause of separatism through the conceptual lens of state sovereignty. In the remainder of this section, the concept of state sovereignty and its constituent claims of embodiment and necessity are clarified. Subsequent sections examine how the institution of state sovereignty has contributed to separatism in the post-colonial states of South Asia. This is achieved through an analysis of the factors associated with separatism in these regions from the perspective of sovereignty's constituent components of embodiment and necessity. In particular, the role of predecessor institutions of sovereignty that pre-date contemporary South Asian states' predatory and discriminatory government policies, economic and social under-development (including demographic concerns regarding a failure by the state to control population movement), and human rights abuses are highlighted as key triggers. In each conflict, these factors manifest in markedly different ways. Nonetheless, the common thread linking them is the rejection of the state's claim to represent the identities and essential interests of all of its citizens equally, thereby rendering the state sub-optimal in comparison with an imagined post-secession state of affairs.

The previous chapter highlighted how most explanatory accounts of separatism have selected either the minority or the parent state as the relevant unit of analysis. In contrast, comparatively scant attention has been paid to the nature of state sovereignty and historical processes of state formation pertaining to the parent state and the successful integration of predecessor institutions of governance. This is remarkable, given that if state sovereignty did not exist, then neither would separatism (at least in the form in which we recognize it). More importantly, it overlooks how sovereignty's conceptualization as a unitary, exclusive property possessed wholly by states maximizes citizens' compliance (upon which the state's legitimacy rests), but sits uncomfortably with the reality of sovereignty's exercise.

To explain, while coercive associations have existed since the beginning of recorded history, the state is distinguished by the ubiquity, breadth and legal-rational justification of its authority. With the exception of lawless or failed states, almost all of the world's population finds itself governed by the institution of the modern state, which exercises a degree of regulatory control historically unprecedented in scope and complexity. The legitimation of this enormous concentration of power rests in a secular discourse of human rights, self-determination and popular sovereignty (Griffiths 2003) embodied in the institution of citizenship that bestows an equality of status upon individuals. In this manner, state sovereignty gives formal expression to citizens' shared values, understandings and aspirations as the optimal means by which individual welfare and the *social product* – i.e., the property, goods, services and values in a community (Sangmpam 2007) – are safeguarded by virtue of the state's ability to enforce binding, non-partisan rules of conduct. Thus, individuals obey, their compliance generating the order and public goods that reaffirm the state as society's sole legitimate representative and guardian, ensuring further compliance in a mutual feedback loop that validates the social contract and legitimacy of the legal-rational state.

However, while the institutions of statehood and state sovereignty may share a common philosophical heritage in the European Renaissance and Enlightenment, the history of their formation varies markedly. The conventional view of sovereignty is of an ontological binary, absolute, indivisible property vested in distinct territorial political communities. In reality, however, sovereignty has numerous, overlapping loci and a long history of being shared, contracted out or surrendered by states to alternative forms of social organization at both local (e.g., chiefs, vigilantes, political associations) and international (e.g., supranational bodies such as the European Parliament, Council of Europe and European Court of Justice) levels (Griffiths 2003). Consequently, the state's authority is frequently dependent upon vestiges of sovereignty that inhere in non-state actors, including predecessor institutions to the state that continue to command citizens' loyalty.

The importance of recognizing sovereignty's incomplete, constantly emergent, non-exclusive character to understanding the causes of separatism is evident when we consider that mobilizing a sub-group behind a separatist agenda requires more than mere dissatisfaction with the status quo. In addition, there must be a deep-seated belief that the alternative jurisdiction of sovereignty proffered by independence from the parent state would better safeguard the group members' identity and common interests. Whereas nationalist theories focus upon the former consideration, greed and grievance theories emphasize the latter. The previous chapter highlighted how, rather than being mutually exclusive, greed, grievance and nationalism are complementary features that may be causally linked to one another in the mobilization of a population behind a separatist agenda. The present chapter develops this insight through an analysis of rational self-interest, remedial justice and national identity from the perspective of state sovereignty. In addition to offering a conceptual framework capable of encompassing these explanatory features, an emphasis on sovereignty is also essential to distinguish separatism from other forms of anti-government mobilization, such as revolution and civil disobedience, that may be rooted in causes similar to those identified by greed, grievance and nationalist theories, but which do not include a claim to territorial sovereignty. Accordingly, because separatism is distinguished and defined by a sub-group's claim to an alternative jurisdiction of territorial sovereignty (and, therefore, state sovereignty is a necessary condition for separatism), it offers an ideal perspective from which to analyze the development and trajectory of separatist movements. Moreover, a focus on the separatist group as the relevant unit of analysis limits possible solutions, given that the demographics, histories and collective identities of groups are notoriously resistant to change orchestrated by external forces. In contrast, because sovereignty is a constantly emergent, dynamic and fluid construct, it is a causal lever more amenable to intercession and capable of generating possible solutions to conflict.

In particular, I shall argue that sovereignty can be understood as comprising two complementary components of *embodiment* (manifestation of citizens' shared values, understandings and aspirations) and *necessity* (as the optimal means of securing a community's welfare through the creation of an environment in which domestic peace and prosperity are enhanced). Accordingly, the moral legitimacy of the state resides in its ability to transcend the inadequacy of individual effort by addressing the problem of human aggression (Agnew 2005) to provide for the common good. Through the promulgation and enforcement of binding rules of conduct, the state reduces transgressions of individual rights and mitigates free-rider problems that plague the provision of public goods, thereby producing a state of affairs that (while not ideal from many individuals' standpoints) is vastly superior to that which would obtain were each individual to act unilaterally. Moreover, because opposing conceptions of the public good and competition for limited social and natural resources engender disagreement, the state must manage this discord in accordance with norms of fairness as it mediates disputes between individuals and society's constituent groups. Thus, the legal-rational legitimacy of state sovereignty rests in its ability not merely to secure an environment superior to counter-factual alternatives, but to do so in a non-partisan manner whereby the costs and benefits of compliance are fairly distributed to create the positive feedback loop of compliance and provision outlined earlier. Citizens obey, their obedience generating the public goods that validate the state's status as the sole arbiter of society's collective interests, affirming its ability to overcome the inadequacy of individual effort, and thereby ensuring the compliance that is a prerequisite to the continued provision of these goods.

While states invariably arrogate to themselves the status of an indivisible political and territorial community, the brute fact is that the concept of state sovereignty does not contain within itself an answer to the question of what the state's relevant territorial jurisdiction is. Consequently, solving the problem of necessity does not resolve the question of embodiment and of how the political community whose interests the state champions is to be constituted. Moreover, efforts by political theorists and states to address this challenge have been particularly unsatisfying. One response has been to invoke a conceptual and ethical 'zero-point' from where the law and political order are constituted in an attempt to reconcile (a) liberal accounts of individual agency, autonomy and self-government that provide the philosophical basis of the legal-rational state and its doctrines of equal citizenship and human rights with (b) the corporate and coercive reality of state sovereignty. The pre-eminent example of this approach is social contract theory, predicated on the fiction of voluntary consent by reference to a pact between the governed and a sovereign to establish a political order by which individuals' natural rights may be more effectively protected. However, reference to individual consent to delineate the community to which the state's sovereignty is to apply (Beran 1987; Gauthier 1994; Wellman 2005) simply begs the question it attempts to answer, since in order to consent to the sovereignty of a state, there must first be a state to consent to (Mayall 2013). In reality, when asked to point to a historical incidence of such a covenant, the best we are able to come up with are referendums on the question of whether or not to secede in Virginia (1861), Texas (1861), Western Australia (1933), Quebec (1995), South Sudan (2011) and Crimea (2014). Indeed, few existing states were created through voluntary contract, and only naturalized citizens expressly consent to the sovereignty of a particular state (the rest of us have these matters determined by morally arbitrary factors such as parentage or place of birth).

Not to be deterred by the shortcomings of political theory, states have attempted to bridge the gap between individual agency and the coercive authority of the state through the structuring of protocols governing statehood, with the result that existing states are the final arbiter of which groups qualify as states. The Treaty of Westphalia (1648) and the Peace of Utrecht (1713) marked the supersession of relations between diverse, feudal conflict-units and the hierarchical claims of Empire and Papacy by formal relations between modern sovereign states (Philpott 2001). Subsequently, international relations were institutionalized in diplomatic protocols, and states became both the architects and the subjects of international law, based on principles of mutual recognition and non-interference. Moreover, the exclusion of rival domestic centers of power through the establishment of bounded territories repressed the independence of the nobility to act as autonomous warlords. Consequently, a clear distinction emerged between the domestic and international spheres, with the result that non-sovereign lords and other corporate actors no longer played any formal or significant role in international relations (Griffiths 2003). Most importantly, states also came to determine both the rules of relations between states and the criteria of statehood, and, therefore, which groups would qualify as states through the principle of mutual recognition (Agnew 2005). This self-regulation might have proven unremarkable had states not afforded existing borders and the position of the state as the pre-eminent international actor the priority that they have. However, due to a fear of setting a precedent that might one day authorize their own dismemberment, existing states have been extraordinarily hesitant to recognize nascent states, even while endorsing propositions that ostensibly require them to do so. Thus, Articles 1 and 55 of the United Nations

(UN) charter affirm the right of all peoples to self-determination, but have been interpreted by states as conferring a right of decolonization tied in time and space to the withdrawal of European colonial administrations and limited by the principle of *uti possidetis juris* (as you possess lawfully), according to which newly formed states retained their pre-independence geographical borders (Mayall 2013).

The outcome of these measures has been to reinforce the importance of statehood while neither reconciling the coercive aspects of state sovereignty with liberal ideals of self-government and autonomy, nor resolving disagreements concerning the justice of existing states' borders. Consequently, the importance of statehood remains undiminished, and it remains a crucial status for groups seeking control over their affairs. Only states can attain representation in the international banking system and the UN, receive International Monetary Fund (IMF) loans, possess inviolable land to attract investment, or be recognized as formal trade partners, members of political/military associations and signatories to economic treaties (Nordstrom 2000). However, while the ubiquity of the state as the dominant international actor speaks to its success, there remains an abiding dissonance between justifications of state sovereignty and the criteria that determine the territorial boundaries of states. Whereas the state's legitimacy is grounded in principles of embodiment and necessity – as the institution best able to represent a community's collective identity and protect its members' individual and collective rights – a group's status as a state is dependent upon recognition by other states (Radan 2010), and this often has nothing to do with the group's ability to represent its citizens' collective identity, provide public goods or maintain order. Consider, for example, the Taliban in Afghanistan, M23 in the Democratic Republic of Congo and the *de facto* government of Somaliland. These groups exercised authority over a geographical area, enforced a code of justice, provided basic services and defended their territory against incursions from rival groups. However, they were all unsuccessful in obtaining the recognition of states, despite the fact that in some cases they exercised greater authority, enjoyed wider public support and were more effective at maintaining order than the internationally recognized government of a state that to all practical purposes continued to exist in name only.

In summary, the thesis advanced here is that separatism does not occur in an institutional vacuum. Rather, the exercise and justification of state sovereignty frame separatist demands by dis-/incentivizing groups to pursue an alternative jurisdiction of sovereignty depending upon the group's characteristics and circumstances. Consequently, even states that are highly effective in maintaining order and regulating competition for the social product may suffer from separatism if a sub-group perceives the state as discriminatory or predatory. This is because separatism is a claim to difference, not merely disadvantage, that challenges the ontological and moral character of the state as equivalent to that of the individual person in classical liberalism, with fixed boundaries and a permanent identity (Jacobson 1998; Skinner 1999). Cognizant of the arbitrary nature of state boundaries and the ever-emergent character of state sovereignty, separatism assumes (and may even manufacture) a dissonant duality of identities that makes a sub-group's political independence from the state the only acceptable outcome.

The states of South Asia and their pre-modern antecedents

A striking feature of most separatist movements is their historical pedigree in the form of political institutions that precede the state and either have not been successfully integrated into the state's institutional fabric or offer a better alternative to it by, for example, continuing to exercise authority at a sub-state level. In societies where the state has failed to abide by the social contract norms of the legal-rational state (typically by acting in a prejudiced or predatory manner), it becomes a sub-optimal solution to the problems of individual security and provision of public goods when viewed through the prism of the counter-factual alternative proffered by predecessor institutions of governance that the state had ostensibly replaced and rendered obsolete. Specifically, if the state has a framework of in/formal but widely agreed rules, conventions, practices and procedures that govern the allocation of resources, distribution of political power and peaceful settlement of grievances, then this may effectively eliminate opportunistic behavior (so-called 'vanity secessions') and the violent expression of grievance. However, in separatist-affected states, this social contract has broken down in consequence of a combination of institutional decay (which sees one group or class benefit at another's expense), inadequate or incompetent economic management, expropriation of land and resources, ethnic rivalry over territory or other resources, and inadequate mechanisms of political representation. The collapse of the social contract – in combination with the lawlessness and political violence that frequently accompany it – further erodes attempts to amalgamate the state's constituent communities into a cohesive political unit. Diminishment in public revenues, diversion of resources to less productive sectors of the economy, increased concentration of political power in the hands of an unaccommodating elite (rather than institutions), and use of draconian security legislation feed the over-centralization of political power and the politicization (or weakening) of state institutions. The result is a vicious cycle of conflict that validates separatist claims of grievance to assist the mobilization of marginalized communities against the state as the rules, conventions and shared understandings that once restrained conflict are eroded (cf. Murshed 2002).

Note that this is *not* to suggest that the root cause of separatist violence is the Western-centric origins of statehood and territorial sovereignty. Kohli (1997) touches upon this issue when he observes that the separation between public and private realms that characterizes many Western states is often unrealizable in developing economies, in which government intrusions into citizens' socio-economic life politicize state institutions, which then become the center of competition for society's elites and constituent groups. Similarly, Njoku (2010) claims that proponents of the ethno-nationalist paradigm – who call for the redrawing of political boundaries to create ethnically (more) homogeneous states as a solution to Africa's problem of recurrent conflict – overlook the reality of ethnic identity in Africa, which, unlike in Europe, is fluid and changeable, with the result that intra-ethnic conflict is as much of a problem as inter-ethnic conflict.

If, however, the misapplication of a Western-centric model of sovereignty to non-Western societies were the main cause of separatism, then we would see many more separatist movements than we do. In addition, numerous Western states also experience separatism, including Spain, Great Britain and Canada. Moreover, it is not the case that separatist groups reject the territorial sovereignty of states, but, rather, that they covet it by attempting to remove themselves from the sovereignty of their parent state to replace it with that of their own. To emphasize, the territorial sovereignty of states may be a Western artifice, but this does not prevent non-Western groups desiring or using violence in their attempts to attain it. Rather, as I shall argue below, separatism occurs when states fail to live up to the hype of sovereignty as a unitary and exclusive property *and* prove unable to deliver the benefits of statehood at least as effectively as alternative institutions premised upon prior configurations of sovereignty.

In the case of South Asia, this dissonance between the theory and the reality of state sovereignty can be traced back to the colonial period, when the British established fixed geographical borders, within which there was held to be an undivided jurisdiction of sovereignty charged with citizens' wellbeing. Consequently, overlooking the multiplicity of existing sovereignties and the subcontinent's extreme linguistic and cultural diversity, the British created an imaginary single sphere of sovereignty whose inhabitants were jointly characterized as the 'natives of India' or 'Indians.' The important point to emphasize is that British attempts to articulate common interests upon which a political community might be constructed through the acceptance of shared goals, a common order, and an informed and participatory citizenry were subsequent to the imposition of political boundaries around a populace that, while they shared the moniker of 'British subject,' possessed no common social or ideological identity. The preference for free trade, introduction of standard measures, and laws of contract and tort established public spaces in which an Indian identity might coalesce. However, these regulations were very much imposed from above and admitted a variety of qualifications and exceptions. The outcome was a curious double standard and creeping discord in which the geographical jurisdiction of *de jure* sovereignty was firmly established, but *de facto* sovereignty was frequently diffuse and derogated to a network of extra-state actors. When the gap between the two grew too large or public, then the British would intervene to reinforce their hegemony and assuage concerns about who was really in charge. For example, in the state of Jammu and Kashmir – which had been sold to Maharaja Gulab Singh in 1846 – the British substantially limited and removed many of Gulab Singh's grandson's (Pratap Singh's) powers over concerns regarding the security of the state's northern frontiers against Czarist influence and the Maharaja's ability to govern effectively after severe famines in 1877 (Lamb 1992; Bhattacharjea 1994; Schofield 1996). Nonetheless, British political and military intervention could not alter the fact that identities are always multiple, contingent and continuously constructed. Nor could it erase tribal, religious, ethnic and other identities or the networks of sovereignty that they sustained and preserved alongside British inventions of sovereignty.

Hansen and Stepputat (2006) have described the colonial world as a twilight zone of multiple, indeterminate configurations of power and authority consisting in large measure of exception and lawlessness, allowing unrestrained violence, exploitation and excessive despotism. At the same time, however, colonial discourses of development and benevolence served as an imaginary canvas on which liberal arguments for the necessity of rights and the rule of law could be articulated but imperfectly applied (Hussain 2003). The subcontinent prior to 1947 epitomized this uneasy arrangement, consisting of a patchwork of regions under direct British rule and those administered by native rulers with varying degree of independence from the Crown, tied together by the poorly defined and haphazardly applied doctrine of Paramountcy. Consequently, liberal discourses of the equality of rights, universal human values, supremacy of law and state sovereignty jarred sharply with the reality of life in pre-1947 India, where the excesses of local princes and courts (which enforced brutal labor and penal regimes under the supervision of colonial administrators) were attended by the frequent use of capital punishment.

Configured primarily to maintain public order by governing communities and collectivities – rather than individual subjects – sovereignty in South Asia was historically fragmented and distributed amongst many, mostly informal, forms of local authority. This configuration continued under British rule and consisted in a series of uneven, overlapping and fragmented entities that papered over their fissures with frequent and excessive violence. This disjuncture remains visible within the context of contemporary South Asian states, which are disproportionately arbitrarily constructed, consisting of a multitude of factious forces, alliances and ethnicities that pre-date the modern state and over which it struggles to produce order and derive coherent structure (Geertz 2004). To emphasize, every notable separatist movement in South Asia and the alternative jurisdictions of statehood they covet are rooted in pre-/colonial structures.

Baloch separatism, for example, can be traced back to 1758, when Nasir Khan of Kalat won sovereign status from the Afghan empire, which was shattered with British annexation in 1884 (Ahmad 2005). The British interest in Balochistan stemmed from a desire to create a buffer zone between India and the Russian empire and allow safe passage from Sindh to Afghanistan through Balochistan. However, the Khan of Kalat was unable to prevent tribal attacks on the British army, which the British regarded as a breach of treaty obligations, leading to Balochistan's dismemberment – the western part went to Iran and the northern areas to Afghanistan, while the remainder was divided into the state of Kalat and three puppet principalities (Harrison 1981). The result was an increase in taxation and the emergence of a large number of tenants and landless laborers. Moreover, the British also imported a new mercantile class from Punjab and Sindh, which monopolized control over the local economy, triggering nationalist sentiments amongst the Baloch (Khan 2009). Consequently, while Baloch economic sovereignty waned, political control (and the tribal institutions in which it inhered) remained very much intact. Subsequently, the British concluded a treaty with the Khan of Kalat, Nasir Khan II, in 1854, whereby the Khan agreed to oppose Britain's enemies and protect British trade with Central and Southwest Asia via Balochistan, which culminated in the Sandeman system in the 1870s that regularized relations between the British and the Sardars (tribal chiefs) by guaranteeing British colonial power, freedom of military movement and the right to unimpeded long-range trade (Siddiqi 2012).

Baloch–British relations during the period from 1876 to partition in 1947 were mostly cordial, as the British sought to pacify the Sardars in order to safeguard freedom of movement and trade without the need for military engagement. To this end, the British preserved and empowered tribal leaders in a process of co-option that included financial support, entrusting the Sardars with administrative functions, guarantees of protection and offers of privilege. Conveniently, this arrangement also preserved intra-tribal feuds, which prevented the unity necessary to challenge British Paramountcy (Ahmad 2005). However, it also meant that at the time of partition, institutions of Baloch sovereignty, while circumscribed, were very much intact. Citing Kalat's status as a princely domain of British Balochistan (and not part of British India), the Khan of Kalat sought a status similar to that of Nepal. As in the case of other princely states seeking independent status (e.g., Jammu and Kashmir), it was also claimed that following the lapse of Paramountcy, full sovereignty returned to the native court, rendering it an independent state. Since the Government of India Act (1935), there had existed a possible route to independence should the British leave, as the lapsing of Paramountcy would return full sovereignty to the princes. However, toward the end of their rule, the British attempted to dismiss this possibility as infeasible and undesirable in order to prevent the Balkanization of the subcontinent (Thomas 1992). In spite of this legal posturing, and both the houses of parliament in Kalat unanimously rejecting the proposal to merge with Pakistan, the Khan of Kalat was forced to sign the instrument of accession, and Kalat was annexed by West Pakistan (Ahmad 2005). Unsurprisingly, Pakistan's feeble attempt to justify this state of affairs by citing the ratification of a proposal to accede to West Pakistan by the municipality of Quetta – a body that was comprised of overwhelmingly non-Baloch settlers – did not prevent an armed insurrection in 1948, led by Prince Karim, the brother of the Khan (Bansal 2006).

This practice of preserving traditional structures of sovereignty to facilitate colonial rule was not confined to Balochistan. For example, the Chittagong Hill Tract (CHT) region of modern-day Bangladesh was ceded to the British East India Company in 1760 but ruled by tribal chiefs who collected revenues for the British, who, in return, did not interfere in the customs and regulations of tribal life. Crucially, this also allowed tribes of the CHT to remain segregated from the Bengalis of the region. This isolation continued when, in 1935, the British government declared the CHT region to be a totally excluded area, with the result that it remained largely isolated from the anti-colonial and anti-British nationalism developing across the Indian subcontinent. This left the tribes – who, with Indian support, unsuccessfully claimed that as Buddhists, Christians, Hindus and animists, the logic of the Two Nation theory that was to be the founding ideology of Pakistan did not apply to them – largely unprepared for merger with Pakistan (Hodson 1969; Phadmis 1981). Despite the CHT's preference to either remain independent or join India, the Boundary Commission charged with demarcating the geographical borders of the successor states to the Raj awarded it to Pakistan in order to maintain the contiguity of East Pakistan's transportation and trade networks. Indeed, the Congress leadership made every effort to include the CHT into India, as evidenced by correspondence between senior Congress leaders, such as Sardar Patel, and Lord Mountbatten.

Similarly, consider the mountainous terrain that makes up India's northeast and which has for decades been destabilized by separatist violence. Today divided into the states of Assam, Nagaland, Manipur, Tripura, Meghalaya, Mizoram, Arunachal Pradesh and Sikkim, the region is notable for its rich ethnic tapestry and bewildering array of ethno-cultural identities. Commercial interests – coupled with a desire to limit trade between Bhutan and Assam and to preserve Burma as a strategic buffer between British India, French Indochina and China – first drew British attention to Assam and neighboring regions (Barbora 2006). The British East India Company conquered Bengal in 1757, with Assam incorporated into the company's holdings in 1826 through a series of wars with Burma (Haokip 2012), and Manipur and Nagaland subsequently also brought within the British sphere of influence (Chasie and Hazarika 2009). Many hill and plains areas were designated 'tribal,' closed to immigration and administered under a complex patchwork of poorly defined territorial and legal jurisdictions. Of the regions that, subsequent to India's creation in 1947, developed violent separatist movements, some had been designated as 'excluded areas' (Barbora 2008), whereas other regions were under direct British control or that of a native ruler largely left alone by the British. For example, discrete treaty relationships with native rulers established the princely states of Bhutan, Nepal, Sikkim, Tripura, Manipur, Cooch Behar and the Khasi states (Lacina 2009). In other regions, a succession of legal measures sought to clarify and consolidate control over the region, including the Frontier Tracts Act (1880), the Backward Tracts Act (1919) and the Excluded and Partially Excluded Areas Act (1936), while allowing native inhabitants a semblance of self-rule in matters related to domestic life that fell under customary law (Barbora 2008).

The inconsistent use of a variety of changing statuses that conferred dissimilar degrees of autonomy upon a range of communities was in keeping with established practice by the British. On the one hand, the British were largely successful in achieving their objectives of securing Anglo-Chinese trade and the tea industry (Vandekerckhove 2009) without creating tensions with the hill tribes, as they carefully avoided any policy that would disturb local land tenure. Indeed, peripheral hill regions remained largely neglected, as the local subsistence economies – foraging, hunting, fishing and *jhumming* (shifting cultivation) – did not easily lend themselves to official regulation (Scott 2009), with the result that 'traditional' actors continued to organize everyday land tenure (Vandekerckhove 2011). On the other hand, however, the imposition of territorial sovereignty clashed with traditional modes of production and failed to secure demographic control (and, therefore, economic sovereignty) for local populations. For example, a 'line system' intended to determine areas permitted to be occupied by outside settlers failed to effectively control encroachment upon traditional landholdings of the indigenous tribes by settlers from the Gangetic plains and (East) Bengal, who came to dominate local economies as traders and merchants. Consequently, in 1942, specified tracts of land were declared off limits for more technologically and economically advanced settlers (Barbora 2006). However, land encroachment continues to be a divisive issue that remains at the heart of several separatist movements in the region. Moreover, laws and practices governing land use, property ownership and control over public resources were often ill-defined, and their construal differed from one community to another depending upon the interpretation of designated persons, such as the village chief (Barbora 2006). Consequently, rather than establishing the authority of external centers of power, British legal-rational tools of governance instead endowed and legitimized traditional, antecedent institutions of tribal authority, while also undermining them, as they failed to secure the essential economic interests of the native populations they were intended to serve. Despite these limitations, however, native institutions, practices and conventions continued to be essential to effective governance in the region. Indeed, as Vandekerckhove (2011) observes, the exercise of public authority has never been exclusively a state affair in the northeast, and successive Indian governments, like their British colonial forebears, have struggled to exercise *de facto* sovereignty, relying on a range of indigenous extra-state actors to enforce their will.

In addition, anti-state agitation and political mobilization under the twin banners of political autonomy and ethno-cultural identity are far from recent developments in the region. For example, the Naga Club was formed in 1918, and in 1929 submitted a memorandum to the Simon Commission demanding that the Nagas be under British control and excluded from proposed changes to the Indian Constitution. Although technically an appeal for continuation of British rule rather than a demand for independence, it is nonetheless regarded by most Naga historians as the first Naga declaration of nationality and demand for independence (Chasie and Hazarika 2009). In 1947, an agreement was signed with the governor of Assam, Sir Akbar Hydari, which gave the Nagas special privileges and rights, including the right to extend the existing agreement or negotiate a new one (Chasie and Hazarika 2009). However, after Sir Akbar's death, the agreement was repudiated by the Assam state government and New Delhi, leading the Naga National Council to declare independence on 14 August 1947 (Chasie and Hazarika 2009).

Other separatist movements in India's northeast also have their origins in political organizations formed prior to, or around, the time of partition – e.g., the Hill Leaders Union (1945) in Assam, the Mizo Common People's Union (1946) and the United Mizo Freedom Organization (1947) (Haokip 2012) – and appeal to contractual and historical factors that pre-date the creation of the modern Indian state. For example, the United Liberation Front of Assam (ULFA), founded in 1979, cites the 1826 Yandaboo Treaty that incorporated Assam into

British India as the end of Assam's independence, which ULFA seeks to restore (Baruah 1994). Similarly, in claims that resonate with those of independence movements in Kashmir and Balochistan, separatists in Manipur cite the region's forcible incorporation into India as grounds for secession; the Maharaja of Manipur was invited to Shillong in 1949 and, when he refused to sign the instrument of accession, was placed under house arrest and held incommunicado until he relented on September 21, 1949 (Haokip 2012).

Analogous circumstances surround the development of violent separatism in the Valley of Kashmir, which, as a constituent component of the former princely and subsequent Indian state of Jammu and Kashmir, was incorporated into the Indian Union after a prevaricating Maharaja was compelled – by either intervention or circumstance, depending upon who is telling the story – to accede to the Indian Union. As a part of the former princely state, the Valley of Kashmir was a predominantly Muslim region that had been governed by a Hindu ruler of the Dogra dynasty since the Treaty of Amritsar (1846), having previously been a part of the Sikh, Afghan and Moghul empires. While it had not been an independent territory since the Kashmiri Sultanate (1346–1586), geographical isolation and official neglect combined to allow the residents of the Valley a substantial degree of institutional autonomy, with the Dogra darbar's emphasis on rapacious tax collection at the expense of social or economic development creating a societal vacuum occupied by indigenous Kashmiri forms of social organization, including an elaborate caste system premised upon occupation. Similarly, religious organization was centered around the local mosque and Mirwaizes (head preachers) as hereditary leaders of sometimes rival communities that were variously wooed or confronted by the Dogra court, depending upon the circumstances of the time (Rai 2004; Zutshi 2004). Inevitably, the intersection of these social and religious structures coalesced around political objectives and the harshness of Dogra rule, as various *Anjuman* (religious societies) supported young Muslim Kashmiris' higher education outside the state. The return of these graduates led to protests regarding Hindu monopolization of government jobs and demands for political and social reform, spearheaded by the Jammu and Kashmir National Conference: the dominant vehicle for the Valley's Muslims to voice their grievances and (post-1947) a party that controlled politics in the state. Thus, despite the lack of a recent history of self-government and Kashmir's status as a distant, ethnically and religiously separate outpost of a mostly negligent ruler, Kashmiris' distinctive identity and traditions provided the basis for the contemporary political identities that permeate contemporary political discourse in the Valley and emphasize a history of suffering and neglect. These factors were given powerful expression in more recent developments in the state, when, in 1987, New Delhi was seen to have set aside a democratically elected government to impose central rule that was often brutally enforced and culminated in the separatist crisis that still affects the region.

Of all South Asia's separatist conflicts, the campaign for an independent Sikh state (Khalistan) that raged in the Indian region of Punjab between the mid-1980s and the mid-1990s arguably has the longest historical pedigree as a community seeking to regain lost independence. As Moghul power declined in the seventeenth century, the Khalsa Sikhs regrouped into 12 *misls* (political units) that were independent but acted in unison when faced with an external threat (Deol 2000). These units coalesced into a 'Sikh Empire' under Maharaja Ranjit Singh (1780–1839), which controlled a vast swathe of territory that is today a part of India, China, Pakistan and Afghanistan. Internal divisions and mismanagement created weaknesses that were exploited by the British in two Anglo-Sikh wars leading to the annexation of the Punjab by the East India Company in 1849. Subsequently, Sikh loyalty to the British during the Indian 'mutiny' (1857–58) saw the political reorganization of the subcontinent. The modern-day Indian state of Punjab, where the separatist insurgency was concentrated, was, prior to 1947, mostly directly administered by the British, but also included a number of small princely states. While Sikhs economically benefited from British rule through land development and military service, internal divisions were also heightened: for example, the Jat class (which today remain dominant in rural areas) constructed colonies (e.g., Lyallpur, Sargodha and Montgomery) along canals built by the British, benefiting from the trade that flowed along these, and the Punjab Land Alienation Act (1900), which limited the transfer and purchase of landed property to agricultural castes largely comprised of Jats (Bal 2005). Significantly, rural–urban divides and the modernization of the countryside were important contributing factors to the development of Sikh separatism in the 1980s: a factor that speaks further to the historical pedigree of institutions and identities that underpin separatist sentiment.

To elaborate, although Sikhs are ostensibly a religious community united by a common faith, language, culture and history, sectarian and economic (class) divisions have historically undermined Sikh political unity and aspirations to reclaim the lost mantle of independent statehood. In contrast, the primary unifying force has been the minority status of Sikhs against the numerically much larger, religiously defined Hindu population. These divisions sharpened in the 1870s when a Hindu group known as the *Arya Samaj* – the ideological forebear of modern Hindu nationalist movements such as the *Bharatiya Janata* Party (BJP) and *Rashtriya Swayamsevak Sangh* (RSS) – mounted a proselytization campaign. In addition to claiming that Sikhs were really Hindus (Deol 2000), the demand was also made by urban Hindus for the official language of government and schools to be changed to Hindi in the Devanagri script, prompting counter-demands from Sikhs for Punjabi in the Gurmukhi script (the language of the Sikh holy scriptures) (Chima 2010). These developments resulted in a reactionary stance by Sikh political and religious organizations, as Sikh identity was redefined to include only *Keshdhari* (unshorn), *Khalsa* (pure) Sikhs in an attempt to purge Sikhism of external influences and promote internal unity (Chima 1994). Emphasis upon religious orthodoxy as the bedrock of Sikh identity gathered institutional and organizational pre-eminence in the Gurdwara Reform Movement of the 1920s. Activists known as *Akali Jathas* (lit. 'immortal group') – a militant order that stretched back to Maharaja Ranjit Singh (Deol 2000) – engaged in a frequently violent campaign to gain control of historic Sikh shrines from *mahants* (hereditary managers) and *Udasis* (a monastic sect). After more than 400 *Akalis* had been killed and 30,000 imprisoned (Deol 2000), the British capitulated and passed the Sikh Gurdwaras and Shrines Bill (1925), which created the *Shiromani Gurudwara Prabahandak* Committee (SGPC) to administer the shrines and defined a Sikh as someone who professed the Sikh faith, believed in the Guru Granth, accepted the Ten Gurus and had no other religion. The SGPC was assisted, and came to be dominated by, the *Shiromani Akali Dal* (soldiers of the immortal), which had been instituted in Amritsar in December 1920 to coordinate the activities of the *Akalis*.

As Chima (1994) highlights, the 1925 Act legitimized Sikh distinctiveness vis-à-vis Hindus and Muslims, but failed to resolve the continuing debate over which sects qualified as 'Sikh.' Moreover, it provided the Sikhs with an unprecedented degree of organizational structure and demarcation from the majority Hindu population (Deol 2000). The SGPC assumed significant spiritual authority through its control of the *Akal Takhat* (the shrine within the Golden Temple complex considered to be the seat of Sikh temporal and religious authority), which enabled it to issue *hukamnamas* (edicts). Moreover, it also gained significant economic resources, as command of the shrines meant control over substantial land and resources (Singh 1998) in the form of large, revenue-generating estates over which the SGPC exercised proprietary rights (Deol 2000). As an indication of the wealth generated by these shrines and estates, the annual budget of the SGPC amounted to more than US$12 million in 1986 (Kapur 1987). Most importantly, however, the 1925 Act set a collision course between the legal-rational state with its modernizing agenda based on Western scientific rationalism, on the one hand, and the political structures of religiously sanctioned dynastic institutions, on the other hand, with the former frequently provoking controversy by attempting to intervene in the latter.

Religious reform was accompanied by political empowerment. Under the Montagu–Chelmsford constitutional reforms in 1921, Sikhs were granted separate electorates in the Punjab legislature. In the 1919–47 period, Sikhs occupied 13 seats in the Council of States and Legislative Assembly, which from 1932 included 33 seats of the 175-seat Punjab Legislative Assembly reserved for Sikhs (Deol 2000). Prior to partition, *Akali* leaders insisted that Sikhs be afforded a separate state in which no religious community would form a majority that could federate with either India or Pakistan. However, they were persuaded to give up this demand in return for promises of special status in an independent India (Deol 2000). Subsequently, this demand was revisited in a 1948 memorandum to the Constituent Assembly that was then engaged in framing the Constitution of India. The *Akalis* demanded special communal representation for Sikhs in the Punjab legislature – at the time, Sikhs constituted 35 percent and Hindus 61 percent of the population of the state that included the present states of Punjab and Haryana (Chima 1994) – and in appointments to government services. If these demands were not acceptable, the memorandum continued, then Sikhs should be permitted to form a separate province comprising the districts in which they formed a majority. The Constituent Assembly refused both demands, which it considered contrary to the spirit of a secular India (Kapur 1987). Nonetheless, the stage had been set for future conflict between the *Akalis* and India – a conflict in which historical, predecessor institutions and identities with a provenance considerably more extensive than that of modern India would play a key role.

The indigenous ethnographic pedigree of the Sikhs of the Punjab contrasts sharply with that of Sri Lanka's Tamil population, which is divided into (a) Sri Lankan Tamils (approximately 12.7 percent of the population), whose ancestors have lived in Sri Lanka for thousands of years, and (b) Indian Tamils (approximately 5.5 percent of the population) descended from Tamils who migrated from India during British colonial rule. Indian Tamils were recruited to work in coffee and then tea plantations in central Sri Lanka, where they still reside, and are politically and socially separated from Sri Lankan Tamils in the north and east (Feith 2013). Prior to the arrival of the British in 1796, there had been three separate kingdoms on the island: Sinhalese kingdoms based around Kandy in the center and Kotte in the southwest, and a Tamil kingdom based in Jaffna in the north, founded in 1215. Although the Tamil kingdom endured until the arrival of the British – a factor in which it was assisted by geography, being separated from the other two kingdoms by vast tracts of jungle (Oberst 1988) – it underwent a series of expansions and declines. Thus, by the time the island was united under British rule, the Tamils of the north and east had evolved a distinct system of governance and ethno-cultural identity. While relations between different ethnic groups under British rule were mostly cordial, as independence loomed, discontent along ethnic lines assumed a heightened significance in the form of debate over ethnic representation on the legislative councils created by the colonial administration in the early twentieth century (Oberst 1988). Moreover, ethnic politics aligned with ideological fissures in the 1930s, as intellectuals who had studied in London returned to form trade unions inspired by Marxist ideology, which found a receptive audience amongst the mostly Tamil workers on tea estates in the island's interior (Rogers 1987). These racial and political divisions were exacerbated by the British, who favored Tamils for civil service and other official positions. The resulting Sinhalese perception of Tamils as a privileged minority meant that independence was seen as an opportunity to restore the Sinhala language and culture to its rightful place, with the consequence that there was little public or institutional resistance to removing Tamil recruits from governmental service (DeVotta 2004).

Mobilization against the parent state

Suppose, then, that we accept that separatist movements have a historical pedigree – real and imagined. Clearly, there are many more groups with a history of self-government, political independence and lost sovereignty than there are separatist movements. The predecessor institutions to the modern, post-colonial states of South Asia provide a focal point for the collective imagining of an alternative political order – which is typically portrayed as a cultural golden age to induce a lament for its return – while also providing a counter-reference to the modern, bureaucratic state that separatists seek to supersede. However, historical imagery in the form of archaeological, artistic and literary representations is generally insufficient to induce a commitment to violent rebellion and the risks that accompany it. Therefore, to make the jump to separatism, there must be a link between past independence and contemporary reality that engenders dissatisfaction with the parent state sufficient to mobilize the population in favor of the alternative jurisdiction of sovereignty proffered by secession. This necessitates demonstrating that the parent state is a sub-optimal solution to the requirements of embodiment and necessity in comparison with the post-secession state of affairs. Consequently, separatism is predicated on a claim of victimhood that, while it may be experienced individually, has a collective component shared by the community's members in a manner that becomes constitutive of their identity.

The post-colonial states of South Asia, like the predecessor and constituent 'nations' that these states inherited, are imagined, because most members do not know their fellow members. Consequently, the constructed, overlapping, imagined and constantly emergent character of sub-/national identities acts as a potential reservoir of dissent. Whether or not these alternative identities coalesce into separatist movements dedicated to the pursuit of alternative jurisdictions of sovereignty depends upon how the members of a minority perceive their position vis-à-vis the parent state. Moreover, a significant determinant in this process of self-perception is government in/action, which, depending upon its consequences for the minority, can dis-/incentivize separatism. This is because government denial or acknowledgment of difference creates a political and legal space for communities to define themselves and their relation to one another and to the state (Tremblay 1996). In the case of South Asia, states have typically disregarded or downplayed inequality and heterogeneity within and between communities for the sake of a unity created through social mobilization and political organization (cf. Deol 2000). Moreover, because processes of unification and nation building have typically viewed sub-state, predecessor institutions of sovereignty as a threat to the narrative of national identity, genuine federalism has been regarded as a threat to national unity and ethnic leaders have had their loyalty co-opted, cajoled or bought.

In some cases, this strategy took the form of a lack of recognition or the legal 'writing out' of prior benefits or acknowledgment of sub-groups. The 1972 constitution of Bangladesh, for example, failed to recognize the existence of sub-national communities, making no mention of the CHT, and instead emphasizing Bengali nationalism, with an emphasis on Bengali language and culture as key principles of the Bangladeshi state. Elsewhere, the state was more interventionist in its attempts to dismantle predecessor structures of sovereignty. In Balochistan, for example, three major tribes – the Bugtis, the Maris and the Mengals – were led by Sardars who did not completely agree with the merger with Pakistan (Aslam 2011) and held considerable sway over their tribal areas and resources. The resulting tension saw the 1955 One Unit Scheme erase formal recognition of Baloch territorial identity by amalgamating Balochistan within the greater province of West Pakistan, which was dissolved in 1970 when Balochistan became a governor's province (Ahmad 2005). Subsequently, Prime Minister Zulfikar Ali Bhutto abolished the Sardari system in 1976 (Ahmad 2005). However, in both cases, central influence failed to erase the deeply rooted political and social institutions and loyalties that became key drivers of separatism.

Similarly, pre-independence efforts in Sri Lanka to preserve a balance of political power between the dominant Sinhalese majority and the sizeable Tamil minority failed to get off the ground. A 1937 proposal by G. G. Ponnambalam, the founder of the Tamil Congress, to prevent any single ethnic group from dominating other groups was rejected by the Sinhalese leadership of the Ceylon National Congress – the predominant political organization of the period. Subsequently, in 1948, a system of single-member electoral constituencies with extra representation for large under-populated districts allowed the Sinhalese to dominate the political system, as Tamils lacked the numbers to block or alter legislation. As Oberst (1988) highlights, this might have been a sustainable arrangement had the Sinhalese majority government resisted the temptation to enact discriminatory legislation against the Tamil (and other) minorities.

In the case of India's myriad separatist movements, most of the pre-1947 formal institutions of political sovereignty were sufficiently emasculated to pose little threat to national integration. Exceptions were the country's northeast and the states of Punjab and Jammu and Kashmir, where India's overt political interference and reliance on military force belied claims of success regarding its secularist nation-building strategy. In the case of all three regions, proximity to a hostile neighbor colored New Delhi's response to local politics. In the northeast, for example, prior to, and immediately after, independence in 1947, groups were already agitating for a very loose federal structure or independent statehood to escape the shackles of Indian nationalism. In India's first parliament – the Constituent Assembly – Assamese leaders proposed a federation with strong, independent states that drew a patronizing and dismissive response from Prime Minister Jawaharlal Nehru (Baruah 2009). Similarly, the Naga National Council (NNC) declared Naga independence a day before India. The declaration, followed by a plebiscite in 1951 on independence from India, a boycott of the first Indian parliamentary election in 1952 (Kikon 2005) and a subsequent declaration of independence in 1956, was followed by a separatist insurgency that was soon replicated in the other northeastern states of Manipur (1964), Mizoram (1966), Tripura (1978) and Assam (1979) (Lacina 2009; Goswami 2011).

The lack of recognition granted to tribal peoples on the geographical, social and economic periphery of a state the size of India is perhaps unremarkable. More notable, and threatening for the standard bearers of Indian identity, has been the failure of secular nationalism to carry the Sikh- and Muslim-dominated regions of Punjab and Jammu and Kashmir in a Hindu-majority polity. In the case of Punjab, a strong tradition of martyrdom and mixing of religion and politics – embodied in the doctrine of *miri-piri* that sanctioned religiously regulated political action – meant that the spiritual wellbeing of the *Panth* (community of believers) depended on the enactment of justice, which in turn derived from the political conditions under which the *Panth* lived (Pettigrew 1987). Consequently, political issues that concerned the essential or common interests of the community (particularly those concerning language and culture) were inherently spiritual and *vice versa*. Indeed, soon after India's independence there was a call for a *Punjabi Suba*, or a state within the Indian republic with a Punjabi-speaking majority: a mainstream demand, given the linguistic reorganization of states occurring at the time. However, it was rebuffed due to concerns regarding Hindu–Sikh relations and the potential security threat of a Sikh-majority state bordering Pakistan (Oberoi 1987). Moreover, Sikhism's political and cultural aspirations were given violent expression only after sustained central intervention under the government of Indira Gandhi. This took the form of empowering revivalist ideologue Sant Jarnail Bhindrinwale as a political counter-force in a Punjabi society experiencing economic and social upheaval due to dislocations in the mainly agricultural economy brought about by new crop technology (the so-called 'Green Revolution') that displaced many small land-holders. The result was a religiously inspired, political and economic activism that quickly adopted an anti-India idiom (Singh 2007).

In Kashmir, similar forces to those in Punjab – lack of investment, large numbers of unemployed graduates and a politically astute generation with wide media access – combined with a historical dispute concerning the region's 1947 incorporation into India to prompt similar expressions of frustration. Jammu and Kashmir's accession to India, complicated by a prevaricating Maharaja who declined to sign the Instrument of Accession to India until faced with a tribal invasion from West Pakistan, sparked the first Indo-Pakistan war. In an attempt to legitimize their position, India's leadership made the state's incorporation contingent upon a plebiscite that was never held – the offer subsequently being withdrawn, as India insisted that state legislative assembly elections and Pakistani intransigence made a plebiscite both unnecessary and impractical. New Delhi maintained an iron grip on the state through significant military deployments and a fiery relationship with the charismatic Kashmiri leader, Sheikh Mohammed Abdullah, whose Jammu and Kashmir National Conference Party dominated politics in the state, retarded the growth of competing parties and prevented the development of a culture of democratic accountability. These factors combined with formal independence under Article 370 of the Indian Constitution (which afforded Jammu and Kashmir a measure of independence from central rule denied other states) to foment anti-India activism in consequence of popular perceptions of election rigging in 1987.

These political statements and violent episodes constitute a repudiation of the embodiment claims of the Pakistani, Sri Lankan, Bangladeshi and Indian states. In India, for example, secular definitions of citizenship that reject the claim that Hindus and Muslims are two separate nations limit the state's ability to give official recognition to the religious and ethnic diversity that characterizes its citizenry – in India's northeast, it is estimated that there are at least 382 culturally distinct and geographically concentrated communities (Baruah 2005). These communities, like those of Punjab's Sikhs and Kashmir's Muslims, inhabit the conceptual and geographical periphery of the imagined Indian nation and have proven problematic for Indian nation building, which since the 1950s has employed colonial notions of wilderness to label the northeast as 'wild,' 'unruly' and, therefore, in need of paternalistic intervention in the form of district councils that, under the constitutional provisions of the Sixth Schedule (Article 3), regulated fundamental aspects of daily life that were the artifacts of pre-modern (i.e., pre-Indian) centers of sovereignty, including land tenure, forest access, shifting cultivation (*jhum*) and village headmen. However, efforts at control and marginalization were of questionable success and often merely added a veneer of central legitimacy to already existing institutions of control, with the newly appointed heads of district councils in many cases being local elites, including former village chiefs.

One explanation for this tension is the yawning gap between the modern machinery of democratic governance (free elections and an independent judiciary) and the lack of change and modernization in India's social structure, which remains mired in caste and other pre-modern structures (Singh 1998). Alternatively, as Chima (1994) suggests, the dynamics of democratic competition may exacerbate the imperative of collective expression by ethnic groups and religious minorities, as peripheral elites attempt to maximize support from their respective communities by rejecting the national idiom propagated by New Delhi in favor of parochial, local identities. Whereas the former explanation allows that economic development and redistribution might bring about greater acceptance of nation-building projects, the latter suggests that ethnic parochialism and center/periphery tension may be built into the democratic system. This diversity of opinion aside, it is clear that the state's claim to embody the essential interests of its citizenry needs to be managed in a continuing process of engagement with minorities – particularly those that are regionally concentrated and have a history of political independence that pre-dates the modern state. In India, for example, policies adopted by successive central administrations conflated Indian and Hindu identity in a putatively non-partisan, secular state to exacerbate national–regional/local tensions. Indeed, Article 25 of the Indian Constitution states that reference to 'Hindu' or 'Hinduism' should be construed as incorporating individuals of the Buddhist, Jain and Sikh faiths. Similarly, a 1995 Supreme Court ruling found that the term 'Hindutva' was permissible in election campaigns as a broad philosophical term equating to Indianization (Deol 2000). For minorities on the political, economic and geographical periphery of the state, such pronouncements, rather than evidencing accommodation, are instead interpreted as validating the claims of Hindu chauvinists who oppose any official recognition of local, minority or non-mainstream identities and interests.

Economic under-development

A common theme linking many of South Asia's separatist conflicts is claims of economic under-development and poverty. However, the causes of this poverty and the nexus with separatist violence are disputed and vary considerably. For example, explanatory accounts of Sikh separatism emphasize a variety of economic-related factors, such as urbanization; consumerism; mass literacy; graduate unemployment; and the so-called 'Green Revolution' whereby new strains of high-yield wheat and a double-cropping pattern caused farming to become steadily un-remunerative due to over-supply, the rising costs of inputs (tube wells, fertilizer, diesel oil and agricultural machinery), electricity cuts, irrigation shortages and other factors (Pettigrew 1987). The central government, with its crop-procurements system, tight control on investment decisions and lack of industrial projects in the state, bore much of the blame for the economic dislocation produced by these changes, which was exacerbated by its decision to reduce Sikh recruitment into the armed forces (a long-standing economic safety valve) (Singh 1998). Unemployment, indebtedness and landlessness also intersected with ethnic factors. Not only was the Indian state associated with a Hindu bourgeoisie, but those at the bottom of Punjabi society had to compete for jobs and other resources with overwhelmingly Hindu migrant laborers (Chima 1994). Demographic evidence in support of the economic determinants of conflict in Punjab is, however, mixed. Whereas some studies suggest that the majority of militants were Jat Sikh youths from farming families of the Gurdaspur and Amritsar districts (Telford 1992), others (e.g., Jeffery 1994) find greater variety amongst the separatists' ranks – including a range of classes and castes across Sikh society – casting doubt upon the saliency of economic deprivation as a motivating factor.

Nonetheless, economic claims formed a central plank of Sikh separatists' agenda. The *Akali Dal*'s 1981–84 mass protests resurrected the 1973 *Anandpur Sahib* Resolution (ASR) – a landmark political statement by the *Akali Dal* – and demanded that all key industries be bought under public sector control; government investment in heavy industry in the Punjab be increased; and the reallocation of river waters of riparian Punjab to other, non-riparian states be halted. Of particular note was the construction of a canal linking the Sutlej and Yamuna rivers that would carry water to the neighboring state of Haryana. *Akali* leaders alleged that the canal would deprive Sikh peasants of vital water resources (Kapur 1987). Although no evidence was produced to substantiate this claim, it struck a chord with ordinary Sikhs, who regularly suffered power blackouts for several hours every day, which caused tube-well motors, fans, air coolers and other electronic equipment to cease functioning (Chima 1994). Other, non-economic demands included the transfer of Chandigarh from Haryana to Punjab; realignment of Punjab's borders to accommodate Sikh-populated and Punjabi-speaking areas contiguous with Punjab; allowing the SGPC to control all Gurdwaras in India; the recognition of Sikh personal law; protection for Sikh minorities living outside Punjab; increased provincial autonomy for all Indian states; and removal of recruitment policies that limited Sikh recruitment to the army (Deol 2000).

Economic deprivation is similarly highlighted as an important causal factor in India's northeast, with one study finding that for every one unit increase in relative poverty, there is a 52 percent increase in the probability of armed conflict within the next year (Vadlamannati 2011). As in the case of Punjab and Kashmir,

New Delhi's failure to ensure adequate economic diversification through industrial development and addressing youth unemployment is a recurring theme (Fernandes 2004). A defining feature of the region is the elaborate system of reservations, land restrictions and reliance on traditional agricultural practices (Lacina 2009), which not only retards economic development through inefficient and environmentally destructive land usage, but also preserves feudal power structures and entrenches the tribal identities that underpin anti-India sentiment. However, it is unclear what kind of industrial development or program of economic modernization would be feasible in such an isolated, mountainous and comparatively resource-poor region. Moreover, effectively addressing perceptions of injustice through programs of modernization will inevitably create tensions with traditional economic structures that are not easily accommodated within modern, state-centric institutions of individual property rights. Of particular note are practices of shifting cultivation and the collective ownership of lands, which place local communities at a significant disadvantage when bargaining for their rights as displaced peoples and engender a deep mistrust of officials, who, with their extraordinary powers, are frequently perceived as enforcers of a rapacious and unjust order (Barbora 2006).

The same considerations are pertinent to Balochistan, which, despite its enormous mineral and energy resources, has some of the lowest scores on indices of social and economic development in Pakistan. In addition to vast depositions of copper, uranium, gold, coal, silver and platinum, Balochistan provides 36 percent of Pakistan's total gas production – a major source of government revenue piped across Pakistan but available to the residents of only four of Balochistan's 28 districts (International Crisis Group 2006). In addition to high unemployment – 33.48 percent, compared to 19.1 percent for Punjab and 19.68 percent for Pakistan overall in 1998 at the outbreak of the current period of separatism (Population Census Organization 1998) – the literacy rate is 26.6 percent (against the national average of 47 percent), only 20 percent of the people have reliable access to drinking water (the same figure for Pakistan is 86 percent), 47 percent of the population live below the poverty line (Ahmad 2005; Pakistan 2005; Khan 2009), incidences of malaria and tuberculosis are 30 times the national average, and the province has the highest child mortality rate (Fazl-e-Haider 2006).

A key consideration in these statistics is their relativity to other provinces in Pakistan. Sentiments of injustice are premised upon distributive and comparative terms. The problem, for example, is not simply that Baloch revenues for its natural gas from the Pakistan government are exceedingly low, but that they are much lower than in other, wealthier provinces. The price paid for 1,000 cubic meters of gas from Punjab is 250 rupees, from Sindh 128 rupees but from Balochistan only 26 rupees (Haye 2005) – one of the lowest natural gas royalties in the world (Duncan 1989; Bansal 2008). Similarly, out of 830 higher civil service personnel in Pakistan, only 181 were Baloch (Noman 1990; Khan 2009). Within their province, the Baloch are similarly under-represented. In 2002, out of 14 government secretaries in Quetta, only four were Baloch; fewer than 500 of

3,200 students at Balochistan University, and only 30 of the 180 faculty members, were Baloch (Weaver 2002). In contrast, despite comprising only 45 percent of Pakistan's population, Punjabis make up 90 percent of the military (Direh *et al.* 2007). The Pakistan government has reluctantly moved to redress this imbalance by adjusting the National Finance Commission Award so that Balochistan's share of national, divisible resources increased in 2009 from 7.17 percent to 9.09 percent (Siddiqi 2012). Nonetheless, sentiments of discrimination, particularly concerning mega projects such as the Gwadar port, remain. Lack of documented land title saw many Baloch allegedly cheated by corrupt officials out of their land, which was then sold to port developers (Ahmed 2008), and also resulted in the loss of trillions of rupees of revenue for the provincial government (Baloch 2004; Bansal 2008). In addition, only 2 percent of the port's revenue is allocated for Baloch – the rest going to the Pakistani and Chinese governments – and all construction contracts and most jobs have been awarded to non-Baloch (Aslam 2011). Moreover, the federal government retains the right to legislate in domains that elsewhere are the preserve of the province, such as tourism, pollution, labor welfare, transfer of property and educational curricula. This is in addition to large military cantonments that deny crucial revenues to the Baloch government, as it has no legal authority to levy entertainment tax or property tax inside the cantonments (Babar 2004; Bansal 2008).

In the case of Sri Lanka, there was no intervening, regional calculus masking Sinhalese animosity toward the Tamil minority. Whereas prior to the 1940s Marxist-dominated trade unions had been the main opposition vehicle to the conservative, nationalist United National Party (UNP), by the time of independence from British rule, religion and ethnicity had become the dominant markers of group conflict. While some (e.g., Rogers 1987) note that pre-independence there were few ethnic or religious riots, arguing that Sinhalese/Tamil polarization was not inevitable, there were warning signs; e.g., the move of the modern town of Anuradhapura by several miles to preserve the 'purity' of the ancient Sinhalese city gave unmistakable voice to sentiments of Sinhalese cultural nationalism. Subsequently, Indian Tamils were denied many of the benefits of legislation passed in the 1930s and 1940s concerning land, voting and citizenship rights. This manifested initially as economic and sociopolitical disempowerment through moves to replace English with Sinhala – e.g., the Sinhala Only campaign that emerged in 1955–56 – to address the disproportionate number of Tamils in professions and government administration. In this manner, Sinhalese cultural nationalism gradually became institutionalized, manifesting the belief that the state had a special duty to the Sinhalese and Buddhism (Puri *et al.* 1999).

More specifically, the effect of government policies on language and education had dire economic ramifications for Tamils – particularly the employment prospects of graduates – and became a key driver of Tamil alienation. To explain, the introduction of universal education was accompanied by the replacement of English as the medium of instruction with *swabasha* (vernacular languages). Consequently, the access of Tamil-speaking children to public sector jobs was restricted, because proficiency in the Sinhalese language was a requirement for public sector employment following the 1956 Official Language Act No. 33 (Sinhala Only Act) (Sørensen 2008). Moreover, from 1971, access to university was regulated on the basis of language, which effectively meant that Tamil speakers had to score higher to obtain a university place, with their numbers in some disciplines dropping by up to two thirds (Chalk 2003; Stokke 2006; Sørensen 2008). Additionally, diminishing terms of trade meant fewer employment opportunities for graduates, which were frequently determined by political and social connections, to which Tamils and the poor had limited access (Rogers 1987). Lack of employment opportunities and investment in the economy of the northeast – plans to develop an industrial processing zone at Trincomalee were abandoned in 1972 (Shastri 1990), while many employers in the region, such as Pesalai Oil and Prima Flour Mills, employed more Sinhalese than Tamils (Sørensen 2008) – led to an exodus of Tamils from Jaffna and the northeast to other parts of the country. Jaffna experienced an increase in its net out-migration rate from 2.3 to 6.0 per 1,000 in the period 1963–71 – the only district on the island to do so (DeVotta 2009). In some instances, this alienation and estrangement, even when given legislative expression, were rolled back; e.g., the Citizenship Act of 1948 and 1951 rendered Tamil plantation workers of Indian origin disenfranchised and stateless, but these rights were restored in the 1970s (Feith 2013). Nonetheless, the economic harm and alienation suffered by Tamils could not be undone. For instance, the government's 1972 proclamation in the constitution of Sri Lanka as a Buddhist theocratic state combined institutional estrangement with economic marginalization, as Tamil recruitment into the armed forces and civil service virtually halted (Rupesinghe 1988). In 1972, these changes led to the formation of the Tamil United Front (TUF), which campaigned for linguistic, ethnic and religious equality. By 1977, the party had been renamed the Tamil United Liberation Front (TULF) and contested the 1977 elections on a campaign for the creation of an independent state (Chalk 2003).

Finally, economic under-development, neglect and predatory policy-making are also frequently cited as factors behind separatism in Bangladesh's CHT. Of particular note is a hydroelectric project – the Kaptai Dam – that was constructed on the Karnafuli River in the Rangamati District. By flooding 400 square miles – including 54,000 acres of arable land, constituting 40 percent of the district's total acreage (Islam 1978; Zaman 1984) – the dam displaced more than 100,000 people, severely disrupting the traditional, agrarian economy, decreasing food production and leading many hills people to migrate across the border with India to Tripura and Mizoram. Subsequently, government rehabilitation and compensation left most families worse off than before the dam (Islam 1978); of an estimated US$59 million, only $2.6 million was distributed, with many alleging that these funds were misappropriated by Bengali officials (Linter 1990). In addition, fewer than 1 percent of the tribal inhabitants of the CHT region were employed in industries generated by the dam – the majority of employees and those controlling local industries being Bengali.

Some commentators (e.g., Murshed 2002) have seen these developments as evidence of the reciprocal, rather than antagonistic, relationship between greed and grievance; war makes poverty reduction difficult to achieve, while the inequities of destitution perpetuate a resentment amongst the poor and a rapaciousness amongst the wealthy that fuel further violence (Aslam 2011). Securing citizens' fundamental welfare through the provision of access to essential services and upholding individual property rights is one of the fundamental duties of a state. However, not all states that fail to discharge their duties in this regard suffer separatism. The counter-factual post-secession state of affairs proffered by separatists must be not only superior to the status quo, but also peculiar to the sub-group of the state's citizenry in whose name the separatist cause is advanced. If not, then the solution would be reform or rebellion – not separation. Natural divisions (such as region, race, religion or culture) assist mobilization against the state, as relative disadvantage is portrayed as emanating from pre-political features not amenable to a negotiated solution, making the reorganization of political boundaries a necessary condition for remedying the condition of injustice. Membership of the sub-group, and how this is defined vis-à-vis the majority population of the parent state, is, therefore, a critical issue in the development of separatism. Without perceptions of difference, separatist claims become specious, as there is no community whose interests require a separate jurisdiction of sovereignty to safeguard. The following section investigates how claims of injustice intersect with assertions of difference, as separatists and the state prosecute their rival claims by reconstituting the sub-group of whom they claim to be the true representatives.

Ethnic dilution and population demographics

If separatism is the consequence of rival claims of embodiment, then this begs the question of who are the sub-group that the state and separatists claim to represent. Moreover, rather than being prior to separatist claims, the constituent individuals and identity of the sub-group are objects of manipulation, as both the state and separatist elites attempt to refashion communities to suit their respective strategic objectives. Indeed, demographic change frequently accompanies – as an intentional strategy or an unintended consequence – socio-economic marginalization, and *vice versa*. For example, unemployment in consequence of lack of development in Sri Lanka's northeast drove many Tamils south in search of employment. At the same time, government efforts to populate Sri Lanka's dry zone – the ancient heartland of the Sinhalese civilization – saw more than 300,000 acres of land distributed to 67,000 allottees by the late 1960s (Gompert 2007). Unsurprisingly, the policy of moving Sinhalese north into traditionally Tamil areas was opposed by Tamils as a calculated strategy of demographic dilution and cultural marginalization (Peebles 1990). There was also a widespread perception amongst Tamils that government spending in the northeast was disproportionately directed to benefit Sinhalese settlers rather than Tamil residents (DeVotta 2004), threatening extinction of the traditional Tamil homeland (Kearney 1987). This characterization in turn validated

Sinhalese perceptions of Tamil criticisms of government policy as being a thinly veiled attempt to justify the creation of a Tamil homeland in the northeast – to them, a patently indefensible concept (Peebles 1990). Indeed, as Feith (2013) highlights, all Sri Lanka's communities perceive themselves as minorities: the 70 percent majority Sinhalese regard themselves as a minority in relation to India (and the state of Tamil Nadu, a very short distance across the Palk Strait, with approximately 72 million Tamils), whereas the Tamils and Moors are clearly a minority in comparison with the Sinhalese. Consequently, policies by each group that led to the geographical concentration of their own community (or dispersion of other communities) were invariably interpreted as hostile acts.

Similarly, in the case of the CHT and Balochistan, demographics combined with the effects of geographical and political distance from the center. While Bengali migration to the CHT had been a long-standing phenomenon, in 1979 the government decided to move landless Bengali families to government-owned *khas* (reserved land) in the CHT region. By the end of 1984, an estimated 400,000 Bengalis had settled in the CHT region, and the Bengali percentage of the CHT's population rose from 2 percent in 1948 to 12 percent in 1962 and then 50 percent in 1991 (Montu 1980). However, the threat to the native culture of the CHT's inhabitants emanated mostly from the economic consequences of this influx rather than demographic dilution *simpliciter*. To explain, much of the land awarded to Bengali migrants had been traditionally farmed by indigenous tribes. Moreover, their superior business acumen and education meant that Bengalis came to dominate local industries such as retail trade, transport and fishing (Montu 1980). In the case of Balochistan, waves of Pashtoon refugees during the Afghan war meant that in many parts of the province the Baloch no longer dominated, while migrants from Punjab and Sindh to the Makran Coast combined with the sale of large swathes of land to outsiders by mafias to demographically and economically marginalize the Baloch in a process similar to that which occurred in Sri Lanka and the CHT (Bansal 2008). Moreover, internal dilution has combined with regional imbalances in the form of Punjabi domination of the organs of state to further evince sentiments of alienation. The population of Punjab exceeds the population of the other three provinces put together; the headquarters of the army, navy and air force, the railways and the Water and Power Distribution Authority are all in Punjab; while Punjabis dominate that most important of national institutions – the army – in a country where military rule has been a recurring phenomenon (Bansal 2006).

It is in India's northeast, however, that demographic factors have exerted the most powerful influence upon separatist mobilization. The radicalization of Assamese nationalism, for example, can be traced back to the influx of illegal migrants from East Pakistan after 1947 and the subsequent war that led to the creation of Bangladesh. At the time of partition, the Assam Congress Party attempted to deal with the immigration issue by unsuccessfully proposing a federation of strong, independent states (Baruah 2009). Subsequently, migrants from India's Gangetic plains, East Pakistan (Bangladesh) and Nepal, seeking to take advantage of the vast tracts of land and employment opportunities in road and railway construction, began to significantly alter the region's demographic balance (Barbora 2008). Tensions over immigration contributed to the Assam Agitation of 1979–84, which ended with the 1985 Assam Accord that attempted to draw a line under the issue by declaring that anybody settled in Assam from Bangladesh after March 25, 1971 was an illegal migrant – not a citizen. However, imperfect implementation meant that the accord failed to stem illegal entry. More egregiously, legislative assembly elections from 1979 have been tainted by the presence of tens of thousands of illegal migrants on electoral rolls (Goswami 2011). In addition to extremely porous borders, lack of official documentation (most people don't have birth certificates or passports) means that a ration card is sufficient to gain inclusion on electoral rolls (Baruah 2009). Illegal immigration has also acted as a lightning rod for protest against the central government due to its economic effects – principally land encroachment and competition for jobs. However, land is arguably the most inflammatory issue, given its close relationship to economic sustenance – many of the population remain farmers, with the result that tribespeople view any threat to land access or ownership as an attack on their identity (Fernandes 2004). These issues were center stage in 1979 at the founding of ULFA, which advocated scientific socialism and self-determination, referred to as *Swadhin Asom* (Independent Assam), through a return to pre-1826 independence when the Treaty of Yandaboo ushered in British rule in Assam (Goswami 2011).

Demographics also intersected with language politics and minority perceptions as a contributing factor in the Khalistan movement. Prior to partition, Sikhs were a territorially dispersed minority in Punjab, and demands of the Sikh elite pertained to representation rather than separate political status (Deol 2000). However, post-1947, Sikhs became a sizeable minority, with the Hindu majority largely concentrated in urban areas. A series of political realignments followed that culminated in the Punjab State Reorganisation Act (1966), whereby southern, predominantly Hindi-speaking regions of the state were spun off to form the new state of Haryana or merged into Himachal Pradesh, leaving a remainder state that was 54 percent Sikh and 44 percent Hindu (Kapur 1987) – in contrast, the pre-partition state was 51 percent Muslim, 35 percent Hindu and 12 percent Sikh (Deol 2000).

These demographic changes had important political implications that saw the resurrection of the language issue in new, and more volatile, forms. Post-partition political agitation in Punjab centered on the Gurmukhi script, which had sacred connotations, but was rejected by Hindu purists, who instead favored the Devanagari script, prompting equivalent demonstrations by Hindu chauvinist organizations (e.g., *Hindi Raksha Samiti*, *Jan Sangh* and *Arya Samaj*) regarding the status of Hindi (Chima 2010). Thus, language, identity, religion and politics (statehood) became increasingly intertwined in an increasingly complex way. Moreover, although a *Punjabi Suba* or Punjabi-speaking (and Sikh-majority) state (Kapur 1987) was eventually attained, bitterness lingered at the length of the struggle, given that the principle of reorganizing states on linguistic grounds had long ago been conceded (Pettigrew 1987). However, Sikh demographic dominance did not translate into political success for the self-appointed standard bearers of Sikh identity – the *Akali Dal* – who were unable to obtain more than 30 percent of the vote in legislative assembly elections between 1967 and 1980 due to the cross-communal support enjoyed by the Congress Party (Kapur 1987). Consequently, in an attempt to improve their electoral fortunes, the *Akalis* adopted a more nationalist, Sikh-based orientation, resurrecting the ASR's definition of the Sikhs as a *Qaum* (nation) and calling for a dramatic devolution of power from the center to the states (Telford 1992).

While there are important differences between the demographic influences summarized here and their contribution to the development of separatism, taken together they illustrate both the importance and the ever-emergent character of group identity. A separatist movement requires a community to function as a bearer of the putative right to independence and provide the sociological basis of the post-secession political unit. Where the fundamentals of community are lacking, they may be imagined and fashioned by elites through articulation of common threats, interests and opportunities that foster sentiments of shared purpose and experience in a process that continues after separation from the parent state. Indeed, it is a matter of significant debate amongst scholars whether communities are more generally prior to, or constituted by, institutions of political rights. While group cohesiveness and distinctiveness may foster a desire for political independence, this does not preclude the possibility that carefully orchestrated claims of independence might also foster bonds of loyalty and shared experience characteristic of the political community whose interests separatist leaders claim to represent.

Examination of these factors within the context of South Asia demonstrates the instability of group identity and the influence of external factors upon it. In India's northeast, for instance, the Naga separatist struggle combined with the Assamese anti-settler agitation (1979–85) to erode the authority of the central state and create a vacuum into which ethnic communities and separatist groups were able to insert themselves. The result was a rise in the profile of competing, ethnically orientated tribal groups at the expense of the inclusive, secularist nation-building project of the Indian state. Moreover, these groups' separatist agendas were a response, not merely to the failed policies of the central government, but also to perceived challenges from neighboring tribes jockeying for the geographic and political space left vacant by the Indian state. For example, the militant Naga leadership of the National Socialist Council of Nagaland (NSCN) expressed strong territorial claims along the eastern border of the Karbi Anglong district of Assam. Contemporaneously, Dimasa political leaders and militants of the *Dima Halim Daoga* (DHD), disappointed by the outcome of the Assamese agitation (1979–85), adopted a more radical agenda for a restored Dimasa kingdom (*Dimaraji*) that included territory in the Karbi Anglong district. This caused a rupture in the Karbi–Dimasa *entente* in the early 1990s and prompted the Karbi militia of the United Peoples' Democratic Front Solidarity (UPDS) to pursue *hemprek kangthim* (Karbi self-rule) (Vandekerckhove 2011). Thus, one group's success in pursuit of its demands created perceptions of threat and opportunity in other groups that prompted counter-demands (and rifts) where previously none had existed. The trend is well identified by Baruah (2005) in examination of the politically active, ethnic groups in the northeast that employ non-constitutional and unlawful means of furthering their political agendas (Asomiya, Naga, Mizo, Kokborok, Khasi, Garo, Hmar and Bodo). Citing the amalgamation of the Chakrii, Keza and Sangtang tribes to form a new tribe of Chakhesang, Baruah highlights the instability of tribal identities and political loyalties that exist in a constant state of flux.

The reformation of tribal identities in the Karbi Anglong also provides a useful illustration of the complex interplay of sovereignty's twin virtues of necessity and embodiment. Through their failure to safeguard the demographic dominance and cultural integrity of the native inhabitants in the northeast – largely by not controlling immigration from Bangladesh and the Indian plains – the Indian state and its local agents failed to meet the minimum standards of necessity, thereby leading inhabitants to resort to alternative centers of authority that pre-dated the Indian state. However, rather than being an organic process, the reconstitution of authority from the national and state level to a local and primordial platform was controlled by tribal elites, many of whom, having received a formal education, had come to occupy hegemonic positions within their respective communities (Baruah 2005). Through negotiation, conflict and alliance with neighboring communities, these elites managed to consolidate the personal networks of patronage on which their power depended. In so doing, however, they also refashioned notions of community, established new social networks, and reformed existing identities and group loyalties. Consequently, the question of *whose* rights are to be protected by the state (embodiment) is often as important as, and inseparable from, the additional question of *how effectively* the state performs this function (necessity). The reformation of group identities in the Karbi Anglong demonstrates how the state's failure to satisfy the requirements of necessity may open a window of opportunity for separatists, not only to create an alternative political order putatively superior to the state in this regard, but also to reconfigure local identities and loyalties according to their own agenda, effectively undoing the hastily crafted project of Indian nation building.

Education, political consciousness and external interference

If separatism is a struggle to mobilize popular sentiment behind a counter-factual alternative jurisdiction of sovereignty, then a key element in this process is education. Historically a vehicle for states and elites to promulgate meanings and invalidate rival claims, in societies that have experienced separatism, education has often proven to be a double-edged sword, as efforts to inculcate the values of national citizenship raise expectations that, when unfulfilled, can fuel anti-government sentiment. Similarly, rising literacy rates amongst impressionable youth, when combined with unemployment, political alienation and ethnic mobilization, have resulted in a descent from political consciousness to activism, extremism and, finally, violence. In the Indian state of Punjab, for example, by

1974, 78 percent of primary school-age children were enrolled in school – the second highest figure of all Indian states – and literacy rose from 27 percent in 1961 to 41 percent in 1981. More tellingly, the number of students enrolled in colleges in Punjab increased from 35,000 in 1964–65 to over 110,000 in the mid-1970s (Telford 1992). However, dislocations in the Punjabi economy attributable to the Green Revolution and a lack of economic diversification left the state heavily reliant on agriculture as the main source of income and employment. Ironically, the division of the state in 1966 exacerbated matters, as government unwillingness to industrially develop a sensitive border state combined with the loss of industry to Haryana and mineral and forestry resources to Himachal Pradesh (Telford 1992). Across all disciplines – with the exception of medicine and veterinary science – unemployment for Punjab's university graduates was up to five times higher than the Indian average (Telford 1992) – a factor that was obscured by the often-quoted refrains of Punjab being India's 'wheat basket' and most prosperous state, with the highest per capita income (Manogaran 1987). Other studies (e.g., Jeffery 1994; Purewal 2000) corroborate these claims, finding that Sikh militants were disproportionately drawn from economically disenfranchised, unemployed Jat cultivators, but question the importance of graduate unemployment, observing that a majority of militants were either school drop-outs or illiterates.

The role of educational institutions, rising literacy levels and mass media is also cited in the case of other separatist movements in South Asia. Ganguly (1997), for instance, notes the dramatic rise in literacy rates, university enrolment, graduate unemployment and media outlets in Kashmir that preceded the 1989 outbreak of violence there, claiming that these factors produced a knowledgeable, politically sophisticated but frustrated generation who, stymied by electoral malpractice and disillusioned with major political parties, turned to separatism and religious fundamentalism – a view shared by others (e.g., Baweja 1994). Similarly, it is alleged that mass mobilization in the CHT was assisted by the large number of educational institutions established there in the 1960s, which raised literacy rates amongst tribespeople above 50 percent and created a politically conscious middle class that opposed the autocratic Pakistani government as ethnic solidarity centered on opposition to central interference in local affairs.

The intuitive claim that increased literacy rates and heightened employment and lifestyle expectations crushed by unemployment and government neglect resulted in an alienated, frustrated and rebellious younger generation with a heightened political consciousness is unremarkable. More noteworthy is the question of why this frustration manifested as separatism rather than, for example, civil disobedience, criminal activity or revolutionary zeal. What additional factors contributed to the development of separatism? In response, it should be noted that many separatist groups did engage in criminal activity and acts of civil disobedience. Nonetheless, it is also true that corruption, electoral malfeasance, unemployment, poverty, rising literacy rates, a burgeoning mass media and the other commonly cited drivers of separatism are not specific to those regions that witnessed separatist violence. Consequently, there must have been additional factors (or something peculiar to the interaction of these different factors) to direct anti-government agitation in a separatist direction. One such factor has already been identified above – that of predecessor centers of sovereignty that retain some contemporary relevance to present-day circumstances and are capable of serving as a wellspring of an alternative political order and return to a glorified past. Another pertinent, but equally overlooked and misunderstood, factor is that of external assistance.

Most of South Asia's separatist movements have received substantial external assistance. While we may debate whether this aid has played a causal or an exacerbating role – the two propositions are not mutually exclusive, and the truth invariably lies somewhere in between – there is little serious debate regarding the importance that this external aid has played vis-à-vis the trajectories and longevity of many separatist movements. Perhaps the most notable example of such assistance is India's 1971 intervention in the conflict between East and West Pakistan that led to the creation of Bangladesh. Other examples include (alleged) aid from the United States, Iran, India and Russia to Baloch separatists (Bansal 2006; Khan 2009); Pakistani aid to separatists in Kashmir, Punjab and India's northeast; Indian assistance to Tamil separatists in Sri Lanka and Bangladesh's CHT; and Bangladeshi, Bhutanese and Burmese aid to separatists in India's northeast. This assistance has taken a variety of forms – diplomatic (mediation, arbitration and the use of international forums); economic (sanctions, inducements and foreign aid); and military (intervention, deployment of peacekeepers, provision of training, sanctuary and weapons). Moreover, it has generally been covert (rather than public) and almost always without the parent state's consent. In other cases, it has consisted merely of turning a blind eye to the presence or activities of separatist groups from neighboring states. For example, Bangladeshi support for separatists in India's northeast consisted mostly of allowing groups from Assam, Nagaland and Tripura to procure small arms through the Cox Bazar area and operate underground camps in the Habibganj, Khagrachari, CHT and Mymensingh areas (Kumar 2004; Goswami 2011). Similarly, Bhutanese support for ULFA consisted in the provision of safe havens and facilitating the procurement of arms, ammunition, funding and travel documents (Saikia 2003; Kumar 2004).

Note, however, that because assistance to separatists is almost always covertly provided, there is frequently no reliable data to settle disputes regarding its nature or extent. Moreover, both the parent state (to deflect blame from its failed policies) and the intervening state (to maintain a veneer of plausible deniability) have an incentive to exaggerate or downplay the nature and scope of foreign assistance to separatist groups. Reasons behind intervention are varied and include aiding co-ethnics/religionists, infliction of economic or military harm on rival states, the pursuit of broader geo-strategic aims – India's assistance to Sri Lankan Tamil separatists is partly explained by a desire to pressure the Sri Lankan government to remain within its non-aligned sphere of influence (Narayanswamy 1994; Joshi 1996; Gunaratna 1997; Chalk 2003) – and domestic political concerns.

In each case, the common thread is the perceived self-interest of the intervening state. The 1983 race riots in Sri Lanka, for example, were significant in internationalizing the conflict, generating widespread media coverage and sympathy for Sri Lankan Tamils in the Indian state of Tamil Nadu. Subsequently, support and training were provided to Sri Lankan Tamil militant groups in India by the Tamil Nadu government and the Research and Analysis Wing (RAW) of the Indian government (Feith 2013). However, Indian involvement changed from an exacerbating force to a mediating one when the flow of refugees from Sri Lanka exceeded 100,000 and the Indian government began to worry about separatist sentiment developing amongst its own Tamil population (Feith 2013). Similarly, Bhutan provided assistance to ULFA in the hope that the group would act as a counter to Ngolops (settlers in southern Bhutan of Nepalese origin), whom Bhutan had previously attempted to evict. However, when ULFA's activities began disrupting the flow of trade between Bhutan and India, and links between ULFA and Nepalese Maoists (who had called for the overthrow of the Bhutanese monarchy) became evident, the strategic calculus no longer favored the continued presence of ULFA in Bhutan (Kumar 2004). Consequently, in December 2003, Bhutan deployed 6,000 military personnel to expel 3,000 ULFA cadres and dismantle more than 30 training camps, forcing ULFA to shift its operations to Burma, Bangladesh and, to a lesser degree, the Chinese province of Yunnan (Goswami 2011).

An additional factor, particularly pertinent to the conflicts in Punjab, Kashmir and Sri Lanka, has been the support of foreign diasporas, i.e., transnational communities that have been dispersed to foreign (host) states but continue to share a common identity and intra-ethnic relations with homeland co-ethnics (Wayland 2004). Diasporas constitute a valuable source of funding, recruitment and publicity, as they exploit freedoms of expression and anti-discrimination laws in host states to publish, organize and lobby for co-ethnics in their homeland (Wayland 2004). With up to one in four Sri Lankan Tamils living abroad (Sriskandarajah 2005), up to 90 percent of the LTTE's funding came from overseas (Chalk 2000). Similarly, the Sikh diaspora is estimated to exceed 17 million, with most having emigrated in the post-colonial era to the United Kingdom, Canada and the United States (Fair 2005), while the Kashmiri diaspora, although substantially fewer in number, contributed important funds to the cause of Kashmiri independence from India (Franchetti and Fielding 2002).

Assistance from external parties enables separatist movements to continue their struggle against the parent state, frequently against overwhelming odds, encouraging rebellion by increasing the separatists' odds of success. It is less clear, however, that such assistance has played a causal (rather than an exacerbating) role. States, in order to deflect blame from their failed policies toward minorities, frequently point the finger at external actors by claiming that separatists are manipulated, controlled or led astray by hostile outsiders. This, however, begs the question of why these communities would allow themselves to be manipulated, controlled or led in such a manner. Without a trigger injustice or underlying sense of grievance, attempts to foment rebellion are unlikely to find fertile ground. For example, in 1965, Pakistan's Operation Gibraltar saw the infiltration of *mujahedeen* across the line of control to Indian-administered Kashmir to sabotage infrastructure, disrupt communications and incite a popular rebellion against Indian rule. However, Kashmiris remained passive in the face of these inducements. In contrast, there is significant agreement amongst scholars and commentators that by the early 1990s, Pakistani training, funding and weapons were playing a key role in the separatist insurgency that wracked Indian-administered Kashmir. Clearly, something had changed since the 1960s – a change that is not explicable solely by reference to Pakistani interference.

Repression and human rights abuses

Perhaps the single most important factor in understanding the radicalization of independence movements and large-scale mobilization behind the cause of separatism is the response of the parent state to demands for greater autonomy. Frequently, what begins as a movement with modest support and demands becomes much more popular and radical on account of the parent state's over-reaction. Accordingly, while it may be inaccurate to identify state-sponsored violence as the primary causal element in understanding the origins of separatism – since doing so begs the question of why the abuses were perpetrated and why separatism (rather than protest, emigration or revolution) was adopted as a response by the aggrieved group – it is equally mistaken to dismiss it as a mere exacerbating factor. Because separatist movements often pre-date large-scale, organized violence by the state, there remains the question of what led to the formation of these groups – a question that state-sponsored violence cannot satisfactorily address. At the same time, however, it does not follow that violent and repressive acts by the state against groups that it perceives as a threat to its territorial integrity are not material to the trajectory of separatist movements. Rather, political, economic, socio-cultural and other factors interact with state and separatist-sponsored violence. Indeed, the resort to violence is a more extreme manifestation of that which defines separatism – i.e., a failure of existing political and legal mechanisms to address a group's grievances and rejection of the status quo. In most cases, separatism (and the violence it engenders) is preceded by failed attempts to peacefully secure the sub-group's interests within established political and legal frameworks.

In Sri Lanka, for example, the *Ilangai Tamil Arasu Katchi* (ITAK), commonly known as the Federal Party, successfully competed in elections on an agenda of an autonomous Tamil linguistic state within a Federal Union of Ceylon, equal status for the Tamil and Sinhalese languages, citizenship for the plantation Tamils of Indian origin and the end of colonization by Sinhalese in predominantly Tamil regions (Peebles 2006). However, the *Swabasha* and Sinhala Only campaigns established a political discourse that saw the two major Sinhalese political parties competing for votes on the basis of which was more anti the demands made by ITAK and other Tamil groups – effectively ruling out any sort of workable compromise. This culminated in the 1956 election of Solomon Bandaranaike, whose first act was to make Sinhalese the sole official language (Feith 2013). The move sparked rioting in Trincomalee and Jaffna that led to in excess of 20 deaths, and subsequently the 1957 Bandaranaike–Chelvanayakam Pact, which provided for regional councils with limited power and recognition of Tamil as a minority language. However, opposition to the agreement from Sinhalese and Tamil nationalists led to its abrogation when Bandaranaike refused to acknowledge the Tamil language and instead reverted to the Sinhala Only policy (DeVotta 2004). The pattern of Sinhalese and Tamil leaders agreeing a compromise that was subsequently undone by Sinhalese chauvinists in the south pressuring their leaders not to honor the agreement convinced many Tamils that non-violent methods of achieving their aims were purposeless. This message was reinforced in the 1958 riots, in which 300–400 Tamils were killed, in addition to widespread rape and looting that contributed to the northward migration of many Tamils. In 1959, Prime Minister Solomon Bandaranaike was assassinated by a Buddhist monk because he was perceived as being too soft on Tamil demands (Feith 2013). Further anti-Tamil riots occurred in 1977–78 and 1981–82. The worst riots, however, which proved to be a turning point in the conflict, occurred in 1983 after the deaths of 13 government soldiers in an LTTE ambush. More than 60 Tamils died in reprisals in the north, and when the soldiers' bodies were returned to Colombo, sustained anti-Tamil riots broke out that lasted for a week and saw Sinhalese attack Tamil homes and businesses – forcing many to flee to the north of the country. While the official death toll was only 367, unofficial estimates put it as high as 3,000 (Peebles 2006). Moreover, there were widespread allegations that the violence was planned and premeditated (Rupesinghe 1988). For example, it is alleged that rioters had electoral rolls provided to them by government officials to identify Tamil properties (Feith 2013).

Most importantly, the violence and subsequent repression of Tamil leaders validated the claims of the LTTE and established it as the dominant Tamil political and military organization. The LTTE had been one of several organizations in the north advocating violence in the cause of Tamil freedom and equality. In its early years, it resembled a small-scale criminal organization that engaged in bank robberies and killings of policemen, rather than a political movement. Its main rival for power was the TULF, which, as the then-dominant Tamil party, was trying to improve the position of Tamils by conventional political means, winning a majority of votes in the northern and eastern provinces (Feith 2013). However, events in the early 1980s saw the LTTE emerge as the pre-eminent vehicle of Tamil nationalism and champion of *Eelam*. As DeVotta (2004) highlights, the seeds of Tamil militancy had been planted decades earlier in dwindling Tamil university enrolments, rising unemployment and the Sinhala Only campaign. However, the movement did not turn violent until the pogroms of the 1970–80s, which saw the Sri Lankan security apparatus swing firmly behind Sinhalese chauvinism. For example, the Prevention of Terrorism Act (1979) allowed security forces to arrest, imprison and leave incommunicado for 18 months without trial anyone suspected of unlawful activity. Its retroactive application resulted in the torture of many young Tamils and was coupled with the emasculation of the judiciary as a countervailing force against government excess, in consequence of the 1972 constitution that granted the legislature power over the judiciary, leading to the coercion or removal of judges deemed hostile to government policies (DeVotta 2004).

The intersection of regional and national politics coinciding with a descent into violence is exemplified in the case of the Punjab, where mobilization behind a separatist agenda was intimately related to events on the national political stage. Singh (1987), for example, attributes the revival of Sikh nationalism in post-independence India to four types of perceived discrimination (constitutional, religious, economic and social). An example of the ability of single issues to transcend these four dimensions is the *Sant Nirankaris* – a minority within Sikhism considered to be heretics by many – whose leader, Baba Avtar Singh, stoked tensions within the *Panth* when he declared himself to be an incarnation of Sikhism's founder, Guru Nanak. What began as an internal religious dispute assumed a political dimension when the *Akalis* claimed that the Congress Party (and urban Hindu elites in Punjab) supported the Nirankaris in an attempt to divide the *Panth* (Chima 2010). Moreover, these perceptions were given voice, and skillfully manipulated, by Bhindrinwale, whose influence derived in large measure from Punjab's national status, which gave events there a significance that extended beyond the state's borders and made violence in the pursuit of political aims a rational course of action.

To explain, the 1966 creation of the present-day state of Punjab had profound effects upon the local political landscape. The Congress Party remained the dominant and most broadly based party, receiving both Hindu and segments of the (mostly rural) Sikh vote, whereas the *Akali Dal* had a comparatively narrower base of support amongst Jat Sikh peasantry and some urban Sikhs. Finally, the BJP – formerly known as the *Jan Sangh* – received the support of urban Hindus. Most importantly, no party was able to obtain a majority of votes in legislative assembly elections during the 1967–85 period (Chima 1994), making coalition government the norm. Thus, the 1966 creation of a Sikh-dominated state failed to ensure political power for the *Akali Dal*, who were forced to reach out to Hindus (mostly the *Jan Sangh*) to obtain political office (Deol 2000), placing them in competition with the Congress Party for Hindu votes (Vohra 1986). Crucial to these developments was the national insecurity of the Congress Party, which in 1967 lost power in half of the states. This coincided with the tendency of Congress leader Mrs Indira Gandhi to maintain power through centralization and the dismissal of popularly elected state governments in a process that prevented any one individual – including Congress Party loyalists – becoming too powerful (Chima 2002). In this vein, supporting Sikh extremists allowed Congress to threaten the *Akali Dal*'s credentials as the self-appointed representative of Sikhism while splitting its support base in Punjab (Chima 2010). The *Akalis*, for their part, had an interest in mobilizing voters around a platform of Sikh nationalism as the most effective means of maximizing votes from moderate Sikhs and distinguishing themselves from the Congress Party. The result was that Punjab's very real economic and political grievances attained a religious coloring due to Sikh leaders lending Punjab–New Delhi and Sikh–India relations a religious dimension not immediately amenable to settlement through simple implementation of the demands of the ASR, such as the handover of territory, extra allocations of electricity or making Chandigarh the capital of Punjab (Pettigrew 1987).

Whereas the *Akali Dal* had enjoyed good relations with the central government when it was a coalition partner in the *Janata*-led central government, relations soured once the Congress (I) came into power in the center, and the *Akali–Janata* coalition fell apart, causing a split between moderate *Akali Dal* (*Longowal*) and radical *Akali Dal* (*Talwandi*) factions (Chima 2010). This coincided with the center's interventionist strategy, as Punjab's issues and problems were recast as national ones by Mrs Gandhi (Chima 1994), who also supported Bhindrinwale – head of the *Damdami Taksal* (Deol 2000) – as a foil to the *Akalis*. Moreover, the Congress (I) allegedly also encouraged radical elements in the *Akali Dal* to resurrect the ASR and call for the creation of an autonomous region in north India with powers mirroring those of a princely state prior to partition (Chima 2010), while also holding anti-*Nirankari* rallies and assisting the *Dal Khalsa* and *Panth Khalsa*, which were openly critical of the claim that Sikh interests could be adequately protected in Hindu-majority India (Chima 2010). Thus, political rivalry became entwined with religious identity as the *Longowal* and *Talwandi* factions of the *Akali Dal* competed for the mantle of guardian of Sikh identity by engaging in ever more radical rhetoric. *Akali* volunteers toured the rural areas to mobilize support behind a list of 45 grievances centered on the core objectives of the ASR and reinforce Sikh communal solidarity – the corollary of which was hostility toward the perceived neglect and indifference of the central government (Kapur 1987). The spearhead of this mobilization was the All India Sikh Students Federation (AISSF), whose membership rapidly increased from 10,000 to 100,000 (Chima 1994) as it organized conferences, study circles, training camps and baptismal campaigns for educated Sikh youth (Telford 1992).

Violence entered this volatile situation in the form of Sikh–*Nirankari* clashes in 1978, followed by the murders of several Hindus, which were blamed by the government on Sikh extremists and Bhindrinwale, who was arrested and subsequently released (Gill and Singhal 1984). Inevitably, due to the *Nirankaris*' affiliation to the Congress Party and Bhindrinwale's strident sermon that preceded the attack on *Nirankaris* (Telford 1992), these events assumed a significance greater than their local impact. Violent demonstrations against merchants selling tobacco, alcohol and other 'vices' by pro-*Akali* mobs, and the assassination of *Arya Samaj* leader Lala Jagat Narain (by the same group responsible for the murder of *Nirankari* guru Baba Gurbachan Singh), added to the tension (Deol 2000). Similarly, the Congress (I) was also implicated in acts of political violence, including the kidnapping of pro-*Akali* members of the Delhi Sikh Gurdwaras Management Committee (DSGMC) and a rampage by police sent to arrest Bhindrinwale for Narain's assassination (Chima 2010). The *Dharma Yudh* (battle for righteousness) launched in August 1982 saw the arrest of over 30,000 protesters in two months (Deol 2000) – more than 200,000 would ultimately be arrested – and was coupled with a campaign of civil disobedience that included non-payment of taxes (Chima 1994), ultimately leading to the imposition of presidential rule in 1983, general breakdown in law and order, and a cycle of tit-for-tat killings.

As in the case of Sri Lanka, Sikh militants found the weight of the state's coercive organs arrayed against them, including extra-judicial killings in fake encounters where *Amritdhari* (baptized) Sikhs were arrested, tortured and murdered. The notoriously inefficient and frequently corrupt Indian judicial system created a perverse incentive for security forces to stage fake encounters to avoid the delays of the legal process (Singh 1998), which, in turn, created a moral vacuum that Sikh extremists could fill as they attended funerals and presented the deceased's families with *siropas* (robes of honor). Moreover, as Chima (2010) highlights, the more Mrs Gandhi and the central Congress (I) government attempted to usurp *Akali* dominance over Sikh institutions, the greater the interest shared by extremists, *Akalis* and Bhindrinwale against the Indian state, as each adopted more radical positions to distance themselves from the central government and assume the mantle of Sikhism's natural advocate and protector (Singh 1998).

The Congress (I) central government, for its part, was also constrained by the fear of religious violence spilling outside Punjab and of jeopardizing voter support amongst Hindus by being seen as too soft on Sikh separatists – concerns that led Mrs Gandhi to declare Punjab a 'disturbed area' and round up more than 4,000 Sikh activists and their supporters (Chima 2010). At the same time, however, Sikh separatism also provided an opportunity for Mrs Gandhi, who, mindful of a Hindu communal backlash building in the rest of the country, buttressed her political credentials by appearing tough on the *Akalis* (Singh 2007). Almost inevitably, anti-Sikh violence did spread beyond Punjab when, in 1984, Sikhs refused to observe a *bandh* (strike) declared by the *Punjab Hindu Suraksha Samiti*, leading to curfews in Punjab's four largest cities and the retaliatory killing of Sikhs in Haryana. This cycle of violence reached its apogee later in 1984 in anti-Sikh riots following Mrs Gandhi's assassination by her Sikh bodyguards (Chima 2010), which was itself 'payback' for Operation Bluestar earlier that year, which had resulted in the defilement of the *Harmandir Sahib* (Golden Temple) and hundreds of deaths (Deol 2000). The 1984 riots caused the death of several thousands of Sikhs and made an estimated 50,000–60,000 homeless – an outrage in which several top leaders of the Congress Party's Delhi Unit were named as organizers and participants (Singh 1985). Subsequent, and widely discredited, commissions and committees charged with investigating the violence exonerated the Congress Party and Delhi police of any responsibility (Kapur 1987).

The escalating cycle of violence, resort to unconstitutional means by the central government to emasculate its opponents, and ascent of separatist groups to a position of political and moral legitimacy that characterized Sikh separatism was also evident in Kashmir. Anti-government violence increased following the perceived rigging of legislative assembly elections in 1987 to ensure the defeat of a broad coalition of opposition groups known as the Muslim United Front (MUF). The elections had been touted as an important step in returning the state to normalcy after the 1984 dismissal of Chief Minister Farooq Abdullah at the behest of Mrs Gandhi. Farooq's dismissal had prompted widespread protests and had been followed by the suspension of the legislative assembly, imposition of governor's rule and then direct rule from New Delhi in 1986. The failure of the 1987 election to restore faith in constitutional government saw a breakdown in law and order, as young and mostly urban graduates and unemployed took up arms in support of independence from India. The transformation of the independence movement from mostly urban, secular and indigenous to rural, Islamist and foreign-controlled in the early 1990s was accompanied by a spike in violence on both sides. Increasingly, separatists were forced to resort to kidnapping and coercion to extort money and food from the local population (Baweja 1995; Ganguly 1997) as support for the conflict waned despite the equally reprehensible actions of many in the security forces, including torture, rape and extra-judicial killings (Asia Watch and Physicians for Human Rights 1993; Amnesty International 1995). Critical to the conflict entering a violent phase with widespread mobilization against Indian rule were excesses committed early in the conflict, including the 1990 Gawkadal massacre, in which at least 50 protesters were gunned down by security forces.

Additionally, there remains the use of the state's legislative apparatus to legalize state-sponsored violence and excess, inculcating a culture of impunity amongst security forces that undermines the legal-rational basis of the state and its claims to necessity and embodiment. The use of draconian security legislation such as India's Terrorist and Disruptive Activities (Prevention) Act (1985) (TADA) and various Armed Forces Special Powers Acts (AFSPA) in accompaniment to state-perpetrated human rights abuses will be discussed in greater detail in the subsequent chapter. Here, it will suffice to note that legislative overkill prefaced human rights abuses at a time when separatist violence, still in its infancy, was very much containable. In addition to federal legislation, state-specific acts have also facilitated crackdowns on separatist groups and anyone deemed hostile to the state, e.g., the Assam Maintenance of Public Order (Autonomous Districts) Act (1953) (Chasie and Hazarika 2009). The use of legislation to provide effective *carte blanche* for security forces in their operations against separatist groups has proven a valuable recruiting tool for separatists, as instances of forced entry, property damage, detention without a warrant and deaths in custody continue to rise (Chasie and Hazarika 2009). Of particular note is India's AFSPA, which comes into force when the state government declares an area 'disturbed' and bestows extraordinary powers on the armed forces to arrest a person on mere suspicion that they are planning a crime (without any incriminating evidence) and excuses military personnel from any criminal or civil responsibility in the cases of suspects' injury or death (Fernandes 2004).

Finally, separatist groups have become embroiled in wider (inter-)state conflicts, prompting severe repression that only hardens their resolve to secede. This is certainly the case with Kashmir and, to a lesser degree, Punjab. As border states on India's frontier with Pakistan (and, in Kashmir's case, China), they occupy a sensitive geo-strategic position that colors events there with a significance that extends beyond the narrow confines of local politics. For example, Kashmir's status as the only Muslim-majority state in secular India means that its retention by India is essential as a demonstration of the success of its founding national ideology. Of particular note within this ideological and geographic context are events surrounding Bangladesh's 1971 war of independence that were to prove pivotal to the Bangladeshi government's policy toward the CHT. During the conflict, the tribes' loyalties were divided between the Pakistan government and *Mukti Bahini* (Freedom Fighters) (Hussain 1971). Subsequently, Bengali freedom fighters began to attack those tribes that had collaborated with the Pakistani regime, engaging in torture and the destruction of property in a campaign of violence that climaxed in February 1972. This prompted the leading political figure from the CHT, Manabendra Larma, to call on President Sheikh Mujibur Rahman (Mujib) to award the CHT its own legislative assembly, limit the migration of outsiders to the region, and provide other constitutional and legislative safeguards for the CHT's autonomy (Ahsan and Chakma 1989). The explicit rejection of these demands, and the suggestion by Mujib that the tribes should forego their ethnic identities by merging with the Bengalis, convinced Larma to form an umbrella party, the *Parbatya Chattagram Jana Samhati Samiti* (PCJSS), with an armed wing, the *Gono Mukti Fouj* (People's Liberation Army) or *Shanti Bahini* (Peace Force) (Shelley 1986). Thus, mobilization against the nascent Bangladeshi state began as a response to a campaign of violence and perceptions of economic and cultural domination as class, ethnicity and post-secession prospects for economic development were blended to define the movement's ideology (Ahmed 1993; Kamal 1995) as it benefited from access to large caches of arms and ammunition left by the fleeing Pakistani Army (Van Schendel 1992).

Conclusion

While the institution of statehood and its corollary of territorial sovereignty may be relatively modern innovations, the search for order and security through the regulation of human conduct is timeless. Similarly, the questions of how a community is to be constituted, and in whose interests it will be governed, have been fundamental problems of human existence throughout recorded history. Accordingly, the state's legitimacy rests on an ability to provide the prerequisites for human security and flourishing at least as effectively as any putative alternative to the territorially bounded, self-defined community that is the state. While this might at first appear an unduly tenuous and abstract foundation upon which to constitute a political order, the high costs of rebellion mean that the state's failure to meet the requirements of embodiment and necessity must be profound in order to mobilize public opinion behind a mass uprising. Consequently, most individuals and groups restrict their activism to non-conformity and civil disobedience through acts such as tax avoidance, criminality and public protest, eschewing the risks of armed insurrection. Only where the perception of grievance is adequately sustained and intense will circumstances favor organized rebellion. In the case of separatist groups in South Asia, the antecedents of separatist violence are varied. However, underlying each of the movements considered here is a perception of grievance with a historical pedigree rooted in

62 Genesis of conflict

political structures that pre-date the parent state. While the origins of this perception vary markedly, the depth of alienation and the ham-fisted response of the parent state, in combination with factors such as external assistance and leadership, combine to make secession a viable and attractive proposition in the minds of many. The following chapter examines how the move to rebellion intersects with a range of factors to guide the conduct of separatists and the parent state in often surprising and contradictory ways.

3 Conduct of conflict

Introduction

The previous chapter explored the implications of state sovereignty for understanding the causes of separatism, advancing the claim that the exercise and justification of sovereignty dis-/incentivize forms of action and therefore cannot be divorced from the question of why groups pursue a separatist agenda. Consequently, in order to adequately explain separatism, it is necessary to first investigate the function, exercise and justification of state sovereignty, since if states did not exercise sovereignty, then separatism, in the form that we understand it, would not occur. The significance of this observation becomes clear when we recognize that separatism does not constitute a rejection of sovereignty, but is instead an attempt to exercise it by redrawing the state's geographical boundaries to exclude the group and its members – a tacit acknowledgment of sovereignty's binary and exclusive character. Here, the analogy with divorce begins to break down, as one can, indeed, get divorced without remarrying or acknowledging the necessity or utility of marriage. In contrast, a group cannot claim a right to secede and form a state of its own (or join another state) without *a fortiori* endorsing the institution of statehood.

This chapter continues this analysis by examining how the institution of sovereignty influences not only the decision to secede, but also the tactics employed in pursuit of this aim. Particular attention is also paid to the interactional and iterative character of separatist tactics vis-à-vis the response of the parent state and how each impacts the other. Returning to the twin attributes of embodiment and necessity introduced previously, the chapter explores the fine line walked by separatists between demonstrating the state's ineffectiveness and redundancy, on the one hand, and alienating their target population, on the other. The indiscriminate use of military force, destruction of essential infrastructure and resulting damage to the local economy enable separatist groups to demonstrate government impotence, thereby questioning the state's claims to necessity, while also creating a void that separatists can fill to validate their claim as the true representatives of the local population. However, this strategy, if not judiciously pursued (and it rarely is), runs the risk of delegitimizing separatist claims through forms of action that, while beneficial to attaining a position of military superiority, may be contrary to the long-term interests of the populace. Similarly, states frequently also employ tactics of 'controlled disorder' to demonstrate their superior military and economic resources, but in so doing often contradict the legal-rational basis of their legitimacy, unwittingly boosting separatist mobilization. Of particular note in the context of South Asia have been the resort to draconian security legislation, the outsourcing of security functions to vigilantes, and the indiscriminate use of military force, which have undermined the legitimacy of the state by empowering local, extra-state sovereignty networks.

As in the examination of the reasons why separatism develops in some groups but not others, it is important to bear in mind the complex inter-linkages between different factors that influence how a conflict plays out. Political, economic, social, cultural and other features influence perceptions of reality and the manner in which actors interpret and respond to events and dis-/incentives. For example, Barbora (2006) notes how the geographical and existential isolation of separatist-affected regions informs a quasi-colonial discourse whereby separatism is often attributed by the parent state to a lack of development and security that can only be remedied through the region's successful reintegration within the national framework. Consequently, those who question the prevailing political order (including, but not limited to, separatists) are frequently portrayed as victims of Machiavellian plots hatched by foreign powers, ethnic entrepreneurs and anachronistic malfeasants hankering for impossible control over imagined or historically defunct political communities. In this manner, even reasonable demands for reform may be delegitimized, as the state dismisses separatism as the handiwork of deviants seeking to destabilize society. In contrast, separatists typically view attempts by the state to reassert its authority as an escalation of conflict that validates their own claims of government malfeasance. The result is a series of counter-claims and tit-for-tat violence described by Barbora (2006) as the 'politics of controlled disorder,' in which armed intervention, instability, the threat of violence, attrition and de-/escalation are the norm. New centers of control and authority emerge from the state security apparatus – individual rights are over-ridden and civilian institutions rendered toothless and irrelevant – as powerful military and political interests usurp authority. India provides perhaps the most compelling example of this process: separatist-affected regions frequently have their legislative assemblies dissolved, central rule is imposed, and former military or intelligence figures are appointed as governors.

The discourse of development that links public funding, governance and loyalty to the state subverts the democratic concept of equal citizenship by portraying residents of separatist regions as marginal, un(der)-developed and on the periphery of civil society both politically and economically. It also entrenches elites, exacerbates corrupt networks of privilege and power through the disbursement of central funds and contracts (many of which are squandered or appropriated by economically dominant actors such as cronies of the ruling elite, the landed aristocracy and other propertied classes) and aggravates the sense of grievance motivating separatist sentiment. Furthermore, the poverty, lack of investment, retarded development and limited economic opportunities that characterize many separatist regions, and which are worsened by separatist violence, serve the economic and political establishment by adding to the enormous pool of cheap labor in South Asian states (Das 2007). Military suppliers, construction contractors and others benefit economically from conflict and have an interest in its continuation. Disorder, lack of effective enforcement of workers' rights, displacement of significant portions of the population (who effectively become domestic economic refugees) and the other consequences of conflict disempower individuals, leaving them (more) vulnerable to mistreatment and exploitation. On a macro level, centralization and the militarization of significant sectors of the economy and public life, combined with an increased developmental role for the state – e.g., in (re)building infrastructure for agricultural and industrial development – also creates dependencies on central funding and administration. This works to the parent state's advantage by tying the region's economic welfare to central government largesse, incentivizing maintenance of the political status quo and rewarding government supporters in separatist-affected regions with positions of influence in centrally funded projects and agencies.

The aim of this chapter is to explore these, and other, linkages between violence and the factors that influence the trajectory of separatist conflict. The following section explores how both states and separatists can benefit from sowing disorder and the perception of powerlessness that it generates. This is followed by a discussion of the use of legislative power by states to address the causes and consequences of separatist violence, including draconian security legislation and the outsourcing of state functions to non-state actors. External assistance and intervention from other states are also examined as being important to understanding both the tactics and the longevity of many of South Asia's separatist conflicts. Finally, internal disputes and violent conflict within separatist movements and between political actors are examined before some concluding remarks.

Return to the state of nature

Although not all separatist struggles are characterized by violence or public disorder, many, particularly those in South Asia, have been. Moreover, numerous violent acts committed by both state and separatist actors appear contradictory to their stated aims. Indiscriminate violence and the destruction of essential infrastructure often confer little long-term strategic advantage, but alienate important public support and invite more severe counter-measures from opponents. At its peak, this cycle of violence can mirror the Hobbesian state of nature from which the state is hailed as providing an effective escape but which, perversely, provides heightened justification for increased repression. Similarly, the success of separatists in establishing an alternative jurisdiction of sovereignty – with many of the public institutions and services characteristic of a functioning state – may engender conflict by heightening the state's fear of replacement and redundancy, leading to further repression and violence. Moreover, the resulting lawlessness reduces incentives for investment in physical and human capital (Lacina 2007) for both public and private sector agencies. On the one hand, lawlessness and government repression may result in an important symbolic and tactical victory for separatists by validating their claim that the state has ceased to occupy a position of moral legitimacy. Retreat by the state also creates a power vacuum that separatists are able to occupy to buttress their claims of legitimacy vis-à-vis the region's inhabitants. On the other hand, however, evocation of pre-political society through the varied imagery of lawlessness and separatist brutality may, under the right circumstances, bolster state authority where there is a widespread belief that the state, through its superior resources, is better able to secure a return to normalcy and provide for the long-term welfare of the region's inhabitants.

To explain, targeted and random violence demonstrates the state's powerlessness to protect both high-value targets and ordinary citizens, creating a physical and ideological space for the separatists to occupy. Consequently, security forces are frequently targeted in densely populated localities where civilian casualties will be maximized to alienate popular support for the government. The declining authority of the state, and the increasingly arbitrary and brutal nature of its repression, combine with the other effects of conflict – including unemployment, diminished economic opportunities, and disruption in essential services such as education, electricity, health care, clean drinking water and physical security – to create an environment reminiscent of Hobbes' state of nature. In Balochistan, for example, effective leadership and easy availability of heavy weaponry have seen violence spread across the province as government installations and personnel are targeted by separatists (Khan 2009). In addition to essential infrastructure – such as gas pipelines, railway tracks, bridges, power transmission lines, telephone exchanges, and military and government installations (Bansal 2006) – the killing of professors and teachers has rendered schools and universities nonfunctional (Siddiqi 2012) as separatists attempt to demonstrate the state's fragility and impotence.

In other cases, minority groups – particularly Hindus, who represent not only a political and economic ruling class but also the Indian state – have been targeted. Fearing violence, Kashmiri Pandits (Hindus) numbering in the tens of thousands left the Valley in the 1990s for refugee camps in Jammu and other locations, where many still languish. Similarly, Hindu traders in Punjab were the victims of extortion, looting, kidnapping and murder at the hands of separatist groups that forced many of them to leave (Bal 2005), mirroring the fate of many Sinhalese in Sri Lanka's northern and eastern provinces, while in the northeast of India since 2005, ULFA and other groups have increasingly targeted Hindi speakers, especially Bengali migrants (Goswami 2011). In discussion of India's northeast, Lacina (2007) notes how inter-communal attacks – in conjunction with local provision of protection, political extortion and crime – feed the cycle of violence, leading to the multiplication of violent organizations. Moreover, she observes, where the rule of law is absent or ineffective, this violence may continue even after mass insurgency has been curtailed, raising the question of to what degree violence is ideologically inspired rather than mere opportunism and criminality. Similarly, Pettigrew (1987) claims that many of the killings in Punjab between December 1983 and June 1984 were a consequence of private vendettas, as political activism degenerated into banditry and criminal activity that turned the local population against the separatists (Puri *et al.* 1999; Chima 2002). Interestingly, Bal (2005), in discussion of the targeting of Hindu traders and business people in Punjab, also observes that after the Hindus' exit, separatists harassed Sikh businesses to extort money in the name of protection. Singh (1998) attributes this descent into criminality – which also afflicted Kashmiri separatist groups (Schofield 1996) – to an absence of coherent leadership and unity amongst the various separatist groups, which lacked any clear objectives or strategy beyond separation from India. The importance of unity and leadership in avoiding the pitfalls of criminality is given additional weight by Sri Lanka's Liberation Tigers of Tamil Eelam (LTTE), which employed often brutal and indiscriminate violence in support of its aims, but whose intolerance of rival centers of power and iron grip on its cadres allowed it to rein in any criminality that might alienate popular support.

Typically, criminality develops over time, as a group's prospects of success diminish and the ideologues who initiated the struggle for independence are incarcerated or killed. In the early stages of conflict, when the violence is more planned and politically motivated, the process is ideational, and individuals in the conflict zone – drawn into the violence as victims, participants and witnesses – are invited to imagine a counter-factual reality of an alternative political order in which the separatists exercise sovereignty. The status of this alternative order as a prerequisite to ending the violence is implicit in the separatists' avowed intention to continue the conflict irrespective of the costs (to themselves and others), until their aims are realized. A key factor in this strategy is the gaps in the effectiveness of state sovereignty that separatists are able to create and exploit. The retreat of state authority from the provision of essential services gives the lie to the state's claim of necessity; life continues – albeit usually not as before – without a descent into the Hobbesian state of nature. The absence of police and state security apparatuses, electricity cuts, food shortages, closure of medical facilities and so forth place strains on the civilian population, but typically do not result in widespread disorder or the breakdown of civil society.

Moreover, as the state retreats, separatists and their affiliated groups emerge to fill the void, to demonstrate both the state's ineffectiveness and their own preeminence. Perversely, this occupation of territorial and institutional space by separatists frequently engenders more government repression, which further alienates the target population from the state. As Deol (2000) observes, because a weakened government has greater difficulty in compromising with minorities, this creates a perverse incentive to take a harder line against opponents and encourage ethnic strife in order to win support from the majority community. Moreover, in addition to the high financial and military burdens that a policy of widespread repression entails, the brutalization of the local population and attendant human rights abuses replicate the methods of the 'terrorists' from which the state ostensibly exists to protect citizens. Consequently, in adopting a policy of repression, the state runs the risk of undermining its legal-rational foundations – effectively 'throwing the baby out with the bath water' – and validating separatist claims vis-à-vis the illegitimacy of state sovereignty (Singh 1996). On the other hand, however, the superior resources of the state to manage both its campaign of repression and the disorder that it engenders, when compared with the relatively meagre resources available to the separatists, mean that the separatists, despite winning the ideological war, may nonetheless fail to obtain victory on the ground.

This process of using violence to sow discontent and disorder with the aim of appropriating state sovereignty is best exemplified by the LTTE, which succeeded in creating a *de facto* state with borders, a functioning civil administration (which oversaw transportation, taxation, banking, broadcasting, education, health, sports, farming, environment and industry), law courts, police, navy and air forces (Feith 2013). These services were funded in large measure by a complex system of taxation, which rivaled that of many developed states and included a range of direct and indirect taxes in areas controlled by the LTTE and the Sri Lankan government. This included income taxes, sharing of resources produced or gathered (e.g., by farmers and fishermen), customs fees on goods being brought into LTTE-controlled territory, vehicle registration tax and a tax on property transactions in Jaffna (Stokke 2006).

Indeed, so effective was the LTTE that it even succeeded in hijacking a deal between the Sri Lankan and Zimbabwean governments for US$3 million worth of mortars by bribing officials to allow their transportation on a freighter that delivered them directly to LTTE cadres (Chalk 2003). This effectiveness contrasted with the inefficiency and corruption displayed by many government institutions, especially law enforcement and the judiciary (Sambandan 2004). Demonstrating that it could simultaneously fight a war against the Indian and Sri Lankan militaries while administering territory, the LTTE was able to convincingly claim (following the withdrawal of Indian peacekeepers) that it had defeated the world's fourth largest army (Feith 2013). These successes, combined with a strict moral discipline amongst its military cadre of no drinking, smoking or premarital sex, assisted the LTTE to demonstrate to Tamils and the international community the feasibility of a separate Tamil state in Sri Lanka (Feith 2013). This public relations success had a positive effect on levels of support extended to the LTTE from Sri Lankan Tamils and diasporas in countries such as Canada and Great Britain, validating the LTTE's cultural concept of citizenship, which it promulgated in contrast to the Sri Lankan state's national citizenship (Sørensen 2008). In this manner, the LTTE's state- and nation-building projects were effectively linked, as the LTTE successfully promulgated a vision of itself as the sole representative of Tamil nationalism. Stokke (2006) eloquently summarizes the complex inter-relationship between the twin factors of embodiment and necessity, and the essential role of violent force in this relationship, that enabled the LTTE to maintain an aura of political and moral legitimacy amongst Sri Lankan Tamils:

In general terms it can be observed that [the] LTTE's state building is closely linked to their political project of representing the Tamil nation and delivering self-determination for it. On the one hand, it is contingent on the discursive framing of [the] LTTE as the sole representative of Tamil nationalism. On the other hand, [the] LTTE's hegemony in Tamil politics is also based on their military capacity to confront the Sri Lankan government and provide a degree of external security, as well as their repressive capacity in regard to internal anti-LTTE political and military forces. Thus, [the] LTTE's state power is contingent on their ability to inscribe themselves in a Tamil national-popular will and their ability to apply force to maintain external and internal security. In other words, the emerging LTTE state formation rests on 'hegemony protected by the armour of coercion.'

Throughout its history, indiscriminate and often brutal violence was a key tool in the LTTE's struggle for supremacy. It ruthlessly assassinated rival Tamil and Sinhalese figures it regarded as a threat (often killing innocent civilians in the process), conscripted child soldiers and persecuted Muslims in the north and east of the country (Feith 2013). These tactics were mirrored by government forces, which frequently failed to differentiate between LTTE cadres and civilians in rebel-controlled areas and treated every Tamil as a real or potential terrorist. The scale, organization and longevity of these practices, which were extended to Tamils living throughout the island, indicate a high degree of planning and centralized control. Government assassination squads operating from notorious white vans roamed the country and systematically eliminated potential recruits and those suspected of sympathizing with the LTTE (DeVotta 2009). This was combined with a culture of impunity in government-controlled areas in the north and east of the country, where extortion, rape, theft, murder and omnipresent checkpoints cowed the local population while restricting the mobility of the LTTE, explaining the relative absence of suicide bombings in the south during the latter stage of the conflict (DeVotta 2009).

While other separatist groups in South Asia have not been as successful as the LTTE in establishing a parallel state, some have come close. Sikh separatists in Punjab, for example, ran *Khalsa panchayats* (local assemblies), which were used by rural populations to settle marriage, land and other disputes – an indication of the ineffectiveness that characterized state institutions (Deol 2000). Similarly, Lacina (2007) observes how in India's northeast, clashes occur due to competition between separatist organizations for access to important smuggling routes and resources, and as a consequence of the provision by these groups of security and vigilante justice in the face of intercommunal brutalities. As in the cases of Punjab and Kashmir, where clashes between different militant groups (which also operated as a kind of 'rent a gang') were common, the ineffectiveness of legal institutions allows extra-state actors to gain power and wealth by filling the void left by the state. Acts such as voter intimidation, land dispossession, and retribution for crimes committed (both real and imaginary) lead to the multiplication of violent groups and reinforcement of the cycle of insecurity and competitive ethnic, religious and economic mobilization that underpins separatism.

Moreover, in their campaign for independent statehood, Sikh separatists initially benefited from the support of elements in the central government due to the contextualization of the struggle for Khalistan within the national political agenda. In addition to splitting the *Akalis*, support for Sikh extremists was also used by Congress Party leader and Prime Minister, Indira Gandhi, to bolster her party's credentials in India's Hindu heartland as the enormous military and other resources of the Indian state were bought to bear on separatists in both Punjab and Kashmir. As states on the geographic and cultural periphery of Hindu India, dominated by religious minorities, both Punjab and Kashmir provided an opportunity for the Congress Party to demonstrate a commitment to its secularist ideology that was frequently squandered through the temptation to mobilize popular sentiment in the Hindu heartland by appearing tough on minorities' demands for greater political independence.

Manipulation by central governments of internal discord and ethnic violence to further their own agenda is not uncommon, while resort to violent tactics by separatists may also be explicated in terms of rational self-interest. Violence (or the fear of it) facilitates group mobilization, recruitment and compliance with the group's edicts, which in turn enhances the group's capacity for collective action, its ability to deliver on past promises and, therefore, the rewards of membership. A landmark study by Puri *et al.* (1999), for example, found that the majority of Sikh militants were either school drop-outs or illiterates, with only around 10 percent having been committed to the cause of Khalistan or motivated by police excesses. Rather, many had joined the movement 'for fun' or to further their private interests by making money and living an adventurous life. While some scholars, e.g., Jeffrey (1994) and Oberoi (1987), have questioned these assertions, others, such as Bal (2005), observed the low socio-economic status of many Sikh militants, noting that their activities soon degenerated into extortions, lootings, kidnappings and murders, the proceeds of which had a very favorable impact on the socio-economic conditions of militants' families. Sikh separatism had its roots in religious revivalism, moderation and abstention from vice – messages that resonated in a society where rapid economic modernization and urbanization had shaken customary norms in the form of alcohol, tobacco, narcotics and lewd cinema (Singh 2007). Like other separatist movements, the Khalistan cause proffered a counter-factually superior alternative to the state by addressing issues of injustice, bias and underdevelopment, which in Punjab manifested as alcoholism, domestic violence and dowry disputes. The separatists' ability to address these issues efficiently and effectively through a parallel system of justice and security stood in stark contrast to the over-burdened and corrupt government courts and highlighted the state's inadequacies (Deol 2000). In conjunction with other policies, such as banning the sale of meat, tobacco and alcohol, the separatists were able to bolster their credentials while denying the government its biggest sources of revenue (Chima 2010).

A key consideration that informs the effectiveness of separatist violence is the response of the state. Whereas a failure to respond sufficiently forcefully may signal a surrender of authority, too strong a response may grant the separatists a degree of legitimacy by signaling that the state considers the struggle for sovereignty to exist on a 'special plane' where normal political and legal constraints do not apply (Lacina 2007). Effective counter-insurgency is acknowledged to be a difficult task that requires security personnel to act as policemen, guerrilla fighters, intelligence officers, peace negotiators and providers of humanitarian aid. This, in turn, requires initiative, motivation, passion, terrain awareness, permanency of tenure, effective knowledge and the ability to build local networks of trust (Gompert 2007). Although South Asian states initially responded poorly to separatist violence, they have shown an ability to adapt tactically and strategically over time. In Punjab, heavy-handed police tactics included extra-judicial killings in fake encounters where *Amritdhari* (baptized) Sikhs were arrested, tortured and murdered, polarizing public opinion against the state and bringing the political mainstream and extremists closer together (Chima 2010). Of particular note are Operation Bluestar (June 8, 1984), in which over 5,000 Sikhs are estimated to have died (Singh 1990; Singh 2007), and subsequent anti-Sikh riots following the assassination of Mrs Gandhi, in which an additional 4,000–5,000 were killed and many more made homeless (Singh 1985). As in the case of Kashmir, Punjab was bought under President's rule (from May 1987 to February 1992), and the state was quasi-militarized through the suspension of normal political processes and draconian law and order measures as virtual civil war conditions prevailed (Singh 1996). Whereas in both regions counter-insurgency operations initially fell to the often poorly equipped and trained Central Reserve Police Force (CRPF), Border Security Force (BSF) and, later, Rashtriya Rifles (RR) (Goswami 2011), these units were augmented with irregular 'hit squads' to infiltrate and liquidate terrorist cells (Singh 1996). In addition, the local law and order agencies were empowered, with police personnel in Punjab increasing from 20,000 in the early 1980s to approximately 60,000 in 1992. At the height of conflict in both states, the summary execution of suspects in faked encounters to avoid the delays of the legal process was common (Singh 1998), while police and militants would often masquerade as each other, engaging in extortion, rape, looting, arson and murder to enrich themselves while attempting to discredit their opponents (Deol 2000). A similar strategy of repression, implemented through massive search-and-arrest operations, was also employed against ULFA in Assam with attendant incidences of torture, deaths in custody, and the curtailment of civil liberties and press freedom (Baruah 1994). Additionally, from 1967 to 1972, 80 percent of the Mizo population (240,000 people) were uprooted from their homes and placed in 102 new villages known as 'protected and progressive villages' to deny insurgents the support and resources necessary to continue their campaign. However, the policy also disrupted traditional agricultural practices and ways of life, causing considerable resentment against the Indian state (Goswami 2011).

In circumstances such as those that prevailed in Punjab and Kashmir at the height of their respective insurgencies, the level of violence and lawlessness can approximate a Hobbesian state of nature. The brutalization of a population in this manner is calculated to induce a degree of war weariness such that any settlement is preferable to the status quo. The difficulty for separatists, however, is that the superior resources of the state give it an advantage by enabling it to offer rewards and incentives to the local population that the separatists cannot match. By providing civilians with benefits (including selective provision of security), the state can obtain a degree of cooperation and compliance beyond that which separatists are able to achieve through coercion. Subsequently, as public support for the separatists wanes and rates of defection climb, the state can demilitarize the region and implement a return to normalcy by, for example, restoring authority to the local police and negotiating with moderate elements amongst the separatists to address grievances. The difficulty with this strategy, as Lacina (2009) highlights, is that the selective provision to, and empowerment of, local actors and elites may promote corruption and localized political violence rather than reduce it. In contrast, Goswami (2011) argues that restraint by state forces and provision of security have built a level of trust between civilians and the army in Nagaland. In other cases, such as Balochistan, the state has pursued harsh measures such as the murder of prominent Baloch political leaders (Fair 2012) and other human rights abuses (Greene 2012), including abduction, torture and extrajudicial execution (Siddiqi 2012), but lacked the resources to adequately follow up this campaign by re-engaging with civil society – or what is left of it – by providing sufficient inducements to re-establish its moral authority (Khan 2009).

Finally, of note has been the state's recourse to sub-state actors to enforce its authority in remote or difficult-to-govern areas. The Indian government's establishment of village defense committees, for example, in far-flung rural areas of Jammu and Kashmir was an attempt to mitigate separatist violence perpetrated in remote locations far from security posts. Villagers were provided with wireless sets, small arms and basic training to defend themselves from separatist attack. This policy was complemented by the co-option of former combatants into the state security apparatus in the form of militants who had been 'turned' to the government side – so-called *Ikhwan* – who were employed as a source of intelligence and enforcement. The historical irony of a post-colonial state enforcing its authority by contracting out essential functions to sub-state actors should not be under-stated. The separatist insurgency in Kashmir has its roots in the pre-independence political artifact of a princely state where the British contracted out sovereign functions to native rulers in return for their loyalty in an arrangement that was formalized under the doctrine of Paramountcy. In the case of Jammu and Kashmir, this resulted in the anomaly of a Muslim-majority region with a Hindu Maharaja who, when forced to make a decision as to whether his state was to become a part of India or Pakistan, prevaricated and then had the decision made for him by tribal invasion and subsequent military intervention. The incorporation of Indian-administered Jammu and Kashmir included Article 370, which provided the state with certain protections and entitlements that afforded it a degree of independence unavailable to other states and territories in the Indian Union in an effective renegotiation of sovereignty. At the same time, however, Jammu and Kashmir's economic sovereignty was significantly compromised by its dependence upon central government handouts as its mostly rural economy languished. Thus, the state's decision at the height of the separatist insurgency to outsource its monopoly on the legitimate use of violence was merely the latest manifestation of a series of incomplete and overlapping sovereignties that had perpetuated conflict in the region for many years. The authority of a native durbar and colonial administration was replaced by that of the Indian state, the Jammu and Kashmir government, and local networks that variously opposed state sovereignty, supported it or had been temporarily co-opted by it, and which frequently structured the lives of ordinary Kashmiris more profoundly than official state institutions.

The use of legislative power to coerce and co-opt

A monopoly on the legitimate use of violence is a corollary of sovereignty that occurs as a consequence of the state's legislative monopoly, which is ostensibly governed by the legal-rational contract between governed and government. The use by the state of its legislative powers in this regard constitutes an ultimately contradictory attempt to legislate extra-judicial methods to combat separatism; the nominally democratic and representative institutions entrusted with upholding the principles of inalienable individual rights, popular sovereignty and equal citizenship enact legislation that underscores their own irrelevance by arrogating sovereign powers to non-representative and undemocratic bodies. Residents of conflict-affected regions do not elect to have discriminatory central legislation or direct rule applied to them, are not free to reject it, and suffer disproportionately from its burdens while having their individual rights circumscribed in a manner that the inhabitants of other regions do not (despite the fact that separatists often export their campaign of violence to high-value targets – particularly capital cities – outside their home region). Thus, the state's virtue of necessity is subverted as violence is perpetuated, and extra-legal violations of individual rights committed, by institutions that derive their legitimacy from the claim that state sovereignty is necessary as a means of enforcing individual rights to ensure prosperity and security. Moreover, the brutal response of separatists to this betrayal only reinforces the state's determination to meet violence with violence, while validating its claim that separatist violence constitutes an existential threat to the state's integrity that requires an extraordinary response.

In India, federal legislation such as the Armed Forces (Special Powers) Act (AFSPA) (1958), Maintenance of Internal Security Act and the Unlawful Activities (Prevention) Act (ULP) (1967), Terrorist and Disruptive Activities (Prevention) Act (TADA) (1985–95) and Prevention of Terrorism Act (POTA) (2002), in addition to state-specific legislation – e.g., the Assam Disturbed Areas Act (1955) and Jammu And Kashmir Disturbed Areas Act (1992) – make it a crime to support secessionist groups and give military and police personnel extraordinary powers to search, detain and use lethal force while at the same time shielding them from judicial review; effectively freeing security forces from fear of being held accountable for their actions and creating a reservoir of extra-legal powers that may be used by office-holders against opponents to settle old scores. Similar legislation was passed in other South Asian states to combat violent separatism, such as the Armed Forces Ordinance (1998), Suppression of Terrorist Activities Ordinance (1975) and Anti-Terrorism Act (1997) in Pakistan, the Prevention of Terrorism Act (1978) in Sri Lanka, and Bangladesh's Anti-Terrorism Act (2009).

The ULP of 1967 constituted the first comprehensive federal legislation to specifically address problems of separatism, and was motivated by the Naga and Mizo armed insurgencies. However, it is the AFSPA (1958) that is the subject of most disapprobation. Moreover, as Chasie and Hazarika (2009) highlight, it is important to understand the legal and operational linkages between ostensibly independent pieces of legislation. The ULP, for example, strengthened AFSPA by defining unlawful organizations and facilitating bans on them while empowering the government to control these groups' use of funds and limiting freedoms of expression, association and movement (Chasie and Hazarika 2009). Moreover, AFSPA can only come into effect after an area has been declared 'disturbed' by either the state or central government, requiring the deployment of the army and other central security forces. It authorizes the armed forces to arrest individuals on suspicion of planning a crime, empowers soldiers to shoot to kill, and then protects them against any prosecution other than by the central government (Fernandes 2004), including in the case of damage to property, detention without a warrant and custodial deaths (Chasie and Hazarika 2009). The outcome of these legislative 'solutions' was to bestow upon the Indian state a permanent counter-insurgency capacity, but also to normalize and embed within its legal fabric rejections of Indian sovereignty that separatist groups could construe as *de facto* endorsement of their claims.

Equally notable have been attempts by the state to alter its legal-rational framework so as to emasculate or incorporate separatist demands constitutionally. Following India and Pakistan's 1947 partition, the specter of secession combined with the difficulty of accommodating unity and diversity within the same polity (Racine 2013): imperatives that clashed with the aspirations of many local communities for greater autonomy. The result has been a series of legal-rational measures adopted by South Asian states to address threats to their territorial integrity, consisting in: constitutionally guaranteed preferential treatment (e.g., Kashmir's special status and Article 370); negotiation; economic incentive (e.g., special economic packages to Punjab); force; and moral argument (claims that minorities are safer in a multicultural, secular state). Pakistan, with its national ideology founded upon the provision of a homeland for South Asia's Muslims, has been particularly loath to recognize sub-groups' socio-cultural or linguistic identity or politically accommodate them on the basis of their ethnicity, preferring instead an emphasis on religious identity to the exclusion of linguistic and ethno-nationalist cleavages (Bansal 2008). Similarly, while Sri Lanka passed the 13th amendment to its constitution to implement the Indo-Lanka Accord, which required the establishment of a provincial council in each of the country's nine provinces and consolidation of the eastern and northern provinces under a single provincial council (Oberst 1988), widespread mistrust and a failure to adequately include the LTTE in the negotiating process effectively ended the peace process.

Once again, it is India that best epitomizes the strategy of legislative accommodation and compromise, born, in no small measure, from its secularist, legal-rational national identity, which attempts to create shared bonds of loyalty amongst a citizenry characterized by remarkable diversity, but which sits ill at ease with the observant, conservative and traditional realities of daily life. On the one hand, this tension can create problems. For example, Deol (2000) highlights how the secularist credentials of India's anti-colonial movements conflicted with the central role that religion continued to play in the lives of most Indians. This tension is exemplified by Article 25 of the Indian Constitution, which states that reference to Hindu or Hinduism should be construed as incorporating individuals of the Buddhist, Jain and Sikh faiths – leading to protests from some of these groups that object to being categorized as 'Hindu.' On the other hand, it is also true that India's secularist ideology has permitted it more flexibility in making concessions to religious and ethnic minorities, e.g., Mrs Gandhi's decision to remove tobacco, liquor and meat vendors from the area surrounding the Golden Temple, and allowing the transmission of *kirtan* by an All-India radio station and Sikhs to carry their *kirpans* on domestic flights (Chima 2010).

Of particular note has been the Indian strategy to grant restive regions statehood. As early as 1947, the interim government had appointed a sub-committee to the Constituent Assembly (the North-East Frontier (Assam) Tribal and Excluded Areas Committee), which recommended the establishment of autonomous district councils to provide representative structures to tribal groups. The recommendation was later incorporated into Article 244 (2) of the Sixth Schedule of the Indian Constitution (discussed below) (Goswami 2011). Subsequently, India's reorganization of states in the 1950–60s along linguistic lines succeeded in defusing Tamil separatism through the creation of the state of Tamil Nadu. Other, similar examples include the Marathi language and the state of Maharashtra, Gujarati and Gujarat, Oriya and Orissa, Telugu and Andhra Pradesh, Kannada and Karnataka, Malayalam and Kerala (Racine 2013). These grants of substantial autonomy (short of independent statehood) worked to defuse sub-national mobilization amongst major language groups. Kohli (1997) attributes this success to the growing salience of *realpolitik* concerns within India's federal political framework, where ethnic mobilization is an ineffective means of addressing the policy matters that occupy state governments. However, this strategy of accommodation came under threat in the 1980s, as Mrs Gandhi actively intervened in state-level politics – manipulating party machinations, dismissing elected governments, imposing central rule and flirting with pro-Hindu themes to recreate a new national electoral coalition – to portray dissenting minorities as victims of outside interference or pre-modern artifacts hankering for a return to past or imagined homelands (Barbora 2006). This boded ill for states, such as Jammu and Kashmir and Punjab, with considerable non-Hindu populations that did not fit within the idiom of increasingly right-wing Hindu populism (Kohli 1997). Consequently, previous arrangements such as Jammu and Kashmir's Article 370 and Article 25 of the Indian Constitution, which, while controversial, had offered a degree of formal autonomy and inclusion to Kashmiri Muslims and Punjabi Sikhs, respectively, now appeared hollow and inadequate.

While the Indian government has refrained from intervening in the structure of political parties in the northeast – unlike Punjab and Kashmir (Misra 2001) – some question whether devolution and the creation of new states has solved (or simply shifted) conflict. Lacina (2007), for instance, points out that modifying state boundaries and creating special autonomy arrangements gives ethnic elites the incentive to seek their own fiefdoms. Similarly, Misra (2001) claims that the creation of new states has encouraged new minorities to rebel (against both the newly created state and the federal government), e.g., Bodo separatism in Assam and Chakma separatism in Mizoram (Misra 2001), while Barbora (2006) highlights how the ambiguity of Indian policy in the northeast frequently undermines effective accountability and democratic practice, opening the door for criminal networks and other sub-state actors to assume positions of authority in newly created states and local administrations.

Indeed, the northeast has seen a bewildering series of agreements and constitutional provisions to address separatist demands and maintain peace, with mixed success. Nagaland, for example, was afforded special status under Article 371 (A) of the Indian Constitution, requiring ratification by the state assembly of any Act of Parliament that affected the religious or social practices of the Nagas. Included within the scope of Article 371 (A) are Naga customary law and procedure, administration of civil and criminal justice, and ownership and transfer of land and resources. Subsequently, statehood was granted to Nagaland in 1963, although disagreement continues over the state's borders due to lingering demands for the inclusion of contiguous Naga-inhabited areas in neighboring states of Assam and Manipur (Chasie and Hazarika 2009). This was followed by the North Eastern Areas (Re-Organization) Act (1971), which granted statehood to Manipur, Meghalaya and Tripura and Union Territory status to Arunachal Pradesh and Mizoram (Goswami 2011), with Mizoram becoming a state in 1986 after the Mizo Accord.

However, in numerous cases, these devolutionary amendments failed to stem conflict or were sabotaged by inter-group rivalry, poor implementation and other problems. Bodos, for example, were encouraged to agitate for greater autonomy after witnessing the success of the Khasis and Garo hill tribes in the southwest of Assam in winning a 'sub-state.' Subsequently disappointed by the 1985 Assam Accord's failure to deal with issues stemming from immigration, a 1993 agreement between New Delhi and the All Bodo Students' Union (ABSU) was not implemented due to protests from other ethnic groups (Bodos are not a majority in any district claimed as the historical homeland of the Bodos) and violence by the Bodo Security Force, which rejected the ABSU's acceptance of an autonomous council rather than a separate state. Indeed, failure to address the issues of immigration and citizenship – which constitute the legal manifestation of the embodiment dimension of sovereignty; i.e., in whose name and interests the state governs – continue to lie at the heart of much of the separatist activity in India's northeast. According to the Assam Accord, immigrants who entered before January 1, 1966 qualified as Indian citizens, those who entered between January 1, 1966 and March 24, 1971 would be disenfranchised for 10 years, and those who came after March 25, 1971 would be deported. These provisions were given legislative expression in the Illegal Migrants (Determinations by Tribunals) (IMDT) Act (1983), which proved both ineffective and incompatible with the state's own legal-rational institutions of governance. To explain, because the IMDT put the burden of proof upon the state to demonstrate, through a lengthy and convoluted process, that an individual is not a citizen, by April 30, 2000, fewer than 0.5 percent of cases had resulted in an individual's deportation. In 2005, the IMDT Act was ruled unconstitutional by the Indian Supreme Court on the grounds that it made available only to persons with disputed citizenship in Assam a quasi-judicial process unavailable to all others resident in India.

The ineffectiveness of the Assam Accord prompted a 2003 agreement with breakaway movements that resulted in the establishment of a Bodoland Territorial Council (BTC), which constituted a further attempt at finding a constitutional solution to the crisis (Lacina 2007). The BTC, also known as the Bodoland Territorial Area District (BTAD), was created under the Sixth Schedule to the Constitution of India, which contains provisions regarding the administration of tribal areas in Assam, Meghalaya, Tripura and Mizoram. However, rather than being a consensual mechanism, the Sixth Schedule is imposed by New Delhi on groups demanding autonomy and secession as a conflict management tool, with the result that it displaces (rather than addresses) the causes of conflict. Consequently, state/sub-group conflict is supplanted by state/new sub-group and sub-group/sub-group conflict as new minorities are created and sub-groups vie for political power and resources. This, as Barbora (2008) points out, is partly because the autonomy proffered by the Sixth Schedule is frequently illusory and ambiguous. For example, it does not address issues pertaining to the control of resources, finances and costs of running autonomous territories, with the result that autonomous councils frequently lack the resources and authority to take steps necessary to resolving the root causes of conflict. In addition, because New Delhi has a stake in the success of power-sharing and devolutionary measures, this sometimes leads it to tolerate repression of local minorities and dissent. Lacina (2009) notes how the state Congress Party in Mizoram has colluded with the Mizo National Front (MNF) to marginalize the main opposition party, the People's Conference, while ethnic minorities such as the Brus and Chakmas have been expelled into Tripura as the state government turns a blind eye to Mizo youth organizations functioning as an extra-legal police force. The result has been increased pressure on resources, heightened ethnic conflict in Tripura, Assam and Manipur, and the mobilization of groups such as the Hmar, who, disappointed with the 1994 treaty that produced the state of Mizoram, have shifted their attacks to Manipur and Assam in support of their claim for a Hmar state or autonomous area (Lacina 2009).

External assistance

Every separatist movement of note in South Asia has benefited from, and been dependent upon, external support. Where this support is provided by states, it may come in the form of overt assistance or, more frequently, through covert intervention using front companies, brokers, intermediaries, extra-state banking systems and other shadow networks that provide the intervening state with a plausible veneer of deniability. In other cases, the intervening state may, through inaction, allow assistance to pass from non-state actors to separatists. For example, many diasporas take advantage of liberal freedoms in their state of residence to mobilize support for the struggle in their homeland (Shain 2002; Ali 2003; Fair 2005; Sökefeld and Bolognani 2011). More direct intervention may include diplomatic methods (mediation, arbitration or the use of international forums); economic intervention (sanctions, inducements and foreign aid); deployment of peacekeepers; covert or public support for one of the warring factions (funds, training, sanctuary and weapons); and military intercession (Heraclides 1990; Enterline and Linebarger 2014). The most notable example of such overt intervention is India's assistance to the *Mukti Bahini* in former East Pakistan, which was decisive in the partition that led to the creation of Bangladesh. India also publicly intervened in the Sri Lankan civil war following the Indo-Sri Lankan Accord of 1987, according to which India would repatriate refugees from the conflict and provide a 16,000–19,000-man Indian Peace Keeping Force (IPKF) (later increased to 40,000). This was to be accompanied by the amalgamation of the northern and eastern provinces into a single Tamil-dominated administrative unit with English and Tamil as the official languages. However, the IPKF became embroiled in an armed conflict with the LTTE that was in part fueled by the government in Colombo, leading India to withdraw in March 1990 (Chalk 2003).

Note, however, that in both cases public intervention was preceded by covert assistance (which is very much the norm in such circumstances). The Indian government, for example, covertly provided materials, weapons, sanctuary and training to the LTTE between 1983 and 1987 (Rao 1988). This was motivated by a concern for India's large Tamil population and its regional ambitions. Of the 975,000 stateless persons created by Sri Lanka's decision not to extend citizenship to Indian Tamil plantation workers, many settled in the Indian state of Tamil Nadu (Das 2012). Subsequently, the governing Congress Party's rapprochements with the two main Tamil Nadu parties, the *All India Anna Dravida Munnetra Kazhagam* (AIADMK) and *Dravida Munnetra Kazhagam* (DMK), elevated the plight of Sri Lankan Tamils to the national political stage (Das 2012). Additionally, India saw assisting Tamil separatists in Sri Lanka as a means of pressuring the Sri Lankan government to remain within its non-aligned sphere of influence (Narayanswamy 1994; Joshi 1996; Gunaratna 1997; Chalk 2003). The change in tactics, from covert support to mediator and peacekeeper, can be explained by a fear that the civil war in Sri Lanka would bring in outside powers (especially the United States or the

Soviet Union), the large numbers of refugees from the conflict arriving in Tamil Nadu, and the fear that the cause of Tamil separatism might spread to India (Taras and Ganguly 1988, Kodikara 1990).

Because most assistance to separatists is provided covertly, it is difficult to accurately measure its scope, quantity and effects. Moreover, just as the intervening party has an incentive to deny or downplay any assistance rendered, the parent state has an incentive to exaggerate the role of outside influences to deflect responsibility away from its failed policies toward the aggrieved minority. The result is often a series of competing and contradictory claims and counter-claims. Pakistan, for example, has alleged that Baloch separatists are supported by external powers – specifically, the Indian and Iranian governments and intelligence agencies – citing the separatists' obvious training, selection of targets and Russian weapons, which are not used by the Pakistani military (Bansal 2008). Indeed, as Siddiqi (2012) highlights, Balochistan's strategic location and enormous natural resources mean that it lies in the middle of a complex nexus that includes Great Powers (the United States and China), regional powers (Iran and India), non-state actors such as jihadist organizations, Baloch nationalist parties and global multinational corporations (Tethyan Copper Company). Explanations for Indian and Iranian intervention include a desire to thwart the development of a large port at Gwadar (which would rival the Chah Bahar port that India is developing in Iran) as a gateway to Central Asia (Bansal 2006). Moreover, a prolonged insurgency that ties down troops in Balochistan would limit Pakistan's ability to project force and might induce it to import petroleum products from Indian refineries (Bansal 2006). On the other hand, however, neither country has an interest in an unstable, violence-wracked, failed state on their border that could destabilize the entire region (Bansal 2006, Khan 2009) or threaten the viability of the Central Asian and Iran–Pakistan–India pipelines – both of which would traverse large tracts of Balochistan (Bansal 2006).

In the case of Pakistan's support for Indian separatists, both the rationale and the evidence are more compelling. Indian secular nationalism and the inclusion of a Muslim-majority state – Jammu and Kashmir – are an affront to Pakistan's founding Two Nation theory and the attendant claim that the security of Muslims in South Asia requires that they be afforded a state of their own. Fomenting rebellion within India is also an effective means for Pakistan to redress the numerical disadvantage of its armed forces and lack of strategic depth vis-à-vis India's much larger military and landmass. In the 1982–92 Sikh separatist insurgency in the Indian state of Punjab, it is alleged that Pakistan provided training and weapons (Chima 2010). Although there is some dispute over whether Pakistani support played an instigating or an exacerbating role (Deol 2000), sealing the Indo-Pakistan border was a key element of India's counter-insurgency strategy (Singh 1996). Similar disagreements characterize the role of Pakistani assistance in Kashmiri separatism. What *is* clear, however, is that from the early 1990s, secular, Kashmiri-centric separatist groups were supplanted by Islamist, Pakistan-orientated and headquartered movements such as *Lashkar-e-Toiba* (LeT), *Jaish-e-Mohammed* (JeM), *Tehrik-ul-Jihad* and *Harkut-ul-Mujahideen*

(Balch-Lindsay *et al.* 2008) in an interventionist strategy that has been well documented (Karim 1999; United States State Department 1999; Swami 2007, 2008). Implicated in cross-border terrorist attacks in India – such as the 2001 attack on the Indian Parliament and the 2008 Mumbai terror attacks – many of these groups have been outlawed by the United States, the United Kingdom, the European Union and other states. Pakistan claims that it has offered only diplomatic and moral support to Kashmiri separatists and affiliated groups, some of which it has recently outlawed (Mills *et al.* 2006). However, while it is clear that official government support for Kashmiri separatists in Pakistan has waned considerably, it is less clear to what degree the powerful Inter-Services Intelligence (ISI), which administers such matters, is prepared to toe the government's line.

Uniting these three separatist movements in Punjab, Kashmir and Sri Lanka is a reliance upon assistance from foreign diasporas. Diasporas constitute a valuable source of funding, recruitment and publicity, as they exploit freedoms of expression and anti-discrimination laws in host states to publish, organize and lobby for co-ethnics in their homeland (Wayland 2004). One estimate put the number of Sri Lankan Tamils living abroad as one in four (Sriskandarajah 2005); between 110,000 and 170,000 lived in the Tamil Nadu province of southern India, and Canada's Tamil population was estimated at between 110,000 and 200,000 persons, with at least a further 200,000 living in Western Europe (Wayland 2004). Another study suggested that overseas contributions made up more than 90 percent of the LTTE's funding (Chalk 2000). Diaspora support was also skillfully manipulated by the television station Tamil Vision International (DeVotta 2009).

In contrast, the Sikh diaspora is estimated to exceed 17 million, with most having emigrated in the post-colonial era to the United Kingdom, Canada and the United States (Fair 2005). Gurdwaras were a key linkage between the diaspora and the Khalistan movement through the collection of funds that were funneled into a variety of organizations (diplomatic, political and military) in support of the Khalistan effort (Axel 2001; Sökefeld 2006). Finally, the Kashmiri diaspora in Britain was an important source of funding for the cause of Kashmiri independence from India (Franchetti and Fielding 2002), as well as a site for the development and articulation of Kashmiri identity beyond the restrictive control of Indian and Pakistani nationalism (Ali 2003). It is worth highlighting, however, that in many cases contributions from diaspora members were coerced. This was particularly true of the Tamil diaspora, as the LTTE threatened relatives or property in Sri Lanka, pressured the diaspora to utilize LTTE front businesses such as catering services for weddings and funerals (La 2004), and kidnapped for ransom diaspora members when they visited LTTE-held areas if they had failed to cooperate (DeVotta 2009). This was in addition to other, illegal fundraising activities by the LTTE, such as trading in gems, human trafficking and (allegedly) smuggling narcotics (Fair 2005).

In northeast India, where a series of groups have used violence in their campaign for greater autonomy from New Delhi, allegations of external interference are commonplace. Some of these regions are now largely conflict free, e.g., Mizoram (1966–76) and Meghalaya (1990s–2004), while in others violence continues, e.g., Assam (1990–), Nagaland (1950s–), Tripura (1978–) and Manipur (1960s–). After the 1962 Sino-Indian war, New Delhi became convinced of the region's strategic value, and worries that the Chinese could promote unrest in the region led India to invest heavily in it (Misra 2001). However, managing relations with (and between) the region's constituent communities is complicated by a bewildering array of tribes with overlapping identities and changing loyalties. In addition, there is some debate as to how many groups are separatist rather than simply criminal enterprises using the rhetoric and symbolism of political activism as a crude attempt to disguise their true motivations in a region beset by drug trafficking and kidnappings (Vadlamannati 2011). India has alleged that many of these groups received external aid from China (in the 1960s and the 1970s), Pakistan (from the 1950s to the present day), Bhutan (to 2003), Bangladesh (to 2008) and Myanmar (to the present day) in the form of arms, training and sanctuary (Bhaumik 1996; Sinha 2007). Bangladeshi support, which mostly came in the form of allowing separatists from Assam, Nagaland and Tripura to procure small arms through the Cox Bazar area and operate underground camps in the Habibganj, Khagrachari, Chittagong Hill Tracts (CHT) and Mymensingh areas, has diminished since Sheikh Hasina came to power in 2008 (Kumar 2004; Goswami 2011). Bangladesh, for its part, alleges that India has supplied arms and funding to separatists in the CHT region that abuts India's northeastern states in an effort to obtain strategic leverage and indicate its displeasure after the assassination in a military coup of pro-India President Sheikh Mujibur Rahman (Balch-Lindsay and Enterline 2000). The recent Indo-Bangladesh rapprochement is attributable to a shared interest in ending tit-for-tat support for insurgents in each other's territory to halt the flow of refugees, reduce cross-border crime and increase investment in the area (Mohsin 2003). An example of this dialogue is increased pressure from New Delhi upon Dhaka to limit assistance to the All Tripura Tiger Force (ATTF) and smaller Tripuri militant outfits, and better border controls with Bangladesh, which borders Tripura on three sides (Lacina 2009). Similar considerations have also curtailed Bhutanese support for the most notorious separatist group in the northeast – the United Liberation Front of Assam (ULFA) – which was forcibly expelled and its training camps dismantled in 2003 by the Royal Bhutan Army (Goswami 2011). Bhutan had initially turned a blind eye to ULFA's presence and allegedly assisted in the procurement of arms, ammunition, funding and travel documents (Saikia 2003; Kumar 2004) in the hope that ULFA would act as a foil to Ngolops (settlers in southern Bhutan of Nepalese origin), which Bhutan had previously attempted to evict. However, when ULFA's activities began disrupting the flow of trade between Bhutan and India and developing links with Nepalese Maoists (who had called for the overthrow of the Bhutanese monarchy), the strategic calculus no longer favored the continued presence of ULFA in Bhutan (Kumar 2004).

The loss of support from Bhutan and Bangladesh has forced separatists in the northeast to rely on Myanmar as a safe haven and source of material support;

both Naga and Assamese groups have benefited from tribal and economic links with non-state actors in Myanmar, e.g., the Kachin National Army (KNA) trained ULFA cadres in the 1980s–1990s (Zartman 1993; Shukla 2005). However, it is unclear to what degree support from Myanmar is in consequence of government policy or an inability to adequately police the border with India and bring groups such as the KNA to heel. While India and Myanmar agreed in 2010 to work together to curb organized crime and drug trafficking, terrorism, smuggling of arms and money laundering – measures partly designed to limit the cross-border operations of ULFA and similar groups – the agreement has yet to be fully implemented. In addition, it is unclear how, even if effectively implemented, the agreement might curtail internal assistance from ULFA to other separatist groups, given the support ULFA has provided to Bodos in northwest Assam and the Rajbanshis on the Assam/West Bengal border (Lacina 2009). Finally, there is the question of ULFA's links with Pakistan and China. The Indian media are rife with largely uncorroborated claims of Chinese assistance, including the sheltering of members of ULFA's leadership (such as vice chairperson and commander-in-chief, Paresh Barua), provision of weapons via ULFA's links with the Myanmar-based Kachin Independent Army (KIA) (Grigoryan 2010; Lintner 2012; *The Times of India* 2014) and the presence of ULFA training camps and bases in China (Trumbore 2003; *India Today* 2009; NDTV 2009). Similarly, it is also alleged that Pakistan's powerful ISI continue to provide arms and training to ULFA cadres as a component of Pakistan's 'network of terror' (Prakash 2008; Hussain 2009; Chakrabarty 2011). While intuitively plausible – fomenting inter-group conflict to occupy the Indian military while destabilizing a strategically vital region of a rival state makes strategic sense – the extent of Chinese and Pakistani support for separatism in the northeast is difficult to substantiate.

Whereas involvement designed to halt a conflict, arrest the flow of refugees or protect co-ethnics might attract little international disapprobation, intervention to fuel a conflict or manipulate it for strategic gain is much less likely to escape criticism and sanction. Consequently, intervening states frequently rely on non-state actors to mask the nature and extent of their involvement. However, the organizations that have acted as vehicles for intervention in South Asia have frequently proven unpredictable and difficult to control. For example, smuggling, trafficking in contraband and people, kidnapping and other forms of criminality are common amongst the various separatist groups in India's northeast, making it difficult for states to support these groups without tarnishing the public legitimacy of their assistance or contributing to the development of similar problems in their own territory. Similarly, many of the groups created and sponsored by Pakistan to facilitate Kashmir's 'liberation,' such as LeT and JeM, have pursued broader objectives pertaining to the creation of an Islamic caliphate and have been implicated in numerous large-scale and high profile terror attacks outside Kashmir. The indiscriminate brutality of these acts has undermined the cause of Kashmiri independence and cast Pakistan's assistance to Kashmiri separatists in a most unfavorable light. It has also placed Pakistan in an unenviable position, where its official claims of offering only diplomatic and moral support for Kashmiri separatism mean it is unable to publicly admonish these groups or assume credit for steps taken to limit their operations.

Finally, reliance on diasporas as a source of fundraising and attacks has also hampered the ability of intervening states to assist and publicly defend separatist movements. Coercion and criminality in fundraising amongst Tamil diasporas were a contributing factor to the LTTE being outlawed by many states, while the bombing of Air India flight 182 in 1985 by Canada-based Sikh separatists with the loss of 329 lives damaged public perceptions of the Khalistan movement and its supporters. In both cases the dispersed, decentralized character of the separatist group and its agents created problems that could not be easily foreseen or countered by the movement's leadership or the intervening state.

Internal discord and fratricide

Finally, it is important to note that neither the state nor separatists are unitary actors, and that the relationship between the two is determined by dominant factions in each. Accordingly, the creation or manipulation of differences and divisions within a separatist movement is an effective strategy for states, and one which they have frequently pursued. Fractionalization reduces separatists' viability and strength by limiting their ability to maintain popular support and effectively deploy resources to confront the state, especially where disunity results in factions violently confronting one another (Chima 2010). Conversely, where separatist groups are able to effectively diminish class, religious, social and other divisions within their target community (in a manner that the parent state could not), then this may garner increased public support.

The LTTE and caste schisms within Sri Lankan Tamil society provide a useful illustration of the benefits of unity and how bridging entrenched divisions within a community may pay dividends. Whereas a rigorous caste system represented a cleavage that had long contributed to disunity, the departure of many belonging to the upper *Vellalar* (farming) caste from the north during the conflict reduced internal divisions and facilitated LTTE control, given its roots in the *Karaiyar* (fishing) caste (DeVotta 2009). The LTTE also addressed gender divides by transforming the standing of women in a traditionally male-dominated, conservative society by discouraging dowry, encouraging the marriage of women whom IPKF and Sri Lankan military personnel had raped, and the integration of all-female units within the military command structure (DeVotta 2009). Nonetheless, regional divisions within Sri Lankan Tamil society did remain, with most LTTE leaders being from the north (so-called Jaffna Tamils) and eastern Tamils disproportionately taxed and pressed into military service. This prompted a split in the LTTE, with the 2004 formation of the *Tamil Makkal Viduthalai Pulikal* (TMVP) to counter the LTTE in the Eastern Province (DeVotta 2009). This split was as much a consequence of personal animus between LTTE leader Vellupillai Prabhakaran and Karuna Amman. Hence, while the TMVP did ally with Sri Lankan military against the LTTE, it is unclear that the Sri Lankan government engineered the split. Moreover, the TMVP has itself been seriously weakened by internal bloodletting. The TMVP president, Kumaraswamy Nandagopan, was assassinated in 2008, while struggles between Karuna and Sivanesathurai Chandrakanthan (Pillaiyan) spilled over into violence, prompting the government to crack down on the group from 2009.

Perhaps the most fragmented separatist movement has been that for Khalistan, with often violent divisions ruthlessly exploited by the Indian government to eventually defeat the campaign for a separate Sikh homeland. Chima (2010) usefully separates these groups into extremists that promoted self-determination through mostly peaceful means (*Akali Dal* (Mann/Baba), All India Sikh Students Federation (AISSF) (Manjit), Sikh Students Federation (SSF) (Mehta/Chawla) and the *Damdami Taksal*) and those that pursued an armed struggle (the old Panthic Committee, Khalistan Commando Force (KCF) (Zafferwal), the new Panthic Committee (Dr Sohan Singh), SSF (Bittu), KCF (Panjwar), Khalistan Liberation Force (KLF), Bhindrinwala Tigers Force of Khalistan (BTFK) (Chhandran), a third Panthic Committee (Manochahal) and *Babbar Khalsa*). The frequent reference to individuals' names to distinguish break-away factions of the same group is an indication of the personal networks of patronage and rivalry behind much of the fractiousness that characterized the cause of an independent state for Sikhs in South Asia. However, these personal rivalries are often characteristic of deeper political, economic and regional divisions within Sikh society.

Moreover, it is also evident that at various junctures these divisions have intersected in a dynamic process to both drive and respond to events affecting the Sikh *Panth*. For example, in 1988, divisions over whether to raise issues of social reform pertaining to dowry and alcohol were, in part, both a cause and a consequence of leadership rivalries and related to divisions between orthodox and modernist interpretations of the Sikh faith that, in turn, had their roots in differing socio-economic classes that dominated different regions of the Punjab. Telford (1992), in particular, highlights the intersection of regional and class divisions within the Khalistan movement, observing that the majority of militants were poor Jat Sikhs from farming families in Gurdaspur and Amritsar, whereas the political classes that dominated the *Akali Dal* leadership were from the richer districts of the Malwa region. Singh (1996) further observes how the lack of horizontal associations that cut across these class and regional divisions resulted in a paucity of organizational structures capable of effectively operating as centers of resistance, opposition and mobilization. The particularity and lack of coordination and control between these different groups help to explain their ensnarement in local feuds, factional enmities, kinship retribution and criminality. Crucially, this meant that rather than maintaining exclusivist, single-purpose ties dedicated to the goal of Khalistan, separatist insurgents instead became mired in the networks of rural society (Singh 1996), employing violent and indiscriminate tactics that precluded the establishment of a sustainable base of mass support (Deol 2000).

The internal divisions of the Khalistan movement and its contextualization within pre-existing, sub-national actors and networks are not unique; similar divisions exist in other separatist-afflicted societies in South Asia. Nor is the link between these divisions and religion specific to Sikhism. For example, similar cleavages between orthodox and heterodox interpretations of Islam coincide with the divide between secularist, pro-independence Kashmiri groups and their more Islamicized, pro-Pakistan rivals – disagreements that New Delhi has skillfully manipulated to prevent consensus in Kashmiri society regarding the region's political future. Similarly, the Pakistani military has been accused of fanning sectarian violence and sponsoring extremist Islamist groups within Balochistan in an attempt to splinter support for an independent Baloch state (Hasan 2012). The fractious nature of these movements contrasts with the relative success of the LTTE in suppressing intra-communal divisions and networks of class and caste that were a distraction from the common objective of independent statehood. Consequently, Sikh separatist groups proved comparatively easy to infiltrate, as local and personal vendettas were skillfully exploited by the police and counter-insurgency forces (Singh 1996). No doubt this infiltration was assisted by the nature of many recruits into their respective movements, who, in the latter stages of the conflict, had not undergone any ideological or counter-surveillance tactics, which resulted in a lack of discipline that facilitated their co-option (Deol 2000). On the other hand, however, it is important to note that the Indian state was itself beset by discord on the question of how best to counteract the Khalistan movement – e.g., Haryana Chief Minister Bhajan Lal's opposition to a settlement with the *Akali Dal* that might negatively impact his own state (Chima 2010). In addition to making Sikh separatist organizations easier to infiltrate, divisions within groups, and rivalries between them, frequently resulted in violence and human rights violations that included members of the public amongst the victims and further alienated public support from the cause of an independent Sikh state (Jodhka 2005). For example, the KLF emerged as a result of Aroor Singh's refusal to accept his removal from the Panthic Committee for initiating contacts with the government. Determined to carve out a niche for itself on an increasingly small playing field, the KLF attempted to make its mark by engaging in increasingly brutal and indiscriminate attacks, including a bus massacre of 24 Hindus (Chima 2010).

However, exploiting and facilitating splits within separatist groups, and fueling rivalries between different groups, may come at the cost of achieving a long-term, negotiated solution by delaying such an outcome or making it more difficult to obtain. Chima (2010), for example, argues that one of the Indian government's main problems in addressing Sikh separatism was disunity amongst the *Akali Dal*. The observation is equally pertinent to Jammu and Kashmir, where a moderate, secular uprising for independent statehood in 1989 was by 1992 transformed into a hardline, Islamic movement that favored union with Pakistan. The splintering of Kashmiri separatism and its domination by Pakistani-sponsored organizations made a negotiated settlement less feasible due to discord amongst these groups on the conduct of negotiations and the desire of some to continue the conflict rather than bring it to resolution. The subsequent creation of an organizational umbrella – the *Hurriyat* Conference – to represent most major Kashmiri separatist groups could not paper over the sharp divisions between its different members and the terms of any negotiations – India rejects the *Hurriyat*'s demand for a tripartite dialogue on the state's future that includes Pakistan (Racine 2013).

In the case of Punjab, the first major initiative to address the crisis was a 1985 agreement named after its chief architects, the 'Rajiv–Longowal Accord,' the principal elements of which were the transfer of Chandigarh from Haryana to Punjab; a commission to examine the transfer of Hindi-speaking areas from Punjab to Haryana; adjudication of the river waters dispute between Punjab and Haryana; completion of the Sutlej–Yamuna canal; reconsideration of center–state relations and governance of Gurdwaras; and empowering the committee examining the anti-Sikh riots of 1984 and other 'special courts' (Chima 2010). The accord was opposed by many Sikhs, who viewed it as a 'sell-out,' prompting a split in the *Akali Dal* in the form of a rival faction (the United *Akali Dal*) led by Bhindrinwale's father, Baba Joginder Singh. This was followed by bomb explosions in Delhi in May 1985, linked to Sikh separatists, which killed almost 80 people, and the assassination of Longowal in August (Deol 2000). Nonetheless, Kapur (1987) argues that the accord achieved a measure of success by bringing the majority of moderate *Akali* leaders back into the political process by convincing them to participate in elections. While there may be an element of truth in this, we should also note that the elections heightened communal divisions (with Sikhs supporting the *Akali Dal* and Hindus the Congress) and could not prevent the state again being placed under President's rule in 1986 and governed directly by the central government (Deol 2000).

Furthermore, the 1985 elections in Punjab, where a boycott of the polls by Sikh parties dissatisfied with the Rajiv–Longowal Accord, such as the *Akali Dal* (U) and AISSF, which left the *Akali Dal* (L) and Congress (I) as the main contenders, mirrors the 1987 legislative assembly elections in Jammu and Kashmir, with similar results. In Jammu and Kashmir, Congress (I) had allied with its traditional political foe, the National Conference (NC), to combat an exaggerated threat from Islamist groups that campaigned under a banner organization, the Muslim United Front (MUF). This allowed the MUF to appropriate the anti-New Delhi, Kashmiri-centric mantle that had previously been the political hallmark of the NC, presenting the NC with a problem similar to that faced by the *Akali Dal*, which, once elected to govern in the Punjab state legislature, could no longer speak the anti-center language of the Sikh militants or radical *Akalis*. The result was a loss of popular legitimacy for the moderate *Akali* groups, which, in the 1989 election, lost out to radical factions led by Simranjit Singh Mann and did not gain a single seat (Jodhka 2005). In the case of Jammu and Kashmir, allegations of election rigging after the announcement of a crushing Congress (I)–NC victory are frequently cited as one of the main reasons for the armed rebellion against Indian rule that erupted the following year. In Punjab, there were similar allegations of collusion: that Congress (I) fielded weak candidates to allow the *Akali* (L) to form the next state government (Chima 2010), with a comparable effect on each party's moral legitimacy in the eyes of many voters. Perhaps more damaging, however, was New Delhi's failure to deliver on the 1985 accord, continuing a theme of symbolic agreements followed by non-implementation (Singh 1996).

There is also the case of India's northeast, with its bewildering array of tribal and ethnic groups, which frequently, despite pursuing an avowedly separatist agenda, clash more with one another than with New Delhi. The Karbi Anglong region of Assam, which until 1854 was part of the Dimasa kingdom, is illustrative of how complex and overlapping allegiances can conflict violently. In June 2000, members of the Karbi ethnic group that dominate the Karbi Anglong attacked Hindi-speaking settlers, who, with the aid of the Central Reserve Police Force (CRPF), later retaliated and killed many Karbi farmers. These events were repeated in 2001–03, in addition to outbreaks of violence between the Karbi and Kuki communities that left thousands displaced over several months of confrontation (Barbora 2008). Elsewhere in the northeast, divisions have occurred for more political reasons. In 1988, for example, a ceasefire split the major rebel group in Tripura, the Tripura National Volunteer Force (TNVF), into dozens of smaller organizations (Lacina 2009). In Nagaland, the National Socialist Council of Nagaland (NSCN) fractured along kinship lines into the National Socialist Council of Nagaland-Isak and Muivah (NSCN-IM), dominated by Nagas from Manipur, and the National Socialist Council of Nagaland-Khaplang (NSCN-K), associated with Nagas from Myanmar. Each faction rejects the other's right to negotiate with the center and has engaged in extreme violence against the other (Goswami 2011), while also claiming that Naga-inhabited areas of other states, including Assam, Manipur and Arunachal Pradesh, should be annexed to Nagaland (Lacina 2009). In Manipur, the United National Liberation Front (UNLF) splintered into two factions, leading to violent clashes that left more than 100 dead. Goswami (2011) attributes this violence to competition for territorial space to facilitate the extortion networks run by both groups. Whereas the fractiousness of some movements has not had a discernible effect on the conflict's overall trajectory, in other cases it has seriously weakened the separatists' cause and resulted in a peaceful solution. In Mizoram, for example, the repeated splintering of the main separatist group, the MNF, resulted in its becoming a spent force compelled to negotiate with New Delhi in a process that yielded the state of Mizoram (Lacina 2007).

Conclusion

The most important difference between separatist and state actors is the relative disparity of resources. Whereas the state commands the legislative domain and has significant resources to compel compliance with its directives, separatists are more reliant on voluntary cooperation. Moreover, the state's resort to coercion to defeat the separatist threat, while a violation of the legal-rational basis of its legitimacy, need not result in the permanent alienation of the inhabitants of separatist-affected regions. Rather, the state's vastly superior resources and staying power mean that once the separatists have been defeated it may elicit voluntary compliance and moral support from victims of its harsh policies. Offering benefits to local populations that the separatists cannot, and exploiting divisions within separatist ranks to promote infighting, undermine separatist claims to be the legitimate representatives of a region's inhabitants. Moreover, the resort to external assistance by separatists in an attempt to counter the advantages of the state frequently requires the surrender of control to external elites, whose interests and aims may differ markedly from their own, and leaves the group vulnerable to allegations of foreign mastery.

Consequently, if separatists are to have any hope of defeating the state, it is essential that they minimize internal divisions, maintain discipline (particularly in their treatment of the local population) and leverage the resources at their disposal to the maximum possible degree. Of all the movements considered here, the LTTE best exemplifies this approach. While benefiting enormously from external aid, leadership of the group remained firmly rooted in the Sri Lankan Tamil community headquartered in their ancestral homeland. Moreover, while the group often employed harsh and brutal tactics, these were for the most part consistently applied and buttressed with effective propaganda campaigns. Perhaps most importantly, the LTTE also provided many of the essential services of a state at least as effectively as they had been provided by the Sri Lankan government, but without any perception of bias or discrimination. These features allowed the LTTE to demonstrate to inhabitants of the territories that it controlled that the LTTE was superior to the Sri Lankan government with reference to the sovereign attributes of embodiment and necessity, requiring the government to defeat the LTTE militarily or concede defeat.

4 Redemption

Introduction

The origins, conduct and conclusion of separatism, while clearly linked, do not follow a linear trajectory. Rather, a movement's chronology often exhibits changes, discontinuities and cleavages that render linkages with its inception tenuous. An example of this is the observation made earlier that the reasons for the formation of a separatist movement and subsequent outbreak of violence often bear little resemblance to contemporary factors driving the conflict. Changes in membership, tactics, available resources, assistance from third party actors and other factors all influence the development of separatist conflicts and their amenability to peaceful resolution. Similarly, we may observe that two of the most effective separatist movements in South Asia – for Khalistan and a Tamil homeland in Sri Lanka – which at various junctures looked close to achieving their aims, were comprehensively defeated. In contrast, other, less inspired and organized groups have managed to continue their struggle or achieved a measure of political independence short of independent statehood that was denied to Sikhs in India and Tamils in Sri Lanka. The only separatist conflict that resulted in an act of secession in South Asia has been the Bangladesh war of independence. However, many of the factors that led to the bifurcation of East and West Pakistan to create Bangladesh – significant military assistance from a much larger, more powerful intervening state and geographic non-contiguity between the parent and nascent states of more than 2,000 km – do not apply to other separatist conflicts.

The purpose of this chapter is to explore the differing outcomes of these struggles and the reasons for the 'success' of various parties to them. The chapter begins with a discussion of Sikh and Tamil separatist movements in India and Sri Lanka that were comprehensively defeated by the parent state and looks at why, despite their often significant strengths and successes, these movements were unable to achieve their aims. This is followed by an examination of conflicts that are continuing (Balochistan, Kashmir, India's northeast and Bangladesh's CHT region) and the reasons behind these movements' longevity.

Clear state victories: Sri Lanka and Punjab

Before exploring the reasons behind the Sri Lankan government's comprehensive military victory over the LTTE, it should be noted that for most of the conflict, the government displayed an inability to effectively combat the group. Chalk (2003) attributes this failure to: (a) poor government communication that failed to effectively combat LTTE propaganda; (b) the application of conventional military tactics to a guerrilla war, including emphasis on superior technology and weight of numbers; (c) inadequate intelligence on the LTTE, compounded by poor training and political interference in the military campaign; and (d) the LTTE's ability to control and normalize the northeast to establish an alternative state. In addition to pursuing a military strategy, the government also engaged in negotiations aimed at depoliticizing Tamil nationalism and bringing Tamil organizations into the political mainstream. For example, Chandrika Bandaranaike Kumaratunga's People's Alliance government sought to devolve limited power to the provinces without granting any special status or guarantee to the Tamil-dominated northeast. A similar strategy was attempted by Ranil Wickremesinghe's United National Front government through peace negotiations and promises of economic development (Matthews 1995). A ceasefire in 2001 was followed the next year by an agreement between the LTTE and the government that resulted in a series of peace negotiations facilitated by Norway. However, negotiations broke down as the ceasefire was increasingly breached (Feith 2013) and it became evident that Tamil demands for territorial sovereignty and self-determination were not being satisfied. From the LTTE's perspective, continuing the conflict to establish a Tamil state in the northeast offered a better chance of realizing their aims by making Tamil self-determination and self-government a *fait accompli* that would eventually force the Sri Lankan government to negotiate with the LTTE as equals.

The deadlock was broken with the 2005 election of Mahinda Rajapaksa as president and his decision to abandon peace negotiations in favor of a military solution supported by increased defense spending and military and diplomatic support from China and India. There is some speculation that the LTTE, fearing that Wickremesinghe's peace plan and increased international involvement was pushing it toward a 'peace trap,' supported Rajapaksa's election campaign by disallowing Tamils to vote in the hope that a victory by the ultra-nationalist Rajapaksa would permit the LTTE to break the ceasefire and justify a return to war. If this is true, the strategy backfired spectacularly, as in 2008, after demanding that all foreign observers leave the northeast, the Sri Lankan government began a determined effort to eradicate the LTTE in a ruthless and bloody campaign (Weiss 2011). Estimates of the death toll in the first four months of the campaign range from 7,000 to 40,000, including many civilians (Baruah 2009; Popham 2010; Weiss 2011).

China, stepping into the breach left by Washington's discontinuation of military aid in 2007 over Sri Lanka's deteriorating human rights record, became Sri Lanka's biggest donor, with aid reaching nearly US$1 billion, including sophisticated weapons and a free gift of six F7 fighter jets (de Silva 2012). China also encouraged its ally, Pakistan, to assist Sri Lanka through the provision of arms and pilot training while also using its veto to prevent the UN Security Council from putting Sri Lanka on its agenda (Popham 2010). Critically, Chinese aid was provided with no conditions over Sri Lanka's prosecution of the war (Pant 2012), freeing the Sri Lankan government to ignore concerns over human rights abuses. In return, China received a boost to its expansionary agenda in South Asia and efforts to construct a 'string of pearls' in the form of deep water ports and other dual use facilities across the Indian Ocean, from Burma to Pakistan, that would be invaluable in the event of a military confrontation with its rival India (Popham 2010). Of particular note was the construction of a port in the Sri Lankan city of Hambantota to complement similar facilities being developed in Gwadar (Pakistan) and Chittagong (Bangladesh). However, China's ambitions suffered a setback with the removal of the Rajapaksa government in 2015 and the decision by the new government of Maithripala Sirisena to halt all US$5 billion worth of Chinese investments pending a formal review.

India had proscribed the LTTE in 1992, after the group's assassination of Indian Prime Minister Rajiv Gandhi in May 1991, due to concern about the spread of Tamil separatism to the Indian state of Tamil Nadu and the LTTE's use of submersibles and aircraft. Additional concerns that led more than 30 other states to proscribe the LTTE as a 'terrorist organization' included its illegal activities (drug smuggling, credit card fraud, human trafficking, money laundering and arms procurements) and speculation regarding the LTTE's links to Al Qaeda (DeVotta 2009). India formally provided only limited financial assistance to the Rajapaksa administration due to the powerful Tamil political lobby (Gokhale 2009) in India and the dependency of the ruling United Progressive Alliance government in New Delhi upon the *Dravida Munnetra Kazhagam* (DMK) party from Tamil Nadu for its survival in Parliament (International Crisis Group 2011). However, there is considerable evidence to suggest that overt and covert assistance to defeat the LTTE went well beyond mere financial help. This included the provision of radars and other non-lethal weapons, ships, intelligence sharing, and assistance with a naval cordon that cut off the LTTE's traditional resupply routes from southern India (Anon 2015). In addition, the Sri Lankan navy leased two warships from the Indian coast guard – the ICGS *Varaha* and ICGS *Vigraha* – which were commissioned as the SLNS *Sagara* and SLNS *Sayurala*, respectively. Other reports indicate that Indian assistance included helicopters, ground-to-air missiles and anti-aircraft guns (Anon 2009). Finally, there is some speculation that Indian forces did take part in anti-LTTE operations, functioning with satellite and artillery units (Brewster 2014) and that an Indian medical team was in reality a wing of the Indian Army performing intelligence-gathering functions. India's interest in ending the conflict can be attributed to a desire to undo Beijing's foray into the Indian Ocean – a region that New Delhi has always regarded as its major defensive perimeter – and the lure of economic opportunities in the reconstruction that would follow the LTTE's defeat.

In addition to external assistance from India and China, the final capture of the last LTTE strongholds in May 2009 and the defeat of the movement are also attributable to LTTE inadequacies and failures. These included the LTTE's intolerance of dissent, high taxation, drafting of civilians for manual labor, and practices of forced conscription (which occasionally included children and the elderly) (DeVotta 2009). In addition, the LTTE was significantly weakened by a split between its northern and eastern wings and the defection of Colonel Karuna. Factors that facilitated the government's military victory include (a) a lack of differentiation between LTTE cadres and civilians in rebel-controlled areas, including indiscriminate shelling expertly calibrated and sanctioned by the uppermost levels of command in the military and government (Popham 2010); (b) a nexus between security personnel and anti-LTTE paramilitary groups amid a culture of impunity that permitted freedom of action ranging from targeted assassinations to random killings designed to instill terror in the Tamil population; (c) an effective propaganda campaign that blunted LTTE counter-claims and included the silencing of journalists critical of the government through death threats, assault, imprisonment and murder; (d) military expansion – the military recruited an additional 3,000 soldiers every month – and effective tactics that included multi-pronged assaults that forced the LTTE to defend its territory on multiple fronts; and (e) the removal of independent witnesses (journalists, non-governmental organizations and human rights observers) from the conflict zone (DeVotta 2009).

In the case of Punjab, similar factors underpin the government's military victory over separatist movements seeking the creation of an independent Sikh state, or Khalistan. However, there are also important differences. For example, being a much larger state with resources at its disposal that vastly outweighed those of Sikh separatists, India, unlike Sri Lanka, did not need to rely on external assistance in order to achieve a military victory. As Kohli (1997) points out, the struggle for an independent Sikh state against such a large and well-organized adversary was always going to be an uphill one. This disadvantage was compounded by other factors, such as the unsuitability of Punjab's topography for guerrilla warfare and the religious, economic and caste divisions that fractured the campaign for Khalistan into rival movements, facilitating infiltration. In addition, Korf (2005) highlights how ethnic bias and political influence in governance structures that regulate access to resources may render formal property rights ineffective, allowing some individuals to illegally acquire benefit streams from resources while others are unable to enforce their entitlements to resources. Unlike Sri Lanka, where there was significant ethnic distance between Hindu Tamils and Buddhist Sinhalese, Sikhism shares historical and doctrinal linkages with Hinduism, while the Indian state pursued an avowedly secularist national ideology that was formally more accommodating to religious minorities. Additionally, Sikhs had a long and proud tradition of military service, while also being well integrated into the economic and financial elite of Indian society. This contrasts with the hostility and alienation that characterized the policies of post-independence governments of Sri Lanka toward the minority Tamils, and highlights how Sikhs had potentially less to lose from the reassertion of Indian sovereignty over their society. Whereas individuals had once chosen to become Sikhs and support the Khalistan movement because it enhanced their lives in in/tangible ways (Singh 1998), once the calculus changed in the opposite direction, they were willing to abandon the goal of independent statehood. Moreover, the departure of members had a self-perpetuating effect, diminishing the movement's ability to engage in collective action (including income-generating activities) and thus adequately reward remaining members, which resulted in further defections and so forth, in a vicious cycle.

The primary tools employed by New Delhi to reduce the attractiveness of being a Sikh and identifying with the Khalistan movement were coercion and hegemony. However, for these to be effective, the costs of remaining a separatist had to be combined with tangible benefits for those who defected by leaving the movement. Notably, a similarly hardline approach by the Indian government in the early stages of conflict had produced the opposite effect and increased Sikh mobilization behind the goal of Khalistan by enhancing communal recognition of the value of martyrdom, hardening the boundaries between Hindus and Sikhs and indirectly raising the costs of abandoning the movement through social disapprobation and violent retribution (Singh 1998). However, once separatist groups' prospects of success and ability to pay rents diminished, then New Delhi's uncompromising approach began to pay dividends. As in other insurgencies, the Indian government's approach was consequently to begin by laying down a blanket of security that prevented separatists from eliciting or coercing cooperation from civilians, depriving the separatist movement of crucial resources and raising defection rates. This was complemented by the modification of official institutions, amnesties, increased investment, land reform, and a public willingness to negotiate and make concessions that reduced separatism's rhetorical appeal and marginalized hardliners (Lacina 2007).

Beginning with the more effective use of coercion and establishment of hegemony, designed to reassert the Indian state's sovereignty over what had by 1992 become a lawless region where the *diktats* of Sikh separatists held sway (Chima 2010), a number of important measures were implemented. These included the reorganization of the Punjab Police through the creation of new senior posts, mass recruitment at constable and special constable levels, and reappointment of K. P. S. Gill as chief of police; strengthening of other security forces, including the Central Reserve Police Force (CRPF), the Border Security Force (BSF) and the regular army; passage of strict, new anti-terrorist legislation, including the National Security Act (1980), the Punjab Disturbed Areas Ordinance (1983), the Terrorist Areas (Special Courts) Act (1984), and the Terrorist and Disruptive Activities (Prevention) Act (TADA) (1985); sealing the Indo-Pakistan border to cut off manpower, weapons and other supplies reaching separatists; and the creation of hit squads intended to infiltrate and kill separatists (Singh 1996). As in Kashmir, where the appointment of hardline governors such as Girish Saxena and Jagmohan had failed to stem the growing insurgency, New Delhi's selection of Siddhartha Shankar Ray, who had been credited with crushing the Naxalite insurgency, as governor of Punjab failed to address the underlying problems driving separatism (Chima 2010). Nonetheless, the Indian state was able to use its overwhelming resources to effectively blunt the operational effectiveness of separatists. Nine additional divisions of the Indian Army were deployed, bringing the peak deployment in Punjab to 120,000 army personnel in 1992, which helped the re-establishment of state sovereignty by assisting law and order agencies, including 53,000 Punjab Police, 28,000 Home Guards, 10,000 Special Police and over 70,000 paramilitary personnel (Singh 1996).

As in other disputed territories, India attempted to buttress its military victories against separatists with a political process designed to establish a return to normalcy through elections. As a tangible manifestation of the legitimacy of state sovereignty (and the principle of popular sovereignty that formally underpins it), the holding of elections, even if not wholly successful, is a critical demonstration of state hegemony in democratic polities. After five years of central rule, state assembly elections were held in 1992, which returned the Congress (I) and were boycotted by all separatist and most moderate *Akali* groups, with a poor voter turnout of only 20 percent (Singh 2007). Rural constituencies returned the lowest number of votes, reflecting the separatists' concentration of power in these areas (Jodhka 2005). This was followed by elections to urban municipal councils in September 1992 and village *panchayats* in January 1993, where turnout averaged 70 and 82 percent, respectively (BBC 2011). The result was a clear demonstration of the growing popular legitimacy, not only of the Congress government in Punjab, but of the electoral process – a clear repudiation of the politics of violence practiced by separatists, whose activities by now had devolved into banditry, private vendettas and criminal activity that alienated the local population (Pettigrew 1987; Singh 1998; Puri *et al.* 1999; Chima 2002).

The growing popular acceptance of the Congress government provided an incentive for the *Akalis* to re-engage in the electoral process, as the alternative of supporting violent groups was by now too costly and unlikely to succeed. In 1994, by-elections were held to the state assembly, with moderate *Akalis* under the leadership of Prakash Singh Badal winning two of the available three seats (Jodhka 2005). There followed a realignment of the parties as the *Badal Akali Dal* disowned militancy and violence, and aligned with the *Bharatiya Janata* Party (BJP) – a pro-Hindu party that had adopted a strict policy against regionalist politics – and the *Bahujan Samaj* Party (BSP), which had some influence amongst sections of dalits of the Doaba sub-region of Punjab (Jodhka 2005). The strategy of abandoning violence and separatism paid dividends, with the *Badal Akali Dal* winning 75 of the available 117 seats in 1997 elections to the state assembly and its partner, the BJP, winning 18. This delivered the Congress Party its worst ever result in the state and, more crucially, replaced the former model of 'confrontational regionalism' with one of 'cooperative federalism,' aligning the *Akalis* with the new reality of national politics at the center, where one party with a super-majority was no longer tenable and coalitions were the new norm (Jodhka 2005). Subsequent elections entrenched a return to political normalcy, with the prior performance of the government – not Khalistan – being the dominant issue, as political discourse eschewed any reference to communal and identity questions (Jodhka 2005). Chima (2002) credits this new reality at the center, where regional political parties are increasingly important in forming ruling coalitions, as a factor in Punjab's rehabilitation and a reason why separatism is unlikely to make a return there. Not only does the new-found national importance of regional parties such as the *Akali Dal* preclude an interventionist central government, such as that which existed under Mrs Gandhi, but it also integrates regional parties into the national political mainstream through alliances with major parties such as the Congress and BJP, while at the same time putting the brakes on major parties' centralizing tendencies and aberrations that occurred in the 1980s, such as the dismissal of popularly elected state governments.

Ongoing conflict: Balochistan, India's northeast, Kashmir and Bangladesh's CHT region

In contrast to the state victories in Sri Lanka and Punjab, the regions of Balochistan and India's northeast continue to seethe with separatist violence, while disturbances and small-scale violent incidents are common in Kashmir. In Balochistan, many of the factors that have underpinned the conflict there remain unaddressed. The Punjabi ethnic group continues to dominate institutions of state, comprising 45 percent of the population but 90 percent of the military and most of the bureaucracy (Direh *et al.* 2007), with the Baloch politically underrepresented and economically discriminated against in their own state (Pakistan Institute of Legislative Development and Transparency 2012). Similarly, issues pertaining to economic sovereignty remain, with Chinese participation in the development of the Gwadar Port and Saindak Copper Mines, and the lack of benefits for ethnic Baloch from these projects continuing to prompt expressions of concern from Baloch leaders (Bansal 2006). While these investments mean that China has an interest in a peaceful, stable and prosperous Balochistan, its sensitivity to foreign criticism and interference over its own human rights record, combined with claims to disputed territories in the South China Sea, Taiwan and Tibet, have prompted a strict doctrine of non-interference, which limits its capacity to leverage Pakistan to effect change in matters pertaining to its domestic affairs. Similarly, India, while having no interest in a failed, collapsing or seriously destabilized Pakistan, is limited in its ability to achieve these ends. On the one hand, the proposed 2,600 km Iran–Pakistan–India gas pipeline would pass through Balochistan and help to supply India's increasing need for energy, providing an incentive for India not to stoke conflict in Balochistan but to do what it can to assist in the development of a peaceful solution there. On the other hand, however, India's criticisms of Pakistan's heavy-handed tactics in Balochistan are blunted by its own human rights abuses in combatting separatist violence and the contextualization of these charges within India's economic self-interest and desire to promote stability for its own, rather than Baloch nationalist or Pakistan's, long-term gain (Khan 2009).

Moreover, it is also abundantly clear that Pakistan has had enormous difficulty reigning in Baloch and other non-state actors, such as ethnic and Islamic fundamentalist groups, that have increasingly challenged its authority. Groups such as the Taliban are, as Khan (2009) points out, a legacy of Pakistan's efforts to counter secular nationalism with religious fanaticism. Moreover, Islamist groups proved a useful, asymmetric mechanism to counter India's numerically superior military and were a foreign policy tool used by Pakistan for many years to foment violence in Kashmir and extend its strategic reach into Afghanistan and other areas of South Asia. Following the Soviet invasion of Afghanistan in 1979, the Pakistan Army and its intelligence service, the Inter-Services Intelligence Directorate (ISI), received a grant of US$3.2 billion over five years that was used to create a range of violent Islamist groups, including the Haqqani network and the Afghan Taliban, which today battle the Pakistan Army (Jalal 1985; Riedel 2008). This contrasts with the Baloch, who, despite their religiosity, have maintained a largely secular political tradition, viewing the Pakistani state as a threat to their ethnic identity but not their religious beliefs. However, this distinction has been challenged by government support of *madrasas* (seminaries) as an expedient substitute for secular education – the budget for the Ministry of Religious Affairs (MRA) that administers the *madrasas* was US$15.4 million in 2006, while the allocation for the secular education ministry was only US$2.56 million (Fulcher 2006). Additionally, in 2002, the government formed an alliance with the conservative religious association *Mutahida Majlis-e-Amal* (MMA) to form the provincial government in Balochistan in 2003. The MMA is dominated by the *Jamiat-e-Ulema-e-Islam (Fazl-ul-Rehman)*, which has been closely linked with the Taliban, leading to charges by Baloch nationalists that the Pakistan government was attempting to 'Talibanize' Balochistan in order to defeat the separatist insurgency (Khan 2009). While the assertion might appear fanciful, within the shadowy context of political life in Pakistan, where secretive government security agencies such as the ISI operate with impunity and have a long record of using religious groups as policy tools, claims such as these are not lacking in credibility.

That the Pakistani military has had such a tough time confronting Baloch separatists should come as no surprise. Political violence in Balochistan has a costly pedigree. In the 1970s conflict, when the military was able to focus on Balochistan without distraction, it still lost over 3,000 of its personnel (Khan 2009). Today, Pakistan's security situation is much more complex. In addition to its arch-foe, India, and often tense relations with Iran, Pakistan has had to contend with other ethnic insurgent groups, such as the *Muhajir Qaumi Movement* (MQM), *Sipah-e-Sahaba* (SSP), *Lashkar-e-Jhangvi* (LeJ), *Tehreek-i-Taliban* (TTP), *Lashkar-e-Toiba* (LeT) and the Pakistan Taliban, and costly operations in the North West Frontier Province–Afghanistan border areas. Suicide bombings increased from a total of 15 between 2001 and 2007 to 358 by November 2013, by which time more than 50,000 people had been killed in terrorist incidents (Abbasi 2013), of whom 17,642 were killed between 2011 and 2013 alone (Ministry of Interior 2014). By 2009, the Pakistan Taliban was in charge of over 30 percent of Pakistan's territory, including most of Khyber Pakhtonkhwa and the tribal areas. This is despite the efforts of Pakistan's 33 intelligence agencies, which employ over 600,000 personnel (Ministry of Interior 2014). Expenditure on security and other effects of violence, such as reduced business activity and investment, have, according to various estimates, cost Pakistan US$180 billion (Abbasi 2012) or 16.13 percent of real GDP per capita growth between 2001 and 2010 (Sultan 2013).

In contrast to Balochistan, separatist conflict in Kashmir has reached a deceptively low level of intensity. From a height of 4,507 fatalities (including separatists, security personnel and civilians) in 2001, violence diminished to 193 fatalities in 2014 (South Asia Terrorism Portal 2016). However, it would be mistaken to conclude on this basis that the Kashmir issue was resolved. Each month, separatist, or 'terrorist,' incidents continue to claim more than a dozen lives. The front pages of newspapers in the state detail incidents, foiled attacks or communal unrest linked to the separatist dispute on an almost daily basis. In 2014, the number of fatalities linked to separatism in Kashmir (193) was second only to that of Assam (305), while at the time of writing there were more separatist-related fatalities (144) in Kashmir than in any other Indian state (South Asia Terrorism Portal 2016). Indeed, there exists still in Kashmiri society a level of antipathy, bordering on hostility, to Indian rule that remains unassuaged despite the steady decline in hostilities.

The tactics employed against the Khalistan movement informed New Delhi's response to Kashmiri separatism. An initially heavy-handed response in the form of authoritarian central rule resulted in numerous state-sponsored atrocities by the CRPF and BSF that revolted ordinary Kashmiris, mobilized public sentiment against the Indian state and have been well documented by international organizations (Amnesty International 1995, 2001, 2008, 2011). In addition to the arbitrariness and injustices highlighted by these reports, India's prosecution of its counter-insurgency campaign in Kashmir bears similarities to those in other regions and is based on experiences in combatting pro-independence movements in Punjab and the northeast. This includes persistent cordon and search operations in which neighborhoods are cordoned off, houses searched and identity parades held; counter-intelligence operations; and attempts to seal off the line of control to halt Pakistani infiltration and assistance to separatist insurgents. While the mountainous topography of the region makes it impossible to completely seal the border, Pakistan's distraction by operations against the Pakistan Taliban and increased international pressure in consequence of Pakistan's sponsorship of internationally proscribed jihadi organizations in Kashmir and Afghanistan have curtailed its desire and ability to lend assistance to violent separatist groups operating in Kashmir. India's strategy was complemented by the outsourcing of security functions to *Ikhwan* – former militants who have been 'turned' and provided with weapons, money and protection by the government (Baweja and Vinayak 1996; Human Rights Watch 1996) – and Village Defense Committees that performed security and intelligence-gathering functions in remote locations such as Doda. Both of these groups, particularly the *Ikhwan*, were criticized as little more than state-sponsored vigilantes, although their local knowledge did prove an important asset as the burden of counter-insurgency operations was shifted from the much-maligned BSF and CRPF to the Jammu and Kashmir Police (JKP). Subsequently, as in other regions, shifts in the composition and tactics of separatist groups alienated public support – which increasingly had to be coerced – although public antipathy toward Indian rule remained.

Politically, the Indian government, as in Punjab and elsewhere, also attempted to use the ballot box in an attempt to demonstrate a return to normalcy in the state. Electoral malpractice in a state dominated by one party – the Kashmiri-centric National Conference – had been a pervasive feature of politics in the state since the 1950s. Unopposed returns in consequence of the disqualification of candidates from rival parties on flimsy grounds (in addition to their detention and beating) and the dismissal of elected state governments by New Delhi had long marred democratic processes in the state. Moreover, the National Conference's intolerance toward rival parties resulted in sustained allegations of abuse of power (Bazaz 1967, 1978; Verma 1994). Its 1983 victory in state assembly elections prompted allegations of vote rigging by the Congress (I), and in July the following year the government was unceremoniously dismissed by the state governor, Jagmohan, in what was popularly believed to be a carefully orchestrated campaign of revenge by Indira Gandhi. Publicly, the dismissal was rather unconvincingly justified by claims that National Conference leader and Chief Minister Farooq Abdullah had consorted with and encouraged secessionist forces, permitted Sikh terrorists to train in Kashmir, and met with Sant Jarnail Bhindrinwale. Subsequent unrest saw the imposition of governor's rule in September 1986 and an accord between the National Conference and Congress (I) that afforded a broad alliance of Islamic groups known as the Muslim United Front (MUF) the anti-center, pro-Kashmiri mantle that had previously belonged to the National Conference. The overwhelming defeat of the MUF, which was preceded by the mass arrests of MUF leaders and election agents prior to the poll, stretched the credulity of the electoral process past breaking point and led many to conclude that New Delhi had once again disregarded democratic procedures in order to cheat Kashmiris of their rightful political inheritance (Bhattacharjea 1994).

Given this history of electoral malpractice – combined with the status of the 1987 elections as a turning point in center–state relations and one of the main catalysts for separatist violence in Kashmir – restoring public faith in the ballot box was a central plank in New Delhi's strategy to rehabilitate relations with the state. However, matters are complicated by the 1947 accession crisis and Kashmir's status as a disputed territory between India and Pakistan; a history of antagonism between the National Conference and New Delhi; the contextualization of Kashmir as India's only Muslim-majority state within broader questions of Hindu–Muslim relations and India's avowedly secular constitution; and Kashmir's lack of integration within the institutional and economic fabric of India. The unfortunate effect of these factors, New Delhi's protestations aside, is that the default position for Kashmir is on India's geographical, cultural and socioeconomic periphery, with numerous unresolved questions regarding the state's rightful status within the Indian Union. While the Indian mainstream might regard Kashmir's integration as a *fait accompli*, for many Kashmiris it is very much an unsettled matter awaiting satisfactory resolution. It was against this background of popular discontent and struggle for recognition that India attempted to use tainted political processes to create a sense of normalcy to bolster its claims to sovereignty over Kashmir.

The 1996 state assembly elections marked the beginning of this process and saw the re-election of the National Conference, which won 57 of the available 87 seats with a turnout of 53.92 percent (Election Commission of India 1997), with *Lok Sabha* elections the same year yielding a turnout of 48.96 percent and the Congress Party winning four of the available six seats (Election Commission of India 1996). However, allegations of coercion and vote rigging persisted, particularly with respect to the legislative assembly poll (Sidhva 1996). The electoral process was given a boost with the removal of the National Conference in favor of a new, Kashmiri populist party, the People's Democratic Party (PDP), which, having won 16 of the available 87 seats, formed a coalition government with the Congress Party in 2002. Following this, elections in 2008 saw the return of the National Conference in coalition with Congress, and in 2014 a PDP–BJP collation was formed after elections the same year. However, dominance of different regions in the state by different parties associated with different religious communities (the Hindu-centric Congress and BJP in Jammu and the Muslim-centric National Conference and PDP in the Kashmir Valley), relatively modest turnout and the boycott of elections by the *Hurriyat* Conference (which acts as an umbrella organization for separatist groups in the state), indicates that the development of an inclusive political process, supported by a civil society that embraces religious and regional difference, remains a distant goal. Today, unrest in the state remains confined mostly to the Kashmir Valley. The most significant event in recent years was the riots in 2010, in which over 100 people lost their lives, which were precipitated by the killing of three civilians whom the Indian Army had initially claimed were Pakistani infiltrators. That the military still feels sufficiently empowered by draconian security legislation to resort to staged encounters is an indication of how little things have changed in the state, the dramatically reduced death toll notwithstanding.

Kashmir's deceptively calm exterior is mirrored in India's northeast, with some regions apparently free of separatist violence while conflict rages in others, with Manipur and Tripura the most afflicted areas (Lacina 2007). Separatist politics and cultural identity remain the main means of mass mobilization for relatively backward, poor and alienated groups to pursue conflicts over land and economic development. The region contains more than 382 culturally distinct, geographically concentrated communities of various sizes and at different stages of development, with new communities forming and others disappearing (e.g., the amalgamation of the Chakrii, Keza and Sangtang tribes into the Chakhesang) in a constantly evolving landscape of changing loyalties and identities. This mobilization is aided by the marginal position of the northeast's inhabitants vis-à-vis Indian national identity construed in Hindi–Hindu–Brahmanical terms (Baruah 2005). This ideological alienation is informed by New Delhi's reliance on military force, the realignment of state boundaries, and special autonomy agreements that have failed to develop institutional capacity in the region or, as in the case of Kashmir, address its reliance on large financial transfers from the center. Moreover, lack of development – compounded by the mismanagement and corruption of much of the aid provided by New Delhi – fosters a lawless environment where, in the absence of opportunities for gainful employment, kidnapping and extortion are lucrative activities that further depress incentives for investment in physical and human capital (Lacina 2007). The result is a vicious cycle of lawlessness, violence and conflict that has seen many 'separatist' groups degenerate into banditry. Attacks on civilians, links with organized crime, and inter-communal/factional violence have supplanted the tactics of an ideologically motivated, organizationally coherent separatist movement united by the shared goal of political independence.

A defining feature of the northeast has been New Delhi's willingness to adjust state boundaries by creating new states out of Assam and to engage in autonomy agreements in an attempt to defuse separatism. Examples include the states of Nagaland (1963), Manipur, Tripura, Meghalaya (1972), Arunachal Pradesh and Mizoram (1987) (Haokip 2012). On the one hand, this strategy has provided groups with real opportunities for cultural autonomy and self-determination, permitting elites a legitimate space in which to carve out spheres of political authority. On the other hand, however, it also bestows legitimacy by placing groups struggling for sovereignty on a 'special plane' where normal political and legal constraints do not apply (Lacina 2007). This results in the elevation of differences within the group granted statehood at the expense of the new minorities created within the nascent political unit, sowing new tensions and conflicts; e.g., the creation of Andhra Pradesh for Telegu-speakers out of the state of Madras prompted demands by Telangana speakers for their own state (Barbora 2006), which were satisfied in 2014 with the creation of the state of Telangana, which prompted more strenuous demands for states of Gorkhaland in West Bengal and Bodoland in Assam. Similarly, the creation of the state of Meghalaya to satisfy the aspirations of the Khasis, Garos and Jaintias did not quell Garo claims that their interests can only be adequately protected in a state of their own (Baruah 2005). Moreover, Lacina (2009) points out how the creation of the state of Mizoram, while apparently ending the separatist insurgency, has established ethnic Mizo hegemony within the state, leading to increased repression of minority communities, vigilantism, the lack of an inclusive democratic process and the expulsion of thousands of Brus, Hmars and Chakmas into Tripura, Assam and Manipur, displacing, rather than resolving, ethnic tensions and other problems in the area and leading to new separatist movements such as that of the Hmar.

It may be argued that the realignment of state borders and devolution of political power to smaller (sub-)units demonstrates the strength of Indian democratic institutions through a willingness to negotiate and compromise that extends as far back as independence from Great Britain. In 1947, the Interim Government appointed a sub-committee to the Constituent Assembly – the North-East Frontier

(Assam) Tribal and Excluded Areas Committee – which recommended providing representative structures at the local level to the tribal population. The recommendation was later incorporated into Article 244 (2) of the Sixth Schedule of the Indian Constitution, which exempts the religious and social practices of the Nagas from federal legislation, prioritizing Naga customary law and procedure in matters pertaining to civil and criminal justice and ownership and transfer of land and resources, subject to ratification of the federal statute by the legislative assembly of Nagaland. These arrangements were parts of a lengthy process of negotiation that included the 1947 Akbar Hydari agreement, the 1964 Naga Peace Mission and the 1975 Shillong Accord (Goswami 2011). Nonetheless, it is also important to acknowledge that this process of negotiation, compromise and devolution was accompanied by the threat and use of state coercion and military power using a 'carrot and stick' approach in which the overwhelming use of military force was interrupted by the offer of talks and lavish development funds in the form of secretive deals (Kikon 2005). Consequently, it would be inaccurate to describe the drawing of state boundaries as consensual or as acquiescence by the Indian state to all, or even the most important, separatist demands.

More crucially, the negotiation and compromise that inevitably accompany realignment of state boundaries may bestow a temporary or 'bargained' character on legal and political institutions that undermines their hegemony (Baruah 1994). Consider, for example, ULFA's activism in a wide variety of political and economic policy areas, including industrial pollution, illiteracy, land management, abuses in the educational system, provision of relief to flood victims, and the control of violence between Hindus and Muslims in Assam following the Ayodhya outrage (Baruah 1994). Participation in (semi-)official processes that address legitimate social and economic issues has conferred upon ULFA a degree of moral and institutional legitimacy at the expense of state institutions, while opening new opportunities for it to influence the lives of citizens. Finally, not all political disputes centering on conflicts of identity are amenable to boundary solutions. As Baruah (2009) highlights, Bodos, Karbis and Dimasas can be given more autonomy within the state of Assam; however, increased autonomy for Assamese cannot be granted in the same way, because, as a non-exclusive ethnic category, 'Assamese' includes these smaller groups.

An often-cited instance of these drawbacks is the appalling law and order situation in the northeast, which sees local politicians frequently targeted by, or in league with, criminal elements in acts of smuggling, extortion, voter intimidation and inter-communal violence. Lacina (2009), for example, argues that the granting of statehood or lesser measures of autonomy has not marked the beginning of political normalization. Rather, she claims, New Delhi tolerates ongoing repression and corruption – which hamper measures that might address mass grievances, such as land reform or poverty relief – if there is an end to attacks on strategic or government targets. While the price for this is increased expenditure (per capita central government grants to the northeast are up to six times higher than the average funding received by other states), the payoff for New Delhi consists in fewer security force fatalities. The Indian government is assisted in this process of harm minimization by the northeast's position on India's ideological and economic periphery (despite its geo-strategic significance) and the outsourcing of security functions to local militia in an arrangement whereby the payoff for local elites is continuation of the status quo and a large measure of impunity (Barbora 2006). Unlike Kashmir (which, as the only Muslim-majority state, is an important demonstration of India's secular nationalism) or Punjab (which is an important commercial and agricultural region), events in the northeast do not hold the attention of the nation. This makes the region and its inhabitants of little electoral significance, reducing the incentive for New Delhi to find a long-lasting solution to the problems there, and enabling it to dismiss continued protest and conflict as deviant behavior in consequence of the region's geographical and existential distance from the nation's heartland (Barbora 2006).

In Assam, negotiations between ULFA and New Delhi, which had begun in 2004 but had been regularly stymied by broken ceasefire agreements, finally bore fruit due to splits within ULFA that saw the so-called 28th Battalion announce a unilateral ceasefire. Mass defections and surrenders, combined with the arrest of much of its senior leadership and closure of its training and supply camps in Bhutan, have severely weakened the organization. In addition, successful interdiction operations by the Indian military have dramatically reduced the infiltration of supplies and insurgents across the border with Bangladesh. While bombings and other violent incidents continue – the most notable being in 2008 in Guwahati, in which 81 persons died – ULFA is clearly on the back foot operationally, with popular support for an independent state predicated on the former Ahom Kingdom also questionable.

Meanwhile, other sub-groups within Assam continue small-scale, violent struggles. A 2001 ceasefire agreement with the Bodo Liberation Tigers (BLT) paved the way for negotiations, which in 2003 led to the creation of the Bodoland Territorial Council (BTC), with about half of the surrendered BLT cadres immediately recruited into the state paramilitary forces. This freed the military to concentrate on the rival National Democratic Front of Bodoland (NDFB), which split in 2008 due to disagreements over whether to negotiate a settlement or continue violence. The NDFB was linked to killings in May 2014 in Narsingbari, in which 33 Bengali-speaking Muslims were killed, and in December 2014, in which 65 tribal people were killed. Other violent separatist groups in the state are either defunct (e.g., the *Dima Halam Daogah*, which laid down its arms in 2003) or inactive (e.g., the Karbi Longri N. C. Hills Liberation Front).

The 'stable but unsettled' status of these groups in Assam mirrors that of Darjeeling, which is a partially autonomous region in West Bengal. The Indian government's creation of the state of Sikkim in 1975 and its reluctance to recognize Nepali as an official language highlighted the conundrum of a separate state of Gorkhaland for people of Nepali origin in northern West Bengal. The demand for political independence has a long pedigree, dating back to a 1907 memorandum by the Hillmen's Association to an audience that included the Viceroy. The proposal was again raised in 1930, in 1941 and shortly before independence in

1947. Violent protests in the 1980s led by the Gorkha National Liberation Front (GNLF) resulted in the establishment of the popularly elected Darjeeling Gorkha Hill Council (DGHC), which exercised legislative and administrative control over matters pertaining to economic development and the management of natural resources. However, due to the DGHC's failure to address economic and social issues in the region and interpersonal rivalries within the GNLF, a breakaway organization, the *Gorkha Jan Mukti Morcha* (GJMM), was formed in 2007. Acts of civil disobedience (rallies, road blockades, general strikes and sieges of government buildings) by the GJMM eventually forced the resignation of the GNLF's founding leader and stalwart Subhash Ghisingh in 2008 as the GNLF surrendered its ascendency to the GJMM. Moreover, as Lacina (2009) points out, the GJMM's tactics of strikes and moratoriums on government offices have established the party's hegemony in the state at the expense of rival parties, genuine public debate and democratic process, as the intolerance of rival parties and thuggery of the GNLF were replicated by the GJMM. The GJMM was implicated in the murder of Madan Tamang, leader of the *Akhil Bharatiya Gorkha* League, in 2010, which was followed by the police shooting dead three GJMM activists in 2011 and a subsequent nine-day strike. Ahead of the 2009 general elections, the GJMM had been encouraged by the BJP's promise to create a state of Gorkhaland. This hope was dashed by the Congress Party's drubbing of the BJP. However, ongoing violence in Darjeeling did result in a pact between the GJMM, the Government of West Bengal and the Government of India that resulted in the formation of an autonomous, elected Gorkhaland Territorial Administration (GTA) with more powers than the preceding DGHC. Subsequent elections in 2012 were dominated by the GJMM. However, it is unclear to what degree the GTA has obviated the appetite for a Gorkhaland state. The sense of neglect and economic under-development that drives separatist sentiment remains largely unaddressed. Moreover, the 2014 creation of the state of Telangana has given new impetus to sub-national movements in India demanding greater independence from central rule. Accordingly, while Darjeeling remains largely violence-free, the question of its final status in the Indian Union is not yet settled.

Turning to areas in which violence remains endemic, Nagaland is the least affected of these regions. After it became a state within the Indian Union in 1963, separatist sentiment continued, spearheaded by the Nationalist Socialist Council of Nagaland (NSCN), which signed a peace accord in 2015 with the government of India. This was preceded by an effective campaign by India to build trust between the army and local peoples, who had tired of the effects of continued conflict and lawlessness. For example, armed separatists would routinely stop public transport vehicles and, using threats of violence, extort payment from passengers. The army's deployment reduced these acts of banditry and other threats to villagers' property (Goswami 2011), earning the army their gratitude and trust. Today, the greatest threat of violence is from enmity between rivals within NSCN, including operations against politicians, civilians and defectors, as opposed to coordinated attacks on government security forces. As in

Punjab, these divisions have assisted the government's anti-insurgency operations, as the NSCN fractured along kinship lines between Nagas from Manipur and Myanmar. However, these splits also call into question the region's future. Aside from the danger to daily life that attacks between these two factions pose, they also threaten to undermine long-term stability, as groups are encouraged to adopt more extreme positions and harden their negotiating stances (Lacina 2007). Underlying these divisions are tribal tensions between ethnic Nagas and Tangkhuls, a Naga tribe that straddles the Indo-Myanmar border. Issues dividing the two groups include the status of the Kuki people living in the Ukhrul district of Manipur, who have close links with Naga tribes, but with whom the Tangkhuls share a fraught relationship; and the role of ethnicity and religion in an independent or autonomous Nagaland. Whereas some groups, such as the NSCN (Isak-Muivah), envisage a greater Nagaland (Nagalim), curiously blending Maoist ideology with Christianity to define the relevant population to whom political authority might be devolved, others, such as the NSCN (Khaplang), adopt a more ethno-centric definition of what it means to be a Naga.

In Manipur, separatist violence continues despite its becoming a state within the Indian Union in 1972, demonstrating that devolution of political authority is not always a panacea to separatism. The United National Liberation Front's armed wing, the Manipur People's Army (MPA), continues as the main protagonist of violent separatism in a state beset by a variety of social and economic maladies, including drug trafficking, unemployment and AIDS (Goswami 2011). As in other regions in the northeast, the struggle incorporates ideological and ethnic dimensions, with conflicts between ethnic groups – particularly Meiteis of the plains areas and hill tribes such as Kukis, Paites, Hmars and Vaiphei – being as common as attacks on government forces and infrastructure. Consequently, because much of the violence is not directed against security forces, various ceasefires with New Delhi have failed to stem the violence, which continues to thrive in an environment of lawlessness and vigilantism (Lacina 2009). Although sizeable deployments of military personnel to the state by New Delhi mean that a military victory by the MPA is untenable, high-profile ambushes of security forces and bombing do generate nation-wide press coverage.

Statehood in 1972 has also failed to stem separatism in Tripura, which is spearheaded by the All Tripura Tiger Force (ATTF) and the National Liberation Front of Tripura (NLFT). Whereas the ATTF is an avowedly ethno-centric, isolationist group whose agenda is centered on the expulsion of Bengali-speaking settlers and land reform, the NLFT's separatist agenda is motivated by a desire to secede from India to create an independent, Tripuri state. Like the NSCN (Isak-Muivah), the NLFT mixes Christianity with ethnic politics and Marxist ideology. Acts by these groups include the massacre of Hindus, kidnapping and other criminal activities. The NLFT has a strong presence in Bangladesh and has benefited from smuggling and the sanctuary provided by an international border. Consequently, India has attempted to obtain the cooperation of Bangladesh in securing the border and pressured Dhaka to limit assistance to Tripuri separatist groups (Lacina 2009). This is part of a broader strategy by India to counter international assistance to separatist groups in the region; e.g., in June 2015, Indian special forces launched a cross-border raid into Myanmar in retaliation for an ambush by NSCN (Khaplang) cadres (Tarapot 2003). In the case of Bangladeshi support for Tripuri separatist groups, the case for cooperation is stronger, given Bangladesh's control over its border areas – an advantage that has eluded Myanmar – and the two governments have recently signaled a willingness to cooperate in coordinated operations and by sharing lists of proscribed organizations and wanted terrorists (Jain 2015).

Finally, there is the case of Bangladesh's Chittagong Hill Tract (CHT) region, in which much of the proposed cooperation between India and Bangladesh to curb militant violence is to occur. Following the restoration of democracy in Bangladesh in 1991, an agreement was signed in December 1997 between the Bangladesh government (led by Prime Minister Sheikh Hasina Wajed of the Awami League) and separatist actors in the CHT. Recognizing the distinct ethnicity and special status of the tribes and indigenous peoples of the CHT, the agreement established a Regional Council comprised of the local government councils of the three districts of the Hill Tracts from the Chakma, Marma, Tripura, Murang and Tanchangya tribes. The intention was for the council to exercise authority over a range of local matters, including law and order, social justice and tribal matters, general administration, disaster relief and development projects. The central government would also be required to consult the council on matters concerning the CHT, while there was to be a central Ministry of Tribal Affairs, to be headed by a representative from the CHT, that would take some responsibility for the redistribution of land and a comprehensive cadastral survey of the region. The agreement was successful in ending organized separatist violence, as many militants surrendered their arms, bringing the main separatist group – the *Parbatya Chattagram Jana Samhati Samiti* (PCJSS) – within the democratic process and allowing the return of many tribal peoples displaced by the violence. However, the agreement was not without its critics, who saw it as compromising Bangladesh's territorial and political integrity while failing to adequately accommodate the interests of Bengali settlers, having been arrived at through a negotiation process conducted in secret.

To date, the accord has yet to be implemented, due to a range of legal and political hurdles. In 2010, the High Court of Bangladesh declared the Chittagong Hill Tracts Regional Council Act of 1998 and sections of the three amended Hill District Council Acts of 1998 unconstitutional because they violated the sanctity of a unitary state (D'Costa 2011). While the legal wrangling continues, violence has returned to the CHT, displacing at least 1,500 indigenous people (D'Costa 2012), with hundreds rendered homeless (Ahmad 2013) and the continued seizure of land belonging to the region's indigenous population (Yasmin 2014). In addition, the accord is opposed by two major political parties – the Bangladesh Nationalist Party (BNP) and the *Jatiyo* Party – that allege it challenges Bangladesh's status as a unitary state and is the handiwork of Indian authorities seeking to weaken Bangladesh. Critics also point to the fact that the accord is opposed by some indigenous groups in the CHT (e.g., the Hill Women's Federation and the *Pahari Chatra Parishad*), while others argue that suzerainty over the CHT is essential for Bangladesh, given the region's economic importance as a center for electricity generation, satellite communications and irrigation (the Karnaphuli, Sangu, Matamuhuri and Halda Rivers rise in or traverse the CHT); the recent discovery of oil and gas reserves in the region; its strategic importance, bordering India and Myanmar; the international dimensions of local politics in the CHT due to the ethnic and religious links tribal inhabitants share with peoples in India and Myanmar; and the criminal activity that pervades the region (Quaider 2015). Prior to the 2010 High Court ruling, these concerns effectively scuppered the Accord's implementation. The Land Commission established by the Chittagong Hill Tracts Land Disputes Resolution Commission Act (2001) found itself at loggerheads with the PCJSS due to the commission's insistence that it first conduct a cadastral survey, meaning that 45,000 applications seeking settlement of land disputes in the hill districts remain pending. Moreover, elections for indigenous representatives from the Hill District Councils to serve on the Regional Council have not been held, meaning that all current members on the Regional Council are government appointees. Consequently, the region remains heavily militarized – a violation of the Accord, which requires removal from the region of all temporary army and security force camps. While the military insists that its presence is required in consequence of the rising numbers of violent incidents between the indigenous population and Bengali settlers, as well as widespread attacks on Buddhists living in the region, the continued military presence and sustained allegations of human rights abuses perpetrated by military personnel only give succor to separatist sentiment (Dowlah 2013).

Conclusion

Given their relative lack of success and increasingly diminutive role on the political stage, one might well wonder why separatist groups in South Asia continue to struggle. Faced with a numerically more powerful and well-resourced adversary, separatists walk a fine line between the competing imperatives of membership, strategy and ideology. A deficiency in just one of these areas is capable of exerting a crippling effect. For example, a shortage of active, committed members can limit a group's chances of success by reducing its ability to enforce edicts, collect rents and appear as a credible alternative to the government. However, a membership that is too large might decrease the aggregate benefits available to members, making it difficult for the group to hold down defection rates. Similarly, an inability to attract the right kind of members or maintain discipline may also affect the group's capacity to obtain a community's voluntary cooperation or collect rents, with a concomitantly negative effect upon its prospects of success. Added to the group's difficulties is the fact that changes to membership, rents and other features do not remain static, but are in a constant state of flux. Consequently, not only must separatist groups get the balance between competing imperatives right, but they must also constantly adjust this equilibrium according to changes in the strategic environment.

In contrast, the state's resources and staying power allow it to outbid and outwait opponents. This also permits the state to alienate the target population in a separatist-affected region through neglect and human rights abuses while nonetheless commanding their longer-term allegiance. Individuals know that, although the state may have serious drawbacks, its ability to impose order, distribute benefits and outbid rivals means that it cannot be easily dismissed. While the state's claims of embodiment – to represent the interests of minority communities fairly and effectively – may ring hollow, its proven ability to provide collective benefits goes some distance in making up for this failure. In contrast, separatists are often held to a higher standard, as they must demonstrate the conceptual and material superiority of a post-secession state of affairs despite its imagined and counter-factual status. The outcome proffered by secession is uncertain and requires that individuals trust separatist leaders to be capable of delivering on their promises. As this trust declines, the commitment of members of the group and the target community evaporates, along with the resources they provide, initiating a cycle of decline. By cutting off resources, leveraging internal splits, expanding military operations and outbidding the separatists on the provision of economic and social goods, the state can create a crisis of confidence amongst the group's membership and support network that becomes self-sustaining. Strategic setbacks increase defection rates, making it harder for the group to maintain momentum and resulting in further losses of territory and authority, causing confidence to wane, defections to surge and the group's struggle to be an increasingly lost cause.

It is little wonder, then, that the separatist movements active in South Asia today are for the most part a pale shadow of their former selves, with graveyards full of the political dreams, and earthly remains, of former adherents. Even in those territories that are still categorized as 'disturbed,' levels of violence are significantly reduced in comparison with earlier years, while other independence movements, such as those in Sri Lanka and the Indian state of Punjab, show little sign of returning. Indeed, most contemporary separatist organizations in South Asia could more appropriately be termed 'criminal enterprises,' with only Balochistan offering a full-blown, ideologically motivated separatist insurgency capable of posing a threat to a weakened and over-stretched military establishment. The following chapter puts this decline in some perspective and offers an alternative explanation for why separatism, but not political violence and activism, is declining in South Asia.

5 Conclusion

Introduction

This book has advanced the thesis that separatism is informed by the concept and practice of sovereignty. Of particular importance is the 'gap' between sovereignty's conceptualization as a binary property possessed exclusively by states, and the reality of its exercise as a shared attribute diffused amongst a range of non-/state actors. In addition, because separatism is not a static phenomenon (but alters over time as a group's membership, objectives and strategic environment change), it is not explicable according to a master narrative or dominant variable. Rather, separatist movements are characterized and driven by a range of divergent features that transform over time. This chapter concludes the discussion by applying these insights to the questions of whether separatism has a future in South Asia and whether the region is moving toward a 'post-separatist' era.

Earlier, it was noted that different separatist groups exhibit a range of descriptive features and 'push' and 'pull' motives that incentivized separation from the group's parent state. The former category of incentive included human rights abuses, economic discrimination and central interference in local matters, whereas the latter referred mainly to perceived benefits of a post-secession state of affairs, such as greater wealth and control over the group's affairs. The 'pull' factors that attract groups to independent statehood – or, more rarely, accession to a neighboring state (as in the case of Kashmir to Pakistan) – are a function of sovereignty and the benefits that it confers. Moreover, just as the composition, ideological convictions, motivations and resources of separatist groups exist in a constant state of flux, the same is true of the institution of sovereignty and its exercise; while the state may be ubiquitous, the control that it exercises over the territory under its jurisdiction is not, and in many ways has over recent decades been substantially altered by forces of economic liberalization and institutional decay.

This chapter explores the implications of this finding to explain the decline of separatist (but not political) violence in South Asia. After summarizing data on death tolls from separatist and political violence in South Asia, the chapter briefly reviews the characteristics of sovereignty before exploring how its conceptualization as a binary property that resides exclusively in institutions of statehood is poorly reflected in the reality of its exercise. While commonly perceived as a binary, non-dependent property possessed exclusively by states, in reality, sovereignty is tenuous, constantly emergent and shared. This disjuncture is evident in both the fanciful moral justifications of state sovereignty and the actuality of its exercise. After exploring some historical and contemporary examples of sovereignty's multi-layered, inchoate and dispersed character from South Asia and elsewhere, this discussion is then related back to the decline of separatist violence in South Asia through the claim that the retrenchment of state institutions and authority has rendered the state a less attractive possession (and target) for political actors and, consequently, significantly reduced the 'pull' factors that incentivize separatism.

Sovereignty as a contingent and contested property

Armitage (2010) has observed that between 1816 and 2001 there were 296 civil wars, of which 109 were fought with the goal of creating a new state, meaning that separatist conflicts comprise more than a third of all wars in the past two centuries. When it comes to calculating the scale and costs of conflict, however, things become more complicated. Determining whether or not a conflict qualifies as 'separatist' is itself far from straightforward, given the multiplicity of actors and motivations for violence that characterize many conflicts. However, it is a comparatively simple undertaking when contrasted with the difficulty of measuring the level and destructiveness of violence over time. Accurate records are frequently not kept or available. Moreover, belligerents have an incentive to exaggerate their successes and downplay their losses. Finally, not all acts of violence in a conflict are motivated by a desire to achieve a movement's stated aims, but may instead be attributable to criminality, personal vendetta and a range of other motives.

Figure 5.1 uses the Correlates of War (COW) dataset to illustrate the changing number of fatalities in separatist violence in South Asia from 1989 to 2014, demonstrating how separatist violence peaked in 2008/9 in the bloody climax to Sri Lanka's civil war and since then has fallen to remarkably low levels. Indeed, as the previous chapter illustrated, only India's northeast and Pakistan's Balochistan continue to exhibit notable levels of violence, whereas other conflicts either have been resolved or are at a low ebb. This is in contrast to intra-state conflict in South Asia over the same period, in which the number of fatalities in 2014 reached an almost record high. Of particular note here are the Taliban's escalating campaign of violence in Afghanistan and Pakistan, and continuing Naxalite violence in India. To summarize, while the number of fatalities from separatist violence in South Asia has declined noticeably, more individuals are dying in other forms of organized sub-state violence by religious and ideological movements. I contend that this decline in separatism, but not in political violence and rebellion, is explicable by reference to changes to state sovereignty that have occurred in South Asia subsequent to decolonization. Specifically, the rolling back of state sovereignty in economic and other spheres has made the

110 *Conclusion*

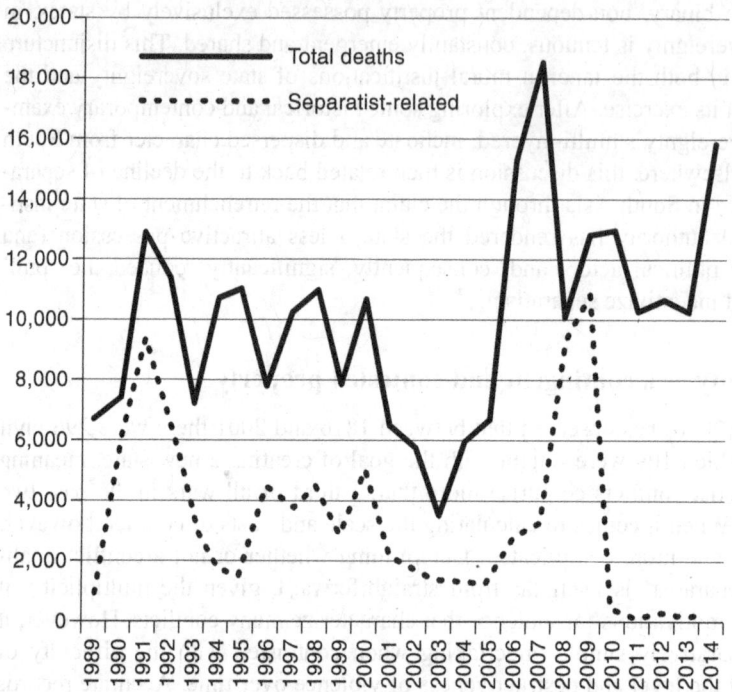

Figure 5.1 Deaths from political violence in South Asia 1989–2014.

state a less attractive target for capture by those who oppose it and its policies. To better understand this process, and the effect that it has had upon antigovernment violence, it is necessary to revisit the concept of sovereignty, which, like the groups that oppose or seek to capture it, has not remained constant over time.

In a conceptual sense, sovereignty is held to inhere in organizational structures and to be generated by actions that constitute or maintain structures of relations (e.g., the passing of legislation) and create roles or identities such as those of taxpayer, immigrant or consumer (Griffiths 2003). While this understanding has changed little over the past two centuries, it serves as an increasingly inaccurate descriptive account of sovereignty's exercise. In Chapter 1, it was noted that sovereignty is distinguished by its territorial delineation, which establishes the exclusive jurisdiction required for the state to achieve its political, social and economic ends (Agnew 2005). For example, some speculate that territorialization facilitates mutual recognition between citizens and sentiments of shared loyalty (both to one another and to the state) by allowing them to commemorate the past, with either celebration or remorse, with reference to a geographical space that is woven together with the image of the state and public authority to create a powerful narrative of belonging and collective agency (Lund 2006). Others hypothesize a link between territorial adjacency and the deliberative nature of democracy, the symbolic content of which is held to rest upon common territorial histories of struggle and social organization (Thaa 2001; Agnew 2005).

Claims such as these – which point to the functionality of territorial sovereignty as an effective means of maximizing morally important goals and values – have formed the main response to moral critiques that challenge the legitimacy of the state's extensive accumulation of power and the ubiquity of its exercise. In addition, geography's fixed, immutable character lends a symbolic permanence to the state, which, like the territory over which it possesses jurisdiction, assumes a natural, unquestionable identity. In this manner, the state is imbued with attributes of agency, neutrality and necessity required to regulate competition for the social product. Accordingly, justification for the state's sovereignty is located in its ability to provide for the common good by addressing the problem of human aggression (Agnew 2005), which, following Hobbes, has historically been reduced to the two dimensions of external security and internal prosperity (Sangmpam 2007).

Through the promulgation and enforcement of binding rules of social conduct, the state reduces transgressions of each individual's rights and mitigates the free-rider problems that plague the provision of public goods, thereby overcoming the inadequacy of individual effort to produce a state of affairs that (while not ideal from many individuals' standpoints) is vastly superior to that which would be attainable if each individual were to act unilaterally to secure his or her own interests. Consequently, as was noted in Chapter 2, the justification of state sovereignty has both deontological elements (as the embodiment of collective interests and a neutral arbiter in conflicts between individuals and groups in society) and teleological aspects (represented by the functional utility of state sovereignty and the counter-factual negative consequences that would obtain in its absence). The two form indistinct sides of the same coin, as the state's neutrality and impartiality permit it to claim to represent common, non-partisan interests, which maximizes voluntary compliance with state edicts that provide order through the regulation of social conduct and relations between groups.

This conceptualization of sovereignty as residing within systems and structures that produce the order required in human affairs has a long historical pedigree in European political thought, stretching back as far as the seventeenth century. Thus, for Hobbes (1588–1679), sovereignty is not the will of a supreme authority over subjects, but various rights to determine the operation of law, organized violence and property. Similarly, Locke (1632–1704) defined sovereignty as the various codes and structures of relations that enable control over domains of life, Machiavelli (1469–1527) emphasized that it is the political order that governs and not the monarch, and Bodin (1530–96) described sovereignty as the power of the Commonwealth that was wielded by the monarch to constitute a domain of law (Griffiths 2003). In each case, recognition of the systems and structures in which sovereignty inheres establishes the domains that constitute its legitimate sphere of application. These structures are both an embodiment of each citizen's welfare, expressed through membership of a political community, and a prerequisite for it, given that the order and regulation of individual conduct that they require would be unobtainable without the coordinating and controlling functions of the state.

The legitimacy of the state's sovereignty is consequently embedded within the functions that the state serves vis-à-vis securing the common interest of individuals in the protection of their rights to a greater degree than could be achieved by individuals acting unilaterally. These claims are instantiated within the divergent and overlapping accounts of the origin of sovereignty developed by different thinkers' descriptions of the conceptual and ethical 'zero point' from where the law and political order are constituted. Whereas legal accounts focus upon a compact of equals and include social contract theories, ethical descriptions rely upon a mutual recognition of others' moral status as individual agents and the need to constitute an order to uphold the rights, duties, privileges and benefits that flow from this status. Some thinkers, such as Hobbes, envisioned a calamitous pre-political order, the 'State of Warre,' from which escape was only possible through the surrender of the sovereignty of the individual to a monarch, while others argued for a mystical or quasi-spiritual origin of royalty (Hansen and Stepputat 2006), such as the divine right of kings or supernatural parentage, as in the case of the Japanese emperor, who, according to legend, was descended from the sun goddess Amaterasu.

Each of these justifications is questionable on ontological grounds in terms of both sovereignty's origins and its daily exercise. Marxists, for example, have severely critiqued claims of state neutrality by seeing the state as a tool of bourgeois oppression and class exploitation, while accounts premised upon supernatural parentage (as in the case of the Japanese emperor) are clearly not amenable to empirical substantiation. However, one need not venture as far as nineteenth-century ideologues or celestial deities in order to observe an element of myth and lack of conceptual clarity in the justification of state sovereignty. Social contract theorists, for example, refer to a pact between the governed and a sovereign in which individuals cede their natural rights in order to establish a political order whereby their civil rights may be more effectively protected. Yet, in reality, only naturalized citizens expressly consent to the sovereignty of a particular state (while the rest of us have these matters determined by morally arbitrary factors such as parentage and place of birth). Consequently, consent theories of political obligation are forced to rely on *tacit* (participation in acts such as voting, not emigrating or receiving state-provided benefits) or *hypothetical* consent (individuals would consent if given the opportunity, as the costs of not consenting would be prohibitively high).

If the contractual or other origins of state sovereignty and the question of why citizens have a duty of obedience to this, and not some other (or no), state remain problematic for political philosophers, then the difficulty also extends to sovereignty's second claim of necessity and the deleterious state of affairs that *would* be produced were the state not to exist. The argument here is a purely teleological one, in which the Hobbesian state of nature is shorn of its historical antecedents and we are invited to envision a return to the state of nature and, recoiling from the implications, acknowledge the need for order in human affairs that can only be satisfied through the territorial jurisdiction of state sovereignty. The problem, in both a conceptual and a very real sense, is that none of these claims are true. Indeed, sovereignty's exercise – as a tenuous, incomplete and contested feature – gives the lie to the claim that it consists in a set of relationships and interactions that are organized, maintained or regulated by a political order with a monopoly on legitimate coercion over a given territory.

To elaborate, competing sources of authority, such as international organizations, social movements, businesses and non-government organizations, daily challenge and recast the sovereignty of the state. For example, multinational corporations and transnational organizations challenge spatial adjacency and the territorial division of sovereignty through a networked system of political authority whereby coercive power and authority emanate from geographically scattered locations (Appadurai 1996; Agnew 2005). While these organizations may have been established by states and depend upon governments for funding, they frequently wield disproportionate influence that smaller and indebted states find insurmountable. In contrast, other examples, such as currency speculators, financial markets and pirates, are not the creation of states, and in many cases exist in opposition to them. Rather than being a new phenomenon, these institutions are the most recent incarnation of an established historical process whereby states have shared, contracted out or surrendered functions of statehood. Consider, for example, 'modern-day privateers' such as military contractors and extra-legal detention centers (Human Rights Watch 2009), the increased role of supranational and foreign courts in judicial regulation within states, and arrangements of 'shared sovereignty,' such as China's two systems of government to incorporate Hong Kong (Griffiths 2003).

In addition, there are a wide range of 'twilight institutions' (Lund 2006) that occupy an intermediary position between state institutions and citizens and, like the state, are premised on claims of common identity defined in terms of geographical space (Humphrey 2004). While these institutions challenge the state's monopoly of legitimate violence by engaging in sovereign practices, they also rely upon its exercise of sovereignty (and gaps within it) to maximize attainment of illicit objectives in an often mutually beneficial and complementary relationship. For example, underworld organizations and their shadow networks exist within the context of state sovereignty and its associated hegemonic discourses of social order, working with the knowledge, tacit consent and assistance of state authorities (Nordstrom 2000). The receipt of bribes and other benefits encourages state officials to create zones of exception where illegal organizations operate with impunity, controlling territories and populations over which the state lacks either the ability or the will to exercise sovereignty. Slum lords, local strong men, quasi-legal networks, private societies and similar organizations have exercised *de facto* sovereignty from colonial times (Hansen and Stepputat 2006) and at various times have been tamed and incorporated into governmental structures (Hansen 2001). Frequently found in developing and post-colonial societies where the rule of law is weak, a common area in which these exceptions manifest is that of property rights, e.g., metropolitan squatter areas and slum cities where land titles are inaccurate or non-existent, and access to entitlements is contingent on a well-connected patron who can channel claims and applications through the state apparatus (Parnell 2003). The problem is exacerbated in conditions of conflict, especially civil war, where the movement of refugees and destruction of registries and documents of title render property rights blurred and unclear, allowing others to encroach on property or resources without legal consequence (Korf 2005).

At issue is the distinction by Abrams (1988) between the state system (tangible, mostly government institutions) and the state as an idea (what is generally expected to comprise the state) (Lund 2006). Similarly, Geertz (2004) suggests that, rather than being beholden to the concept of the homogeneous nation-state as the essential form of modern power, we should instead recognize that the identity and practices of states cannot always be derived from, or reduced to, any cultural logic. State sovereignty is, thus, recast from an ontological binary concept possessed exclusively by states, to a tentative and always-emergent form of authority grounded in violence to evince loyalty, fear and legitimacy (Hansen and Stepputat 2006). According to this understanding, the state's sovereignty is a matter of degree – never definitively formed, but waxing and waning in a constant process of (re)formation – sometimes in competition with, and at other times complemented by, alternative or illicit centers of sovereignty. Moreover, these non-state institutions that exist in the vacuum between state/society and public/private realms may exercise sovereignty in the form of political power and public authority, blurring the boundaries between non- and state sovereignty. Lund (2006) gives the example of the incoherence and incapacity of many African states that possess multiple parallel structures and alternative sites of authority (chiefs, vigilantes, political factions, hometown associations, neighborhood groups) that defy any notion of a unitary, rational state. Similarly, Nordstrom (2000) cites what he terms 'extra-state' networks that work through and around formal state representatives and institutions. Comprised of shadow linkages and extra-state actors, these networks forge economic policies, operate within political realms, fashion foreign policy and have sophisticated systems of enforcement and dispute resolution that are governed by codes of conduct and rules of behavior embedded in social and cultural systems that echo the national cultures of states. While not states, they share many of the attributes of states, including sovereignty (Nordstrom 2000). Consequently, public authority is an amalgam of power exercised by a variety of local institutions interspersed with that of external institutions conjugated with the *idea* of a state, rather than the state as a coherent institution; government institutions that claim to be an embodiment of state authority may issue formal rules and regulations, but these are often renegotiated or negated by corruption, political networks and powerful alliances with, and within, the same institutions.

This multi-layered, emergent, pluralistic reality in which sovereignty emanates from a variety of sources (in competition with and complementary to that of the state in a sometimes hostile, and at other times mutually beneficial, arrangement) produces a range of favorable and destructive outcomes. For example, undeclared earnings from legal and illegal activities leave a serious gap in taxation revenue and expose individuals to dangerous and harmful practices in unregulated workplaces. A 2010 report estimated that the British government missed out on £42 billion in earnings due to the so-called 'black economy,' consisting of il/legal activities from which earnings are undeclared (Morris 2010). The size of the Spanish black economy was estimated to be equivalent to 19.2 percent of official GDP, with estimates for other European countries ranging from 8.1 percent in Switzerland to 32.6 percent in Bulgaria (Mallet and Dinmore 2011). In addition, new markets, looser border controls and developments in communications technology have opened up a range of profitable activities that exist outside effective government regulation and in parallel to official, regulated markets. The people-smuggling industry, for instance, is estimated to have generated at least US$5 billion in US–Mexico traffic alone in 2003, while a similar figure of €4 billion was estimated for Europe (Padgett 2003). More recently, the global cybercrime industry was estimated to be worth $12.5 billion in 2011 (Kleczynski 2012). Other examples of the scale and value of extra-state, illegal networks are not difficult to locate; e.g., the UN estimated in 1997 that the illegal drug industry was worth around US$400 billion (United Nations Office on Drugs and Crime 2005), the financial value of the illegal trafficking of small arms and light weapons is estimated to be worth US$1 billion a year (Council on Foreign Relations 2012), and a 1998 study found that 20 percent of the world's financial deposits were in unregulated banks (Lopez and Cortwright 1998).

These criminal enterprises, the revenues they generate and the power structures they sustain do not exist outside the legal economy or state institutions. Rather, they permeate it in the form of laundered capital, which translates into formal economic and political power as illicit business people engage in legal activities. Japan's property bubble, which collapsed in 1989, was partly attributable to organized crime syndicates known as *Yakuza*, whose extensive links with politicians, banks and construction companies saw ineffective banking regulation and speculative investments precipitate a rise and fall in property and share prices that led to more than two decades of economic stagnation (Parry 1996). So pervasive was the influence of these criminal groups that they were able to play a significant role in the selection of Japanese Prime Minister Noboru Takeshita in 1987 (McCarthy 1993). Indeed, the junctures between lawful and unlawful centers of sovereignty are frequently impossible to delineate. Il/legal commodities, capital and power permeate each other, as everyday goods traverse international channels of production and distribution that intersect with official channels, non-formal systems, quasi-legal grey markets and undisputedly illegal enterprises. Goods such as arms, computers and medicines that enter states and war zones outside formal economic channels constitute profits for legitimate businesses in the world's industrial centers that combine with laundered capital to form an important source of liquidity in the global financial system (Nordstrom 2000). A UN official estimated that laundered criminal proceeds worth

US$352 billion were the only liquidity available to banks in sufficient quantities to save the international banking system from collapse in 2008 (Syal 2009). This is in addition to informal, extra-state banking systems that are common in Asia and transmit fortunes through family and ethnic linkages, business partnerships and gangster associations (Nordstrom 2000). Alternatively, consider the electronic marketplace Silk Road, where buyers and sellers traded electronic cash ('bitcoins') for illegal drugs, pornography and weapons that were distributed to purchasers through postal systems and courier firms (Robinson 2012). In both cases, these illegal and unregulated industries bypass government regulation and taxation, but rely on technology and services developed and provided by government and privately owned companies that derive benefit from illicit activities in the form of additional income or traffic. Similarly, conflict diamonds and rare earth minerals are examples of industries worth billions of dollars that exist in the shadow of the sovereignty of states but which are essential for 'legitimate' goods such as mobile telephones and other electronic and industrial products. Through contracting arrangements, by acting as a conduit for il/licit materials and funds, and as suppliers of legal hardware to illegal enterprises, the state and legal businesses profit from extra-state networks.

Is separatism a spent force in South Asia?

The important point to note is that state sovereignty and extra-state networks are characterized by reciprocity and shared interests. A complex interplay and cycle of influence consisting in mutual benefit and hostility, common aims, competing claims and rival outcomes allows extra-state networks to benefit from government weakness, incompetence, corruption and largesse despite their stated interests and intentions being antithetical. Examples of sovereignty's constantly emergent, contested and fungible character in South Asia include the outsourcing of essential functions of governance and intrusions of market forces into the practice of state sovereignty, as well as the abandonment of swathes of territory and functions to sub/non-state actors. These realities contrast with the traditional view of sovereignty as absolute, indivisible and exercised within the fixed territorial boundaries of individual states (Agnew 2005), reconfiguring it into a multi-layered property with numerous, overlapping loci dispersed and contested by a mélange of hybridized and shape-shifting groups (Geertz 2004). Moreover, these disjunctures were evident in the predecessor institutions of South Asian states, which were held together by loose, poorly defined and frequently violent bonds that endure in contemporary South Asia as regional, ethnic and ideological fault lines.

Influenced by their own status as an island nation, British colonial officials established fixed geographical borders within which there was held to be an undivided jurisdiction of sovereignty that belied the subcontinent's extreme linguistic and cultural diversity. Despite these portrayals of unity and claims of absolute sovereignty, zones of authority and exception persisted, justified by considerations such as the perceived danger of interfering in religious practices, unreliability of local agents, special problems of 'tribal' zones and the need to keep onside with the native rulers of princely states, which in 1947 numbered 562. Thus, while the preference for free trade, introduction of standard measures, and laws of contract and tort established public spaces that were defined and regulated by the state, these admitted a variety of qualifications and exceptions. Where the gap between sovereignty's rhetoric and the reality of its exercise grew too great or too public, then the British would intervene to reinforce their hegemony and assuage concerns about who was really in charge. For example, in the state of Jammu and Kashmir – which had been sold to Maharaja Gulab Singh in 1846 – the British substantially limited and removed many of the powers of Gulab Singh's grandson, Pratap Singh, after severe famines in 1877 and concerns pertaining to security of the state's northern frontiers against Czarist influence (Lamb 1992; Bhattacharjea 1994; Schofield 1996).

Following the departure of the British, sovereignty in the subcontinent changed, from a dispersed property that was loosely bound to a colonial power through the doctrine of Paramountcy, to that of emergent nation status. Consequently, the anti-imperialist struggle against a colonial occupier was transformed into a tussle for recognition and control by local communities against the successor states to the British Raj. Enduring local sovereignties with lengthy historical pedigrees combined with nationalist discourse, political mobilization, poverty and ethno-religious rivalry to produce an explosive cocktail and potential for rebellion. The nascent states of South Asia attempted to paper over these fissures through coercion and the purchase of loyalty (Geertz 2004). Enormous power was concentrated in the hands of political elites to forge a unifying discourse of nationhood and common interest, security legislation was enacted to suppress dissent, and the media and school curricula were employed to promulgate a national culture that addressed the question of *whose* self-determination the state was intended to embody and protect (Mayall 2013). In this manner, the fractious forces, alliances and ethnicities that comprised the misshapen building blocks of the newly independent states of South Asia were hewn into shape through a series of measures that included vestiges of colonial rule.

This concentration of power and its often arbitrary use conflicted with limitations upon the unilateral actions of power-holders inherent in the principle of popular sovereignty that provided the moral legitimacy of South Asia's independence movements and the post-colonial states that they inherited. Standards of justice in governance render impermissible the use of state power to disproportionately benefit different social classes, ethnic groups or sects in the division of the social product. Rather, shared collective interests and associated notions of fairness such as 'equality of opportunity' require that division of the social product follow from agreed decision-making procedures consistent with claims of individual freedom and equality of rights and opportunities. Moreover, effective implementation of these principles requires a robust institutional framework that is insulated from political and social competition between society's constituent groups, their rival interests and competing formulations of the common good (Steinberg and Saideman 2008). The legitimacy of state institutions and procedures, therefore, rests in their ability to adjudicate between competing interests in a non-partisan manner that enables the participation of rival social actors in the decision-making process without privileging any particular group or conceptualization of the common good. Thus, the legitimacy of state institutions that regulate and distribute the social product requires a degree of trust in their neutrality between the social actors that constitute society. This, in turn, pre-supposes a degree of ubiquity, unity and control on the part of the state: that the state is the only (or best) 'game in town' when it comes to ensuring the provision and equitable distribution of the social product. Where these mechanisms are absent or inadequate, the legitimacy of the state is questioned as its neutrality is eroded. The problem, however, is that the state is not the only game in town. Rather, as we have seen, because sovereignty is diffuse, multi-layered and non-exclusive, there are a significant number of competitors to the state that exercise sovereignty, both in complement and in competition to it, and significantly influence the production and distribution of the social product. Where the state is unable to effectively control these extra-state networks, then the neutrality and objectivity of decisions concerning the social product begin to appear tainted and public confidence suffers. Left unchecked, this institutional decay results in a 'winner takes all' melee in which competition for state power becomes an objective of society's constituent groups and political processes are reduced to a zero-sum game.

In South Asia, as in many developing states, the state proved incapable of meeting the standards of neutrality required to adjudicate between societies' rival actors and factions. In addition, because of its dominating position and enormous concentration of power, the state became a prize to be captured. This was due primarily to three factors. First, the scope of state ownership and participation in the economy bestowed access to a range of resources, infrastructure and industries with significant rent-generating capability. Examples include defense contacts and the outsourcing of security functions to non-state actors such as *Ikhwan*, village defense committees and other extra-judicial, quasi-vigilante forces; enormous construction contracts and land purchases, including Pakistan's Gwadar Port and Bangladesh's Kaptai Dam; labyrinthine regulatory requirements and taxes that differed significantly between and within states, and the practices of smuggling and bribery that they sustained; and the infiltration of the legislative, judicial and military branches by criminal elements – approximately one third of India's parliamentary members have outstanding criminal charges against them (Alfred 2014; Varghese 2014).

Second, the state's extensive apparatus of coercion (matched by an absence of countervailing institutions to ensure the security force's political neutrality and legal accountability) meant that power-holders possessed significant ability to perpetuate and extend their control through an extensive security apparatus. Examples include the use of anti-terrorism and security legislation that gives security forces wide-ranging powers and effectively shields them from criminal responsibility for the consequences of their acts, such as India's Armed Forces (Special Powers) Act (AFSPA) (1958), the Maintenance of Internal Security Act and the Unlawful Activities (Prevention) Act (ULP) (1967), the Terrorist and

Disruptive Activities (Prevention) Act (TADA) (1985–95), the Prevention of Terrorism Act (POTA) (2002), Pakistan's Suppression of Terrorist Activities Ordinance (1975) and Anti-Terrorism Act (1997), Sri Lanka's Prevention of Terrorism Act (1978) and Bangladesh's Anti-Terrorism Act (2009).

Third, marginalized groups were prevented by power-holders from participating effectively in political and economic decision-making processes. Gerrymandering, rigging of elections, censorship, outlawing political parties, designating rivals as 'terrorist groups' and other similar tactics meant that the political activism of ethnic and religious minorities occurred outside constitutional and institutional limits and frequently developed a violent, anti-government/state agenda (Sangmpam 1992). Examples include the repeated dismissal of democratically elected state governments in India (most notably in Punjab and Jammu and Kashmir), Indira Gandhi's declaration of a state of emergency in 1975–77, and unopposed returns (where only one candidate contested an electorate, thereby eliminating voter choice) in India, Pakistan and Bangladesh. In such a state of affairs, the political arena becomes closed and hostile as the outcome of competition for the social product becomes increasingly pre-determined, and participation in the political process for some groups is rendered pointless. With little to gain from continued participation in conventional politics, these groups seek to either modify the rules of the 'political game' through (the threat of) violence or step outside them as the established channels of political participation become politicized in power-holders' favor (Sangmpam 1992, 2007).

These are the 'push' and 'pull' factors of separatism. While some, such as Chima (2002), have examined these with respect to specific conflicts and the likelihood of violence returning, the future trends of separatism in South Asia have not been widely addressed amongst scholars. Moreover, there has been little consideration of how reconfigurations in state sovereignty have disincentivized the pursuit of independent statehood for sub-state minorities. Clouding the picture further is the difficulty discussed earlier that, while violent separatism appears to be waning in South Asian states, sub-state political violence and rebellion against the government are expanding. One explanation for this phenomenon is the changes in sovereignty that have occurred since the states of South Asia obtained their independence. As explained earlier, in the years following the departure of the British, there was an overriding emphasis on the narrative of national unity and construction of a common identity based upon shared interests and universal values that saw the state take center stage in citizens' lives and political discourse. This was combined with an intolerance of sub-national groups, particularly those that possessed the history, population and resources to perceive themselves as 'total societies' with a complex division of labor sufficient to sustain ambitions of territorial sovereignty (Kohli 1997). Extending beyond mere neglect, this suspicion frequently manifested in a tendency to disregard democratic norms by interfering in local politics through the dismissal of democratically elected state governments, vote rigging, human rights abuses and other actions that violated the legal-rational basis of the state's legitimacy. Economically, the state also loomed large in citizens' lives through heavy government control and extensive regulation in the form of strong protectionist measures, intervention in labor and financial markets, extensive bureaucratic control, and nationalization of key industries such as electricity generation, steel-making, telecommunications and insurance, resulting in government monopolies with large rent-generating capacity. Moreover, the state's extensive apparatus of coercion meant that power-holders possessed significant ability to perpetuate and extend their control through intelligence-gathering, law-enforcement and military networks. Consequently, control of the state became the *sine qua non* of civic engagement, whereby politics was reduced to a high-stakes 'winner takes all' game, as marginalized groups perceived little benefit from 'playing by the rules of the game,' which they perceived as unfairly rigged against them and instead resorted to extra-constitutional methods to advance their agendas.

Increasingly, however, processes of economic and political deregulation, combined with institutional decay, have rendered the state a passive observer in some arenas and geographical locations. The corollary of this development is that the waning of state sovereignty has been accompanied by a diminishment in the appeal of independent statehood and, therefore, one of the pull factors behind separatism. In India, for example, tariffs and interest rates were reduced, many public monopolies were ended, and foreign direct investment (FDI) increased from US$132 million (Singh and Ranawana 1996) in 1991–92 to US$31 billion in the first half of 2015 (Fingar 2015). Other South Asian states have followed a similar course. For example, Pakistan has reduced electricity subsidies and amended its taxation legislation by eliminating numerous loopholes that existed in the form of special exemptions or Statutory Regulatory Orders (SROs). However, continuing violence and instability have severely hampered economic growth, with FDI falling from a peak of US$5.4 billion in 2007–08 (Sherani 2014) to US$825 million in 2014–15 (Pakistan Board of Investment 2015). In Bangladesh, limited economic reforms have seen FDI increase from approximately US$200 million in 1996 to more than US$900 million in 2010 (Bangladesh Board of Investment 2011) as the textile and agricultural sectors experienced substantial growth. For Sri Lanka, deregulation involved investment incentives to foreign and domestic capital, a shift in the composition of public spending and trade policy premised on export-led growth (Embuldeniya 2000) ensuring respectable rates of economic growth during the war years until 2000 of 4.5 percent per annum (O'Sullivan 2001). With the sclerotic, moribund controlling influence of central rule relaxed, private enterprise and wealth creation have flourished in South Asia since the 1990s, replacing government employment as the main avenue of economic and social advancement. For the region as a whole, per capita gross national income (GNI) has increased from US$779 in 2006 to US$1,496 in 2014, while over the same time period, the number of days required to start a business has dropped from 31.4 to 15.7 (The World Bank 2015), and 800,000 jobs were added each month between 2000 and 2010 (The World Bank 2011).

At the same time, the role of the state as a provider of order and security has been severely tested in some regions. While in India (e.g., Punjab and Jammu and Kashmir) and Sri Lanka (the northeast), previously lawless or hostile regions have been bought to heel, pockets of resistance still remain. In India, Naxalite guerrillas continue attacks in the states of Karnataka, Chhattisgarh, Orissa, Andhra Pradesh, Maharashtra, Jharkhand, Bihar, Uttar Pradesh and West Bengal, while a large security presence remains in Sri Lanka's northeast. In contrast, large parts of Pakistan remain effectively beyond the central government's remit. Most affected are the Federally Administered Tribal Areas (FATA), comprised of seven tribal agencies and six frontier regions that are loosely tied to the federal government through the Frontier Crimes Regulation legislation. With a history of significant independence from central rule, these regions have been the scene of major military clashes between the Pakistan Army, local militias and outlawed organizations (including Al Qaeda), with the death toll from 2003 to 2016 being almost 60,000 (South Asia Terrorism Portal 2016). Equally concerning has been the politicization of the judiciary and law-enforcement agencies, media censorship, and infiltration of organs of the state by criminal enterprises. In Bangladesh, the governing Awami League has used the International Crimes Tribunal, which was established in 2009 to investigate and prosecute genocide suspects for crimes committed in the 1971 war of independence, as a weapon against rival parties such as the *Jamaat-e-Islami* and Bangladesh Nationalist Party, with a number of party members sentenced to death. This is part of a broader process of institutional decay and political violence in which journalists and bloggers have been threatened and killed, mostly by Islamic extremists, for what they write. Similarly, in Sri Lanka, journalists and other government critics were threatened and subjected to violence under the Rajapaksa regime (2009–15), while in Pakistan, journalists, government critics and social commentators perceived as 'liberal' have all been the target of extreme violence by outlawed jihadi groups. The most high-profile victim of this campaign of violence was the governor of Punjab, Salman Taseer, who was murdered, ostensibly for his opposition to Pakistan's blasphemy law.

Finally, there is the problem of the many mafias that have a strong presence in certain localities, political parties and industries (such as property, construction and film). Across economic, political and social spheres in South Asia, there exists a range of intersecting cliques and cabals, often dominated by family dynasties, practicing a pernicious authoritarianism that sustains generations-old client–patron networks. Caste, ethnic, class, family and other divisions, in conjunction with corruption, poverty and a lack of universal education, impede the development of a meritocratic culture in which offices and institutions (rather than individuals) dominate. Instead, advancement and reward are often dependent upon informal linkages and transactional arrangements. Nowhere is this more evident than in the political realm, where party candidates form alliances with criminal syndicates that assist with voter mobilization and raising the funds necessary to contest elections (Ghosh 1997; Sharma 1999). In addition, individual 'rogue' candidates with underworld connections also bring a 'Robin Hood aura,' illegal funds and a network of supporters; all of which are valuable commodities to political parties. Indeed, a recent study in India found that candidates accused of minor crimes had success rates of 19–25 percent, compared with only 7 percent for 'clean' candidates (Vaishnav 2014).

In conclusion, the replacement of central planning by market forces and the development of non-state networks of sovereignty that assist, oppose and supplant the sovereignty of the state in various arenas means that the state and government office no longer hold the allure that they once did. Individuals and organizations can accumulate wealth and influence official decisions without winning political office or attaining statehood. The dispersion of sovereignty across a range of in/formal and il/legal networks has opened a range of avenues for actors to perform functions, exercise power and command obedience in a manner that was once the preserve of government actors. Consequently, when political rebellion does occur, it is generally not with the aim of establishing a new jurisdiction of state sovereignty through an act of secession, but, instead, of carving out zones of exception, changing official policy or substantially weakening the ability of the government to impose its edicts. The allure of independent statehood is, for most groups in South Asia, a thing of the past.

Conclusion

Having gained independence, the societies of South Asia were not free to establish an alternative model of governance that rejected principles of statehood and territorial sovereignty. Not only did the departing colonial authorities determine the geographical boundaries of successor states through institutions such as the Boundary Commission, but the development of a substitute exemplar of sovereignty premised, for example, on a loose confederation of sociologically independent collectivities (rather than territorially defined political units) was not an available option. In order to be eligible for international aid, recognized as formal trade and treaty partners, and adequately and equally represented in transnational associations such as the United Nations, it was necessary to adopt the mantle of statehood. In their attempts to construct a unifying national identity that bound their geographically, culturally and socio-economically disparate constituent groups together, the nascent states of South Asia also had to contend with antecedent networks of sovereignty. Possessing histories that pre-dated the formation of the state, many of these communities were not effectively incorporated into the fabric of the state. Consequently, absent a framework of agreed rules, conventions, practices and procedures that governed the allocation of benefits (including resource rents), the distribution of political power and settlement of grievances were frequently determined by opportunistic, violent and extra-constitutional mechanisms that over time became an established feature of political discourse. In addition, the state's resort to force to quell violent rejections of its sovereignty aggravated the causes of conflict through the collapse of public revenues, diversion of resources to military sectors, increased concentration of political power in the hands of an unaccommodating elite, and human rights abuses that validated separatist claims to assist mobilization against the state. This resulted in the exacerbation of perceptions of grievance that had fueled the initial outbreak of violence and erosion of the rules, conventions and shared understandings that had restrained the violent expression of these perceptions (Murshed 2002).

Well-institutionalized states with accommodating leaders that provide a clearly defined scope for regional and sub-state elites to achieve tangible gains increase the opportunity costs of rebellion. However, the separation between public and private realms and development of strong, impartial institutions to police this separation is often difficult to obtain in developing states, such as those of South Asia, that are charged with establishing their own legitimacy while also achieving economic development. Consequently, there is a tendency in these states to over-politicize society through the reorganization of citizens' socio-economic life, thereby rendering state institutions the center of competition for the society's elites and constituent groups (Kohli 1997).

Over-politicized, weakly institutionalized states also tend to perceive regional elites and extra-state networks as threats, responding repressively toward them and lowering the opportunity costs of rebellion. Thus, by failing to address perceptions of grievance and responding repressively to group mobilization, the state corroborates claims of prejudice and makes conflict more likely, as those not served by the state have less to lose by opposing it. Rebellion may take a variety of forms, ranging from lawful protest and civil disobedience to criminality and armed insurrection. Separatism is distinguished from these forms of rebellion by a claim of territorial sovereignty. It occurs where an aggrieved group is sufficiently populous and possesses a historical and cultural provenance such that it can perceive itself as a complete society capable of performing the functions of statehood at least as well as the parent state – so-called 'sub-national' minorities. However, because not all sub-national minorities possess the leadership, resources and pre-requisites of mobilization to sustain an insurgency, many do not rebel.

Because the functions and authority of states in South Asia have diminished due to the increased role of non/extra-state actors and networks, the allure of statehood (and therefore separatism) is substantially less than in the period immediately following decolonization. This, it should be emphasized, does not mean that South Asia does not suffer from significant challenges, or that separatism might not make a comeback. Resource depletion, corruption, sectarian conflict, food insecurity, inter-state rivalry and other maladies possess considerable potential to destabilize the region. Whether sub-national minorities once again perceive secession as a feasible solution to these problems will, in large measure, be determined by the continued evolution of sovereignty in South Asia. The surrender, contracting out and devolution of state functions to non/extra-state actors and networks has diminished the attraction of statehood for potential challengers, which perceive greater opportunity in pursuing alternative centers of influence in areas such as emerging markets, government outsourcing and criminal enterprises. This, however, may change. The religious and cultural identities that sustain sub-national communities, while not fixed and subject to change, will not merely disappear. Their propensity to challenge the state for the mantle of sovereignty will, in large measure, be determined by how the state exercises its sovereign powers and the changes that occur to these powers over time. An example exists in the member states of the European Union (EU), which surrendered monetary control to the European Central Bank, border and immigration control to the collectivity of states in the Schengen Area, and substantial statutory and regulatory jurisdiction to European courts and councils. Migration and economic crises have recently placed great strain upon these arrangements, with some states, and many Europeans, demanding greater control over their own affairs, effectively asking that the 'nation' be put back into the 'nation-state.' Were this to occur, then it is difficult to conceive of separatist-inclined minorities such as the Basques and Catalans not seizing on the opportunities of devolution to once again hoist the flag of nationalism and independent statehood. Indeed, frustration with Spain's inability to contend with many of the consequences of the 2008 financial crisis – a matter in which Spain's freedom to act was significantly constrained by its EU membership – is one of the driving reasons behind Catalonia's bid for independent statehood.

Similar considerations apply to South Asia and the reforms that underpinned economic liberalization there, which are still comparatively new and not without controversy. A series of crises that tested or resulted in the rolling back of these reforms would have the potential to reinvigorate dormant national identities, enmities and grievances. States, therefore, need to remain cognizant of both the opportunity costs for sub-national minorities of remaining a part of the state, and factors that assist mobilization by sub-national minorities against the state. Crises and rapid change have the potential to act as national unifying forces by forging a common purpose and shared interest in overcoming adversity. If not properly managed, however, they can also create division and mistrust while lowering the opportunity costs of exit and rebellion. The economic inequalities and dislocations that have accompanied rapid urbanization and development in the economies of South Asia have thus far cut across sub-national divisions and failed to act as a rallying point against the state. However, unforeseen developments and skillful manipulation by ethnic entrepreneurs could see these inequalities adopt a religious or regional contextualization that once again threatens national unity. Successfully confronting the threat will require governments to resist the temptation to respond with unnecessary force, mobilize sentiment in the national heartland against the minority, or interfere in democratic processes to undermine regional elites.

Bibliography

Abbasi, A. (2012). "37 pc Baloch Favour Independence: UK Survey." *The News*. Karachi. August 13.

Abrams, P. (1988). "Notes on the Difficulty of Studying the State." *Journal of Historical Sociology* 1(1): 58–89.

Agnew, J. (2005). "Sovereignty Regimes: Territoriality and State Authority in Contemporary World Politics." *Annals of the Association of American Geographers* 95(2): 437–461.

Ahmad, A. (2013). "Bangladesh in 2012: Economic Growth, Political Underdevelopment." *Asian Survey* 53(1): 73–83.

Ahmad, Q. S. (2005). "Balochistan: Overview of Internal and International Dimensions." *Pakistan Horizon* 58(2): 27–40.

Ahmed, A. (1993). "Ethnicity and Insurgency in the Chittagong Hill Tracts Region: A Study of the Crisis of Political Integration in Bangladesh." *Journal of Commonwealth & Comparative Politics* 31(3): 32–66.

Ahmed, M. (2008). "The Great Land Robbery." *The Herald*. Karachi. June.

Ahsan, S. A. and B. Chakma (1989). "Problems of National Integration in Bangladesh: The Chittagong Hill Tracts." *Asian Survey* 29(10): 959–970.

Alfred, C. (2014). "India's New Parliament Has the Most Members Facing Criminal Charges in a Decade." *The Huffington Post*. May 23.

Ali, N. (2003). "Diaspora and Nation: Displacement and the Politics of Kashmiri Identity in Britain." *Contemporary South Asia* 12(4): 471–480.

Alter, P. (1989). *Nationalism*. London, Edward Arnold.

Amnesty International (1995). *India, Torture and Deaths in Custody in Jammu and Kashmir*. New York, Amnesty International.

Amnesty International (2001). *Impunity Must End in Jammu and Kashmir*. ASA20/023/2001. London, Amnesty International. Retrieved May 26, 2016, from www.amnesty.org/en/documents/asa20/023/2001/en/.

Amnesty International (2008). *Annual Report 2008 – Enforced Disappearance Update*. London, Amnesty International.

Amnesty International (2011). *A 'Lawless Law': Detentions under the Jammu and Kashmir Public Safety Act*. London, Amnesty International.

Anon (2009). "India's Help Significant in Defeating Tigers – Sri Lanka Minister." *Tamil Guardian*. London. April 1.

Anon (2015). "Indian Troops Assisted Sri Lankan Military during War: Karuna." *Colombo Mirror*. Colombo. August 30.

Appadurai, A. (1996). "Sovereignty without Territoriality: Notes for a Post-National

Bibliography

Geography." In: *The Geography of Identity*. P. Yaeger, ed. Ann Arbor, University of Michigan Press: 40–58.

Arambam, L. (2001). "On Ethnicity, Conflict and Development in Manipur." *Manipur Research Forum* 1(4).

Armitage, D. (2010). "Secession and Civil War." In: *Secession as an International Phenomenon: From America's Civil War to Contemporary Separatist Movements*. D. H. Doyle, ed. Athens, GA, University of Georgia Press: 37–55.

Asia Watch and Physicians for Human Rights (1993). *The Human Rights Crisis in Kashmir: A Pattern of Impunity*. New York, Asia Watch.

Aslam, R. (2011). "Greed, Creed, and Governance in Civil Conflicts: A Case Study of Balochistan." *Contemporary South Asia* 19(2): 189–203.

Axel, B. K. (2001). *The Nation's Tortured Body: Violence, Representation and the Formation of a Sikh 'Diaspora.'* Durham, Duke University Press.

Ayres, R. W. and S. Saideman (2000). "Is Separatism as Contagious as the Common Cold or Cancer? Testing International and Domestic Explanations." *Nationalism and Ethnic Politics* 6(3): 91–113.

Azam, J.-P. (2001). "The Redistributive State and Conflicts in Africa." *Journal of Peace Research* 38(4): 429–444.

Babar, F. (2004). "Nibbling Away at Autonomy." *The Dawn*. Karachi. October 21.

Bal, G. (2005). "Violence, Migration and Entrepreneurship: Punjab during the Khalistan Movement." *Economic and Political Weekly* 40(36): 3978–3986.

Balch-Lindsay, D. and A. J. Enterline (2000). "Killing Time: The World Politics of Civil War Duration, 1820–1992." *International Studies Quarterly* 44(4): 615–642.

Balch-Lindsay, D., A. J. Enterline and K. A. Joyce (2008). "Third-Party Intervention and the Civil War Process." *Journal of Peace Research* 45(3): 345–363.

Baloch, A. H. (2004). "Bringing Development to Balochistan." *The Dawn*. Karachi. December 13.

Bangladesh Board of Investment (2011). *Survey Report, Statistics Department of Bangladesh Bank and Foreign Direct Investment in Bangladesh (1971–2010)*. Dhaka, Bangladesh Board of Investment.

Bansal, A. (2006). "Balochistan: Continuing Violence and Its Implications." *Strategic Analysis* 30(1): 46–63.

Bansal, A. (2008). "Factors Leading to Insurgency in Balochistan." *Small Wars & Insurgencies* 19(2): 182–200.

Barbora, S. (2006). "Rethinking India's Counter-Insurgency Campaign in North-East." *Economic and Political Weekly* 41(35): 3805–3812.

Barbora, S. (2008). "Autonomous Districts and/or Ethnic Homelands: An Ethnographic Account of the Genesis of Political Violence in Assam (North-East India) against the Normative Frame of the Indian Constitution." *International Journal on Minority and Group Rights* 15(2): 313–334.

Baruah, A. (2005). "Conflicts & Communities: A Northeast India Perspective." In: *Inter-Ethnic Conflict in Northeast India*. G. Phukon, ed. Delhi, South Asian.

Baruah, S. (1994). "The State and Separatist Militancy in Assam: Winning a Battle and Losing the War?" *Asian Survey* 34(10): 863–877.

Baruah, S. (2009). "Separatist Militants and Contentious Politics in Assam, India: The Limits of Counterinsurgency." *Asian Survey* 49(6): 951–974.

Baweja, H. (1994). "The Mind of the Militant." *India Today*. December 31.

Baweja, H. (1995). "The Hostage Crisis." *India Today*. September 15.

Baweja, H. and R. Vinayak (1996). "A Dangerous Liaison." *India Today*.

Bazaz, P. N. (1967). *Kashmir in Crucible*. New Delhi, Pamposh.
Bazaz, P. N. (1978). *Democracy through Intimidation and Terror*. New Delhi, Heritage.
BBC (2011). "Sri Lanka's Killing Fields."
Beran, H. (1987). *The Consent Theory of Political Obligation*. London; New York, Croom Helm.
Bhattacharjea, A. (1994). *Kashmir: The Wounded Valley*. New Delhi, UBSPD.
Bhaumik, S. (1996). *Insurgent Crossfire: North-East India*. New Delhi, Lancer Publishers.
Brancati, D. (2006). "Decentralization: Fueling the Fire or Dampening the Flames of Ethnic Conflict and Secessionism?" *International Organization* 60: 651–685.
Brancati, D. (2009). *Peace by Design*. New York, Oxford University Press.
Brasted, H. and Z. Ahmed (2015). "The Political Economy of Pakistan's 'War on Terror'." In: *The Political Economy of Conflict in South Asia*. M. J. Webb and A. Wijeweera, eds. Houndmills, Palgrave Macmillan: 114–131.
Brewster, D. (2014). *India's Ocean: The Story of India's Bid for Regional Leadership*. Abingdon, Routledge.
Chakrabarty, R. (2011). "ISI trained Ulfa, Says Outfit's 'Foreign Secretary'." *The Times of India*. August 9.
Chalk, P. (2000). "Liberation Tigers of Tamil Eelam's (LTTE) International Organization and Operations – A Preliminary Analysis." Commentary No. 77. Canadian Security Intelligence Service. March 17.
Chalk, P. (2003). "The Liberation Tigers of Tamil Eelam Insurgency in Sri Lanka." In: *Ethnic Conflict & Secessionism in South & Southeast Asia: Causes, Dynamics, Solutions*. R. Ganguly and I. Macduff, eds. New Delhi, Sage: 128–165.
Chasie, C. and S. Hazarika (2009). *The State Strikes Back: India and the Naga Insurgency*. Washington, DC, East-West Center.
Chima, J. S. (1994). "The Punjab Crisis: Governmental Centralization and Akali-Center Relations." *Asian Survey* 34(10): 847–862.
Chima, J. S. (2002). "Back to the Future in 2002?: A Model of Sikh Separatism in Punjab." *Studies in Conflict & Terrorism* 25(1): 19–39.
Chima, J. S. (2010). *The Sikh Separatist Insurgency in India: Political Leadership and Ethnonationalist Movements*. New Delhi, Sage.
Collier, P. (2005). "Rebellion as a Quasi-Criminal Activity." *Journal of Conflict Resolution* 44(6): 839–853.
Collier, P. and A. Hoeffler (1998). "On the Economic Causes of Civil War." *Oxford Economic Papers* 50(4): 563–573.
Collier, P. and A. Hoeffler (2000). "Greed and Grievance in Civil War." Research Working Paper 2355. Washington, DC, World Bank.
Collier, P. and A. Hoeffler (2002). "On the Incidence of Civil War in Africa." *Journal of Conflict Resolution* 46(1): 13–28.
Collier, P. and A. Hoeffler (2005). "Resource Rents, Governance and Conflict." *Journal of Conflict Resolution* 49(4): 625–633.
Collier, P., A. Hoeffler and D. Rohner (2009). "Beyond Greed and Grievance: Feasibility and Civil War." *Oxford Economic Papers* 61(1): 1–27.
Council on Foreign Relations (2012). "The Global Regime for Transnational Crime." International Institutions and Global Governance Program.
Crawford, J. (2006). *The Creation of States in International Law*. Oxford, Clarendon Press.
Cuffe, J. and D. S. Siroky (2013). "Paradise Lost: Autonomy and Separatism in the South

Caucasus and Beyond." In: *Secessionism and Separatism in Europe and Asia: To Have a State of One's Own*. J.-P. Cabestan and A. Pavković, eds. Abingdon; New York, Routledge: 37–52.

Cunningham, K. G. (2011). "Divide and Conquer or Concede: How States Respond to Internally Divided Separatists." *American Political Science Review* 105(2): 275–297.

D'Costa, B. (2011). "Bangladesh in 2010: Digital Makeover but Continued Human and Economic Insecurity." *Asian Survey* 51(1): 138–147.

D'Costa, B. (2012). "Bangladesh in 2011: Weak Statebuilding and Diffident Foreign Policy." *Asian Survey* 52(1): 147–156.

Das, C. (2012). "With Nowhere to Go, Insurgents Take Refuge in Burma." *Khabar South Asia*. June 26.

Das, R. J. (2007). "Looking, but Not Seeing: The State and/as Class in Rural India." *Journal of Peasant Studies* 34(3–4): 408–440.

de Silva, K. M. (2012). *Sri Lanka and the Defeat of the LTTE*. Gurgaon, Penguin.

De Soysa, I. (2002). "Paradise Is a Bazaar? Greed, Creed, and Governance in Civil War, 1989–99." *Journal of Peace Research* 39(4): 395–416.

Deol, H. (2000). *Religion and Nationalism in India: The Case of the Punjab*. New York, Routledge.

DeVotta, N. (2004). *Blowback: Linguistic Nationalism, Institutional Decay, and Ethnic Conflict in Sri Lanka*. Stanford, CA, Stanford University Press.

DeVotta, N. (2009). "The Liberation Tigers of Tamil Eelam and the Lost Quest for Separatism in Sri Lanka." *Asian Survey* 49(6): 1021–1051.

Direh, D., A. Marchylo, M. Urban and M. Wyszomierska (2007). "Pakistan Risk Assessment Brief: Based on CIFP Risk Assessment Methodology." Retrieved April 1, 2013, from www4.carleton.ca/cifp/app/serve.php/1117.pdf.

Dowlah, C. (2013). "Jumma Insurgency in Chittagong Hills Tracts: How Serious is the Threat to Bangladesh's National Integration and What Can be Done?" *Small Wars & Insurgencies* 24(5): 773–794.

Doyle, D. H. (2010). "Introduction: Union and Secession in the Family of Nations." In: *Secession as an International Phenomenon: From America's Civil War to Contemporary Separatist Movements*. Athens, GA, University of Georgia Press: 1–16.

Duncan, E. (1989). *Breaking the Curfew – A Political Journey through Pakistan*. London, Penguin Books.

Election Commission of India (1996). *Statistical Report on General Elections, 1996 to the Eleventh Lok Sabha*. New Delhi, Election Commission of India.

Election Commission of India (1997). *Statistical Report on General Election, 1996 to the Legislative Assembly of Jammu and Kashmir*. New Delhi, Election Commission of India.

Embuldeniya, D. K. (2000). "Economic Reforms and the Corporate Sector in Sri Lanka." *Contemporary South Asia* 9(2): 165–179.

Emizet, K. N. and V. L. Hesli (1995). "The Disposition to Secede. An Analysis of the Soviet Case." *Comparative Political Studies* 27(4): 493–533.

Enterline, A. J. and C. Linebarger (2014). "Win, Lose, or Draw: Third Party Intervention and the Duration and Outcome of Civil Wars." In: *What Do We Know about Civil Wars?* T. D. Mason and S. Mitchell, eds. Lanham, Rowman & Littlefield: 93–108.

Fair, C. C. (2005). "Diaspora Involvement in Insurgencies: Insights from the Khalistan and Tamil Eelam Movements." *Nationalism and Ethnic Politics* 11(1): 125–156.

Fair, C. C. (2012). "Balochistan." United States House of Representatives, Committee on Foreign Affairs, Oversight and Investigations Sub-Committee.

Fazl-e-Haider, S. (2006). "Social Development in Balochistan." *The Dawn*. Karachi. January 23.
Fearon, J. D. and D. D. Laitin (2000). "Violence and the Social Construction of Ethnic Identity." *International Organization* 54(4): 845–877.
Fearon, J. D. and D. D. Laitin (2003). "Ethnicity, Insurgency, and Civil War." *American Political Science Review* 97(1): 75–90.
Feith, D. (2013). "Separatism in Sri Lanka." In: *Secessionism and Separatism in Europe and Asia: To Have a State of One's Own*. J.-P. Cabestan and A. Pavković, eds. Abingdon; New York, Routledge: 164–177.
Fernandes, W. (2004). "Limits of Law and Order Approach to the North-East." *Economic and Political Weekly* 39(42): 4609–4611.
Fingar, C. (2015) "India Grabs Investment League Pole Position." *Financial Times*. September 29.
Franchetti, M. and N. Fielding (2002). "British Muslims are the Second-Largest Benefactors of Kashmiri Terrorist Groups." *Times of India*. January 15.
Fulcher, R. (2006). "Balochistan's History of Insurgency." *Green Left*. November 30.
Ganguly, S. (1997). *The Crisis in Kashmir: Portents of War, Hopes of Peace*. Cambridge, Cambridge University Press.
Gauthier, D. (1994). "Breaking Up: An Essay on Secession." *Canadian Journal of Philosophy* 24(3): 357–372.
Geertz, C. (2004). "What Is a State If It Is Not a Sovereign? Reflections on Politics in Complicated Places." *Current Anthropology* 45(5): 577–593.
Gellner, E. (1983). *Nations and Nationalism*. Ithaca, NY, Cornell University Press.
Ghosh, S. K. (1997). *Indian Democracy Derailed: Politics and Politicians*. New Delhi, APH.
Gill, S. S. and K. C. Singhal (1984). "The Punjab Problem: Its Historical Roots." *Economic and Political Weekly* 19(14): 603–608.
Gokhale, N. (2009). *Sri Lanka: From War to Peace*. New Delhi, Har Anand.
Gompert, D. C. (2007). "Heads We Win: The Cognitive Side of Counterinsurgency (COIN)." Occasional Paper. Santa Monica, CA, RAND Corporation.
Goswami, N. (2011). "Armed Ethnic Conflicts in Northeast India and the Indian State's Response: Use of Force and the 'Notion' of Proportionality." Heidelberg Papers in South Asian and Comparative Politics. Heidelberg. Working Paper No. 60.
Greene, M. (2012). "Hidden War Embodies Pakistan's Struggle." *Financial Times*. May 25.
Griffiths, M. (2003). "Self-Determination, International Society and World Order." *Macquarie Law Journal* 3: 29–49.
Grigoryan, A. (2010). "Third Party Intervention and the Escalation of State Minority Conflicts." *International Studies Quarterly* 54(4): 1143–1174.
Gunaratna, R. (1997). *International and Regional Security Implications of the Sri Lankan Tamil Insurgency*. Colombo, Bandaranaike Centre for International Studies.
Gurr, T. R. (2000). *Peoples versus States: Minorities at Risk in the New Century*. Washington, United States Institute of Peace Press.
Gurr, T. R. and B. Harff (1994). *Ethnic Conflict in World Politics*. Boulder, CO, Westview.
Hagendoorn, L., E. Poppe and A. Minescu (2008). "Support for Separatism in Ethnic Republics of the Russian Federation." *Europe-Asia Studies* 60(3): 353–373.
Hale, H. E. (2000). "The Parade of Sovereignties: Testing Theories of Secession in the Soviet Setting." *British Journal of Political Science* 30(1): 31–56.

Hale, H. E. (2008). "The Double-Edged Sword of Ethnofederalism: Ukraine and the USSR in Comparative Perspective." *Comparative Politics* 40: 293–312.

Hansen, T. B. (2001). *Wages of Violence: Naming and Identity in Postcolonial Bombay.* Princeton NJ, Princeton University Press.

Hansen, T. B. and F. Stepputat (2006). "Sovereignty Revisited." *Annual Review of Anthropology* 35: 295–315.

Haokip, T. (2012). "Political Integration in Northeast India: A Historical Analysis." *Strategic Analysis* 36(2): 304–314.

Hardin, R. (1995). *One for All: The Logic of Group Conflict.* Princeton, Princeton University Press.

Harrison, S. S. (1981). *In Afghanistan's Shadow: Baluch Nationalism and Soviet Temptations.* New York, Carnegie Endowment.

Hasan, S. S. (2012). "Sectarian Militancy Thriving in Balochistan." *The Dawn.* April 11.

Haye, F. A. (2005). "National Integration." *The News.* Karachi. January 21.

Hechter, M. (1975). *Internal Colonialism: The Celtic Fringe in British National Development.* Berkeley, University of California Press: 1536–1966.

Hechter, M. (1992). "The Dynamics of Secession." *Acta Sociologica* 35: 267–283.

Hegre, H. and N. Sambanis (2006). "Sensitivity Analysis of Empirical Results on Civil War Onset." *Journal of Conflict Resolution* 50(4): 508–535.

Heraclides, A. (1990). "Secessionist Minorities and External Involvement." *International Organization* 44(3): 341–378.

Hodson, H. V. (1969). *The Great Divide.* London, Hutchinson.

Hoeffler, A. (2011). "Greed versus Grievance: A Useful Conceptual Distinction in the Study of Civil War?" *Studies in Ethnicity and Nationalism* 11(2): 274–284.

Hooghe, L. (1992). "Nationalist Movements and Social Factors: A Theoretical Perspective." In: *The Social Origins of Nationalist Movements.* J. Coakly, ed. London, Sage: 21–43.

Horowitz, D. L. (1985). *Ethnic Groups in Conflict.* Berkeley, University of California Press.

Human Rights Watch (1996). "India's Secret Army in Kashmir: New Patterns of Abuse Emerge in the Conflict." *Human Rights Watch Asia Report* 8(4).

Human Rights Watch (2009). "Secret 'Black Jails' Hide Severe Rights Abuses: Unlawful Detention Facilities Breed Violence, Threats, Extortion." New York. November 12.

Humphrey, C. (2004). "Sovereignty." In: *A Companion to the Anthropology of Politics.* D. Nugent and J. Vincent, eds. Oxford, Blackwell: 418–436.

Humphreys, M. and J. M. Weinstein (2008). "Who Fights? The Determinants of Participation in Civil War." *American Journal of Political Science* 52(2): 436–455.

Huntington, S. (1993). "The Clash of Civilizations?" *Foreign Affairs* 72(3): 22–49.

Hussain, H. (1971). "Problems of National Integration in Bangladesh." In: *Bangladesh: History and Culture.* S. R. Chakravarty, ed. New Delhi, South Asian.

Hussain, N. (2003). *The Jurisprudence of Emergency. Colonialism and the Rule of Law.* Ann Arbor, University of Michigan Press.

Hussain, W. (2009). "Ethno-Nationalism and the Politics of Terror in India's Northeast." In: *South Asia: the Spectre of Terrorism.* P. R. Kumaraswamy and I. Copland. eds. Abingdon; New Delhi, Routledge.

India Today (2009). ULFA Admits Having Camps in China. November 19.

International Crisis Group (2006). "Pakistan: The Worsening Conflict in Balochistan," South Asia Report, no. 119. September 14.

International Crisis Group. (2010). "War Crimes in Sri Lanka." Retrieved October 14, 2015, from www.crisisgroup.be/flash/sl/sl.html.

International Crisis Group (2011). "India and Sri Lanka after the LTTE." Asia Report No. 206. Brussels. June 23.

Islam, S. N. (1978). "The Karnafuli Project: Its Impact on the Tribal Population." *Public Administration* 3(2): 31.

Islam, S. S. (2015). "The Economics of Conflict in the Chittagong Hill Tract Region of Bangladesh." In: *The Political Economy of Conflict in South Asia*. M. J. Webb and A. Wijeweera, eds. Houndmills, Palgrave Macmillan: 12–31.

Jacobson, N. (1998). "The Strange Case of Hobbesian Man." *Representations* 63: 1–12.

Jain, B. (2015). "Inside Story: Over 100 Northeast Militants May Have Been Killed in Army's Myanmar Operations." *The Times of India*. June 10.

Jamil, I., S. Askvik and T. N. Dhakal (2013). "Understanding Governance in South Asia." In: *In Search of Better Governance in South Asia and Beyond*. I. Jamil, S. Askvik and T. N. Dhakal, eds. New York, Springer.

Jeffrey, R. (1994). *What's Happening to India? Punjab, Ethnic Conflict and the Test for Federalism* (Second Edition). London, Macmillan.

Jenne, E. K., S. M. Saideman and W. Lowe (2007). "Separatism as a Bargaining Posture: The Role of Leverage in Minority Radicalization." *Journal of Peace Research* 44(5): 539–558.

Jodhka, S. S. (2005). "Return of the Region: Identities and Electoral Politics in Punjab." *Economic and Political Weekly* 40(3): 224–230.

Joshi, M. (1996). "On the Razor's Edge: The Liberation Tigers of Tamil Eelam." *Studies in Conflict & Terrorism* 19(1): 19–42.

Kalyvas, S. N. (2003). "The Ontology of 'Political Violence': Action and Identity in Civil Wars." *Perspectives on Politics* 1(3): 475–494.

Kamal, S. (1995). *Nationalist Movement in North East India and Bangladesh*. Kingston, Queen's University.

Kapur, R. A. (1987). "'Khalistan': India's Punjab Problem." *Third World Quarterly* 9(4): 1206–1224.

Karim, A. (1999). "Pakistan's Aggression in Kashmir: 1999." *Asian Journal on Terrorism and Internal Conflicts* 2(4).

Kaufman, C. (1996). "Possible and Impossible Solutions to Ethnic Civil Wars." *International Security* 20: 136–175.

Kearney, R. N. (1987). "Territorial Elements of Tamil Separatism in Sri Lanka." *Pacific Affairs* 60(4): 561–577.

Khan, A. (2009). "Renewed Ethnonationalist Insurgency in Balochistan, Pakistan: The Militarized State and Continuing Economic Deprivation." *Asian Survey* 49(6): 1071–1091.

Khan, M. G. A. (1970). *Raiders in Kashmir*. Karachi, Pak Publishers.

Kikon, D. (2005). "Engaging Naga Nationalism: Can Democracy Function in Militarised Societies?" *Economic and Political Weekly* 40(26): 2833–2837.

Kleczynski, M. (2012). "Don't Forget The Cyber Criminals." *Forbes*. May 9.

Kodikara, S., Ed. (1990). *South Asian Strategic Issues: Sri Lankan Perspectives*. New Delhi, Sage.

Kohli, A. (1997). "Can Democracies Accommodate Ethnic Nationalism? Rise and Decline of Self-Determination Movements in India." *Journal of Asian Studies* 56(2): 325–344.

Korf, B. (2005). "Rethinking the Greed–Grievance Nexus: Property Rights and the Political Economy of War in Sri Lanka." *Journal of Peace Research* 42(2): 201–217.

Kukathas, C. (1995). "Are There Any Cultural Rights?" In: *The Rights of Minority Cultures*. W. Kymlicka, ed. Oxford, Oxford University Press: 228–256.

Bibliography

Kumar, P. (2004). "External Linkages and Internal Security: Assessing Bhutan's Operation All Clear." *Strategic Analysis* 28(3): 390–410.

La, J. (2004). "Forced Remittances in Canada's Tamil Enclaves." *Peace Review* 16(3): 379–385.

Lacina, B. (2007). "Does Counterinsurgency Theory Apply in Northeast India?" *India Review* 6(3): 165–183.

Lacina, B. (2009). "The Problem of Political Stability in Northeast India: Local Ethnic Autocracy and the Rule of Law." *Asian Survey* 49(6): 998–1020.

Lamb, A. (1992). *Kashmir: A Disputed Legacy*. Karachi, Oxford University Press.

Lichbach, M. I. (1990). "Will Rational People Rebel against Inequality? Samson's Choice." *American Journal of Political Science* 34(4): 1049–1076.

Linter, B. (1990). "Tribal Turmoil." *Far Eastern Economic Review*. April 5: 24.

Lintner, B. (2012). *The Great Game East: India, China and the Struggle for Asia's Most Volatile Frontier*. New Delhi, Harper Collins.

Lopez, G. and D. Cortwright (1998). "Making Targets 'Smart' from Sanctions." International Studies Association, Minneapolis.

Lujala, P., N. P. Gleditsch and E. Gilmore (2005). "A Diamond Curse? Civil War and a Lootable Resource." *Journal of Conflict Resolution* 49(4): 538–562.

Lund, C. (2006). "Twilight Institutions: Public Authority and Local Politics in Africa." *Development and Change* 37(4): 685–705.

MacCulloch, R. and S. Pezzini (2007). "Money, Religion and Revolution." *Economics of Governance* 8(1): 1–16.

Mallet, V. and G. Dinmore (2011). "Europe: Hidden Economy." *Financial Times*. June 8.

Manogaran, C. (1987). *Ethnic Conflict and Reconciliation in Sri Lanka*. Honolulu, University of Hawaii Press.

Mason, T. D. (1996). "Insurgency, Counterinsurgency, and the Rational Peasant." *Public Choice* 86(1–2): 63–83.

Mayall, J. (2013). "Sovereignty, National Self-Determination and Secession: Reflections on State-Making and Breaking in Asia and Europe." In: *Secessionism and Separatism in Europe and Asia: To Have a State of One's Own*. J.-P. Cabestan and A. Pavković, eds. Abingdon; New York, Routledge: 20–34.

McCarthy, T. (1993). "Japan's Crime Incorporated: The Years of the Bubble Economy Lured Japan's Yakuza Gangs to Muscle into Big Business." *The Independent*. January 17.

McGarry, J. and B. O'Leary (1993). "Introduction: The Macro-Political Regulation of Ethnic Conflict." In: *The Politics of Ethnic Conflict Regulation: Case Studies of Protracted Ethnic Conflicts*. J. McGarry and B. O'Leary, eds. London, Routledge: 1–40.

Mills, M., G. G. van de Bunt and J. d. Bruijn (2006). "Comparative Research: Persistent Problems and Promising Solutions." *International Sociology* 21(5): 619–631.

Ministry of Interior (2014). *National Internal Security Policy 2014–2018*. Islamabad, Government of Pakistan.

Misra, A. (2001). "The Politics of Secessionist Conflict Management in India." *Contemporary Security Policy* 22(2): 49–68.

Mitra, S. K. (1995). "The Rational Politics of Cultural Nationalism: Subnational Movements of South Asia in Comparative Perspective." *British Journal of Political Science* 25(1): 57–77.

Mohsin, A. (2003). *The Chittagong Hill Tracts, Bangladesh: On the Difficult Road to Peace*. Boulder, CO, Lynne Rienner.

Montu, K. (1980). "Tribal Insurgency in Chittagong Hill Tracts." *Economic and Political Weekly* 15(36): 1510–1512.

Morris, N. (2010). "Black Economy Leaves £42bn Hole in Britain's Tax Accounts." *The Independent*. London. September 17.

Murshed, S. M. (2002). "Conflict, Civil War and Underdevelopment: An Introduction." *Journal of Peace Research* 39(4): 387–393.

Narayanswamy, M. (1994). *Tigers of Lanka: From Boys to Guerrillas*. New Delhi, Konarak.

NDTV (2009). "ULFA: Moving to Safe Haven in China?"

Nielsen, K. (1998). "Liberalism, Nationalism and Secession." In: *National Self-Determination and Secession*. M. Moore, ed. New York, Oxford University Press: 101–133.

Njoku, R. C. (2010). "Nationalism, Separatism, and Neoliberal Globalism: A Review of Africa and the Quest for Self Determination since the 1940s." In: *Secession as an International Phenomenon: From America's Civil War to Contemporary Separatist Movements*. D. H. Doyle, ed. Athens, GA, University of Georgia Press: 338–360.

Noman, O. (1990). *Pakistan: A Political and Economic History since 1947*. London, Kegan Paul International.

Nordlinger, E. A. and S. P. Huntington. (1972). *Conflict Regulation in Divided Societies*. No. 29. Cambridge, MA, Center for International Affairs, Harvard University.

Nordstrom, C. (2000). "Shadows and Sovereigns." *Theory, Culture & Society* 17(4): 35–54.

O'Sullivan, M. (2001). "Sri Lanka: Civil Strife, Civil Society, and the State 1983–1995." In: *War and Underdevelopment*, Volume II. F. Stewart and V. Fitzgerald, eds. Oxford, Oxford University Press.

Oberoi, H. S. (1987). "From Punjab to 'Khalistan': Territoriality and Metacommentary." *Pacific Affairs* 60(1): 26–41.

Oberst, R. C. (1988). "Federalism and Ethnic Conflict in Sri Lanka." *Publius: The Journal of Federalism* 18(3): 175–194.

Ostby, G. (2008). "Polarization, Horizontal Inequalities and Violent Civil Conflict." *Journal of Peace Research* 45(2): 143–162.

Padgett, T. (2003). "People Smugglers Inc." *Time*. 12 August.

Pakistan Board of Investment. (2015). "Foreign Investment." Retrieved January 3, 2016, from http://boi.gov.pk/foreigninvestmentinpakistan.aspx.

Pakistan Institute of Legislative Development and Transparency (2012). "Balochistan: Civil Military Relations." PILDAT Issue Paper.

Pakistan, State of (2005). "Report of the Parliamentary Committee on Balochistan." No. 7. November.

Pant, H. V. (2012). *China's Rising Global Profile: The Great Power Tradition*. Eastbourne, Sussex Academic.

Parnell, P. (2003). "Criminalizing Colonialism: Democracy Meets Law in Manila." In: *Crime's Power: Anthropologists and the Ethnography of Crime*. P. Parnell and S. Kane, eds. London, Palgrave Macmillan: 197–220.

Parry, R. L. (1996). "Yakuza Settle Bad Debts with a Bullet as Japan Bubble Bursts." *The Independent*. February 4.

Pasha, H. A. (2014). *Economy of Tomorrow: A Case Study of Pakistan*. Islamabad, Friedrich Ebert Stiftung.

Paul, T. V. (2014). *Pakistan in the Contemporary World*. Oxford, Oxford University Press.

Pavković, A and P. Radan, *Creating New States. Theory and Practice of Secession*. Farnham & Burlington VT, Ashgate Publishing, 2007.

Pavković, A. and J.-P. Cabestan (2013). "Secession and Separatism from a Comparative Perspective." In: *Secessionism and Separatism in Europe and Asia: To Have a State of One's Own.* A. Pavković and J.-P. Cabestan, eds. Abingdon, Routledge: 1–19.

Peebles, P. (1990) "Colonization and Ethnic Conflict in the Dry Zone of Sri Lanka." *Journal of Asian Studies* 49(1): 30–55.

Peebles, P. (2006). *The History of Sri Lanka.* Westport, CT, Greenwood Press.

Pettigrew, J. (1987). "In Search of a New Kingdom of Lahore." *Pacific Affairs* 60(1): 1–25.

Phadmis, U. (1981). "Woes of Tribals in Bangladesh." *Times of India.* January 5.

Philpott, D. (2001). *Revolutions in Sovereignty: How Ideas Shaped Modern International Relations.* Princeton, Princeton University Press.

Popham, P. (2010). "How Beijing Won Sri Lanka's Civil War." *The Independent.* London. May 23.

Population Census Organization (1998). "Demographic Indicators – 1998 Census." Retrieved April 5, 2013, from www.census.gov.pk/DemographicIndicator.htm.

Prakash, V. (2008). *Terrorism in India's Northeast: A Gathering Storm.* New Delhi, Kalpaz.

Purewal, S. (2000). *Sikh Ethnonationalism and the Political Economy of Punjab.* New Delhi, Oxford University Press.

Puri, H., P. S. Judge and J. S. Sekhon (1999). *Terrorism in the Punjab: Understanding Grassroots Reality.* New Delhi, Har Anand.

Quaider, S. (2015). "Bangladesh Raids Militant Training Camp in Remote Area of Chittagong." *Reuters.* February 22.

Racine, J.-L. (2013). "Secessionism in Independent India: Failed Attempts, Irredentism, and Accommodation." In: *Secessionism and Separatism in Europe and Asia: To Have a State of One's Own.* J.-P. Cabestan and A. Pavkovic, eds. Abingdon; New York, Routledge: 147–163.

Radan, P. (2008). "Secession: A Word in Search of a Meaning." In: *On the Way to Statehood, Secession and Globalisation.* A. Pavkovic and P. Radan, eds. Aldershot, Ashgate: 17–32.

Radan, P. (2010). "Lincoln, the Constitution, and Secession." In: *Secession as an International Phenomenon: From America's Civil War to Contemporary Separatist Movements.* D. H. Doyle, ed. Athens, GA, University of Georgia Press: 56–75.

Rai, M. (2004). *Hindu Rulers, Muslim Subjects: Islam, Rights, and the History of Kashmir.* Princeton, Princeton University Press.

Rajagopalan, S. (2008). "Peace Accords in Northeast India: Journey over Milestones." Policy Studies. Washington DC, East-West Center. 46.

Rao, V. P. (1988). "Ethnic Conflict in Sri Lanka: India's Role and Perception." *Asian Survey* 28(4): 419–436.

Regan, P. M. and D. Norton (2005). "Greed, Grievance, and Mobilization in Civil Wars." *Journal of Conflict Resolution* 49(3): 319–336.

Riedel, B. (2008). "Pakistan and Terror: The Eye of the Storm." *Annals of the American Academy of Political and Social Science* 618: 31–45.

Riker, W. H. (1964). *Federalism: Origin, Operation, Significance.* Boston, Little, Brown.

Robinson, M. (2012). "The eBay for Drugs: 'Silk Road' Website Allows UK Drug Users to Buy Cocaine and Heroin by Mail Order from All Over the World." *The Daily Mail.* November 19.

Roeder, P. (2009). "Ethnofederalism and the Mismanagement of Conflicting Nationalisms." *Regional & Federal Studies* 19: 203–219.

Rogers, J. D. (1987). "Social Mobility, Popular Ideology, and Collective Violence in Modern Sri Lanka." *Journal of Asian Studies* 46(3): 583–602.

Rogowski, R. (1985). "Causes and Varieties of Nationalism: A Rationalist Account." In: *New Nationalisms of the Developed West: Toward Explanation*. E. Tiryakian and R. Rogowski, eds. Boston, MA, Allen & Unwin.

Rotberg, R. I. (1999). *Sri Lanka's Civil War: From Mayhem toward Diplomatic Resolution*. Washington, DC, Brookings Institution.

Rupesinghe, K. (1988). "Ethnic Conflicts in South Asia: The Case of Sri Lanka and the Indian Peace-Keeping Force (IPKF)." *Journal of Peace Research* 25(4): 337–350.

Saideman, S. M. and D. Lanoue (2005). "The (Exaggerated) Perils of Democracy: Analyzing Democracy's Influence on Different Forms of Communal Dissent." American Political Science Association. Marriott Wardman Park, Omni Shoreham, Washington Hilton, Washington, DC.

Saideman, S., D. Lanoue, M. Campenni and S. Stanton (2002). "Democratization, Political Institutions, and Ethnic Conflict: A Pooled, Cross-Sectional Time Series Analysis from 1985–1998." *Comparative Political Studies* 35: 103–129.

Saideman, S. M., B. K. Dougherty and E. K. Jenne (2005). "Dilemmas of Divorce: How Secessionist Identities Cut Both Ways." *Security Studies* 14(4): 1–30.

Saikia, J. (2003). *Terror Sans Frontiers: Islamic Militancy in North East India*. Urbana, IL, University of Illinois at Urbana-Champaign.

Sambandan, V. S. (2004). "History from the LTTE." *Frontline* 21(3). Retrieved May 18, 2016 from www.frontline.in/static/html/fl2103/stories/20040213000206000.htm.

Sangmpam, S. N. (1992). "The Overpoliticized State and Democratization: A Theoretical Model." *Comparative Politics* 24(4): 401–417.

Sangmpam, S. N. (2007). *Comparing Apples and Mangoes: The Overpoliticized State in Developing Countries*. Albany, NY, State University of New York Press.

Saxton, G. D. (2005). "Repression, Grievances, Mobilization and Rebellion." *International Interactions* 31(1): 87–116.

Schofield, V. (1996). *Kashmir in the Crossfire*. London, Tauris.

Scott, J. C. (2009). *The Art of Not Being Governed: An Anarchist History of Upland Southeast Asia*. New Haven, Yale University Press.

Shain, Y. (2002). "The Role of Diasporas in Conflict Perpetuation and Resolution." *SAIS Review* 2(2): 115–144.

Sharma, M. L. (1999). "Organised Crime in India: Problems and Perspectives." *Resource Materials Series* 54(1): 82–129.

Shastri, A. (1990). "The Material Basis for Separatism: The Tamil Eelam Movement in Sri Lanka." *Journal of Asian Studies* 49(1): 56–77.

Shelley, M. R. (1986). "Nation Building and Political Development in Bangladesh." In: *Nation-Building in Bangladesh: Retrospect and Prospects*. M. A. Hafiz and A. R. Khan, eds. Dhaka, Bangladesh Institute of International and Strategic Studies.

Sherani, S. (2014) "Falling FDI Inflows." *The Dawn*. October 17.

Shukla, V. (2005). *India's Foreign Policy in the New Millennium*. New Delhi, Atlantic.

Siddiqi, F. H. (2012). "Security Dynamics in Pakistani Balochistan: Religious Activism and Ethnic Conflict in the War on Terror." *Asian Affairs: An American Review* 39(3): 157–175.

Sidhva, S. (1996). *Guns and Votes*. Frontline.

Singh, A. (1985). *Punjab in Indian Politics*. Delhi, Ajanta.

Singh, A. and A. Ranawana (1996). "Conflict of Interest Local Industrialists Issue a Broadside against Multinationals." *Asia Week*. Retrieved January 3, 2016, from http://edition.cnn.com/ASIANOW/asiaweek/96/0412/nat1.html.

Singh, G. (1987). "Understanding the 'Punjab Problem'." *Asian Survey* 27(12): 1268–1277.
Singh, G. (1996). "Punjab since 1984: Disorder, Order, and Legitimacy." *Asian Survey* 36(4): 410–421.
Singh, K. (1990). "Preface." In: *Blue Star over Amritsar*. H. Kaur, ed. Delhi, Ajanta.
Singh, N. (1998). "Cultural Conflict in India: Punjab and Kashmir." Global, Area, and International Archive. Retrieved January 26, 2012, from http://escholarship.org/uc/item/8v28z2gq.
Singh, P. (2007). "The Political Economy of the Cycles of Violence and Non-Violence in the Sikh Struggle for Identity and Political Power: Implications for Indian Federalism." *Third World Quarterly* 28(3): 555–570.
Sinha, S. P. (2007). *Lost Opportunities: 50 Years of Insurgency in the North-East and India's Response*. New Delhi, Lancer.
Skinner, Q. (1999). "Hobbes and the Purely Artificial Person of the State." *Journal of Political Philosophy* 7(1): 1–29.
Smith, D. E. (1979). "Religion, Politics, and the Myth of Reconquest." In: *Modern Sri Lanka: A Society in Transition*. T. Fernando and R. N. Kearney, eds. Syracuse, NY, Maxwell School of Citizenship and Public Affairs: 83–99.
Snyder, J. (1999). *When Voting Leads to Violence: Democratization and Nationalist Conflict*. New York, Norton.
Sökefeld, M. (2006). "Mobilizing in Transnational Space: A Social Movement Approach to the Formation of Diaspora." *Global Networks* 6(3): 265–284.
Sökefeld, M. and M. Bolognani (2011). "Kashmiris in Britain: A Political Project or a Social Reality." In: *Pakistan and its Diaspora: Multidisciplinary Approaches*. M. Bolognani and S. M. Lyon, eds. New York, Palgrave Macmillan: 111–131.
Sorens, J. (2005). "The Cross-Sectional Determinants of Secessionism in Advanced Democracies." *Comparative Political Studies* 38: 304–326.
Sorens, J. (2010). "The Politics and Economics of Official Ethnic Discrimination: A Global Statistical Analysis, 1950–2003." *International Studies Quarterly* 54: 535–560.
Sørensen, B. R. (2008). "The Politics of Citizenship and Difference in Sri Lankan Schools." *Anthropology & Education Quarterly* 39(4): 423–443.
South Asia Terrorism Portal (2016). "Fatalities in Terrorist Violence in Pakistan 2003–2016." Retrieved February 12, 2016, from www.satp.org/satporgtp/countries/pakistan/database/casualties.htm.
Spencer, J. (1990). *A Sinhala Village in a Time of Trouble: Politics and Change in Rural Sri Lanka*. Delhi, Oxford University Press.
Sriskandarajah, D. (2005). "Tamil Diaspora Politics." *Diaspora* 1: 3–7.
Steinberg, D. A. and S. M. Saideman (2008). "Laissez Fear: Assessing the Impact of Government Involvement in the Economy on Ethnic Violence." *International Studies Quarterly* 52: 235–259.
Stepanov, V. (2000). "Ethnic Tensions and Separatism in Russia." *Journal of Ethnic and Migration Studies* 26(2): 305–332.
Stephens, B. (2008). "The Most Difficult Job in the World: Pakistan's President on Terrorism, India and His Late Wife." *The Wall Street Journal*. October 4.
Stewart, F. (2005). "Horizontal Inequalities: A Neglected Dimension of Development." In: *Wider Perspectives on Global Development*. Unu-Wider, ed. London, Palgrave Macmillan.
Stokke, K. (2006). "Building the Tamil Eelam State: Emerging State Institutions and Forms of Governance in LTTE-Controlled Areas in Sri Lanka." *Third World Quarterly* 27(6): 1021–1040.

Sultan, M. (2013). "Terrorism and the Macroeconomy: Evidence from Pakistan." *Defence and Peace Economics* 25(5): 1–23.

Swami, P. (2007). *India, Pakistan and the Secret Jihad: The Covert War in Kashmir, 1947–2004*. New York, Routledge.

Swami, P. (2008). "The Well-Tempered Jihad: The Politics and Practice of Post-2002 Islamist Terrorism in India." *Contemporary South Asia* 16(3): 303–322.

Syal, R. (2009). "Drug Money Saved Banks in Global Crisis, Claims UN Advisor." *The Observer*. December 13.

Taras, R. and R. Ganguly, eds. (1988). *Understanding Ethnic Conflict: The International Dimension*. New York, Longman.

Telford, H. (1992). "The Political Economy of Punjab: Creating Space for Sikh Militancy." *Asian Survey* 32(11): 969–987.

Thaa, W. (2001). "Lean Citizenship: The Fading Away of the Political in Transnational Democracy." *European Journal of International Relations* 7(4): 503–525.

The Times of India (2014). "Ulfa Chief Calls Deputy from China." *The Times of India*. February 3.

The World Bank (2011). *Conflict, Security, and Development*. Washington, DC, The World Bank.

The World Bank (2011). *More and Better Jobs in South Asia*. Washington, DC, The World Bank.

The World Bank (2015). *World Development Indicators*. Washington, DC, The World Bank.

Thomas, Raju G. C. 1992. Reflections on the Kashmir Problem. In *Perspectives on Kashmir*, edited by R. G. C. Thomas. Boulder, Westview Press.

Toft, M. D. (2003). *The Geography of Ethnic Conflict*. Princeton, NJ, Princeton University Press.

Tolumin, S. (1990). *Cosmopolis: The Hidden Agenda of Modernization*. Chicago, Chicago University Press.

Treisman, D. (1997). "Russia's 'Ethnic Revival': The Separatist Activism of Regional Leaders in a Postcommunist Order." *World Politics* 49(2): 212–249.

Tremblay, R. C. (1996). "Nation, Identity and the Intervening Role of the State: A Study of the Secessionist Movement in Kashmir." *Pacific Affairs* 69(4): 471–497.

Trumbore, P. F. (2003). "Victims or Aggressors? Ethno-Political Rebellion and Use of Force in Militarized Interstate Disputes." *International Studies Quarterly* 47(2): 183–201.

United Nations Office on Drugs and Crime (2005). *World Drug Report 2005*. Vienna, United Nations.

United States State Department (1999). *Patterns of Global Terrorism: 1998*. Washington DC, United States State Department.

Vadlamannati, K. C. (2011). "Why Indian Men Rebel? Explaining Armed Rebellion in the Northeastern States of India, 1970–2007." *Journal of Peace Research* 48(5): 605–619.

Vaishnav, M. (2014) "It's Criminal, How Indians Vote." *The Times of India*. February 2.

Van Schendel, W. (1992). "The Invention of the 'Jummas': State Formation and Ethnicity in Southeastern Bangladesh." *Modern Asian Studies* 26(1): 95–128.

Vandekerckhove, N. (2009). "'We Are Sons of This Soil': The Endless Battle over Indigenous Homelands in Assam, India." *Critical Asian Studies* 41(4): 523–548.

Vandekerckhove, N. (2011). "The State, the Rebel and the Chief: Public Authority and Land Disputes in Assam, India." *Development and Change* 42(3): 759–779.

Varghese, J. (2014) "186 Indian Members of Parliament Have Criminal Cases Including Murder and Rape." *International Business Times*. 19 May.

Verma, P. S. (1994). *Jammu and Kashmir at the Political Crossroads*. New Delhi, Vikas.

Verma, P. S. (1995). "Zilla Parishad and Panchayat Samiti Elections in Punjab: Revival of Political Activity." *Economic and Political Weekly* 30(22): 1321–1328.

Vohra, S. (1986). "Demand for Khalistan." *Economic and Political Weekly* 21(40): 1738–1739.

Walter, B. F. (2006). "Information, Uncertainty, and the Decision to Secede." *International Organization* 60(1): 105–135.

Wayland, S. (2004). "Ethnonationalist Networks and Transnational Opportunities: The Sri Lankan Tamil Diaspora." *Review of International Studies* 30(3): 405–426.

Weaver, M. A. (2002). *Pakistan in the Shadow of Jihad and Afghanistan*. New York, Farrar, Straus and Giroux.

Weingast, B. R. (1995). "The Economic Role of Political Institutions: Market-Preserving Federalism and Economic Development." *Journal of Law, Economics, and Organization* 11(1): 1–31.

Weinstein, J. M. (2005). "Resources and the Information Problem in Rebel Recruitment." *Journal of Conflict Resolution* 49(4): 598–624.

Weinstein, J. M. (2007). *Inside Rebellion: The Politics of Insurgent Violence*. Cambridge, UK, Cambridge University Press.

Weiss, G. (2011). *The Cage: The Fight for Sri Lanka and the Last Days of the Tamil Tigers*. Sydney, Pan Macmillan Australia.

Welch, C., Ed. (1967). *Political Modernization: A Reader*. Belmont, CA, Wadsworth.

Wellman, C. H. (2005). *A Theory of Secession: The Case for Political Self-Determination*. New York, Cambridge University Press.

Widmalm, S. (2002). *Kashmir in Comparative Perspective: Democracy and Violent Separatism in India*. New York, RoutledgeCurzon.

Wimmer, A., L.-E. Cederman and B. Min (2009). "Ethnic Politics and Armed Conflict: A Configurational Analysis of a New Global Data Set." *American Sociological Review* 74(2): 316–337.

Wood, J. R. (1981). "Secession: A Comparative Analytical Framework." *Canadian Journal of Political Science* 14(1): 109–135.

Yadav, Y. (1993). "Political Change in North India: Interpreting Assembly Election Results." *Economic and Political Weekly* 28(51): 2767–2769, 2771–2774.

Yasmin, L. (2014). "The Tyranny of the Majority in Bangladesh: The Case of the Chittagong Hill Tracts." *Nationalism and Ethnic Politics* 20(1): 116–132.

Young, R. A. (1994). "How Do Peaceful Secessions Happen?" *Canadian Journal of Political Science* 27(4): 773–792.

Zaman, M. Q. (1984). "Tribal Issues and National Integration: The Chittagong Hill Tracts Case." In: *Tribal Cultures in Bangladesh*. M. S. Qureshi, ed. Rajshahi, Institute of Bangladesh Studies.

Zartman, I. W. (1993). "The Unfinished Agenda: Negotiating Internal Conflicts." In: *Stopping the Killing: How Civil Wars End*. R. Licklider, ed. New York, New York University Press: 20–36.

Zutshi, C. (2004). *Languages of Belonging: Islam, Regional Identity and the Making of Kashmir*. New York, Oxford University Press.

Index

Abdullah, Farooq 59
Abdullah, Sheikh Mohammed 41
Afghanistan 28, 31, 36, 96–7, 109
Africa 29–30, 114
Akali Dal 37–8, 43, 50, 57–9, 70, 84–6, 94–5
All India Sikh Students Federation (AISSF) 58, 84–6
Anandpur Sahib Resolution (ASR) 43, 50, 57–8
Article 370, 41, 72, 74, 76
Arunachal Pradesh 33, 76, 87, 100
Arya Samaj 36, 49, 58
Assam 22, 33–5, 40, 48–53, 60, 71–7, 81–2, 87, 97, 100–2

Balochistan: history of separatism 31–2, 39, 48, 66, 72, 89, 95–7; economy 44; foreign interference 79; Punjabi domination of 44–5, 48
Bandaranaike, Solomon 55–6
Bangladesh 1, 22, 74, 91, 118–21; Chittagong Hill Tract 2, 12, 32, 46, 53, 61, 81, 89, 105–6; constitution of 39, 41; creation of 1, 3, 48, 53, 61, 78, 89; and northeast India 48–9, 51, 53–4, 81, 102, 104–5
Bharatiya Janata Party (BJP) 36, 57, 94–5, 99, 103
Bhindrinwale, Jarnail Singh 20, 41, 58–9
Bhutan 22, 33, 53–4, 81, 102
Bluestar, operation 59, 71
Bodoland 77, 100–2
Bru 77, 100
Buddhism 32, 42, 45–6, 56, 75, 92, 106

Canada 4, 6, 8, 30, 54, 68, 80, 83
Chakma 76–7, 100, 105
China 33, 36, 60, 75, 79, 81–2, 90–2, 95, 113

Christianity 32, 104
Chittagong Hill Tract 12; history of conflict 32–3, 39, 46, 48, 61, 81, 105–6
Congress Party (India) 33, 50, 57–9, 70, 77–8, 86, 94–5, 98–9, 103
Council of Europe 25
counter-insurgency 71, 74, 79, 85, 97
crime: connection with separatism 66, 69, 81–2, 100, 121–2; cyber 115; legislation 73–4

Damdami Taksal 58, 84
Darjeeling 102–3
decolonization 2, 5, 9, 28, 109, 123
devolution of power 11–12, 75, 100–1
Dharma Yudh 58
diaspora 2, 11, 15, 19, 22, 54, 68, 78, 80–3

East India Company 32–3, 36
education 35, 45, 48, 51–2, 66, 68, 96, 101, 121
European Court of Justice 25
European Parliament 25
European Union 124

foreign intervention in separatist conflicts 11, 18, 53–5, 78–83, 103, 106

Gandhi, Indira 41, 57–9, 70–1, 75, 95, 98, 119
Gandhi, Rajiv 91
Garo 51, 76, 100
Green Revolution 41–3, 52
grievance versus greed 12–17, 20, 25–6, 47
Gwadar Port 45, 79, 91, 95, 118

Hinduism 32, 35–7, 40–3, 49, 57–9, 66–7, 70, 72, 75–6, 85–6, 92–4, 98–9, 101, 104

Hmar 51, 77, 100, 104

immigration *see* migration
India 1–2, 22, 30–5, 40, 53, 64, 73–5, 79–81, 89–91, 106–7, 109, 120–2; Balochistan 95–6; Bangladesh relations 78, 81, 105–6; economic deregulation of 118–19; Kashmir 6, 19–20, 35, 41, 52, 54, 66–7, 72–3, 79, 86, 97–9; Myanmar relations 82, 106; national ideology of 6, 40–3, 51, 60–1, 79, 80; northeast regions of 13–14, 20, 33, 40–1, 44, 46, 48–51, 53, 66, 69, 71, 75–7, 81–2, 87, 95, 99–102, 103–5; reorganization of states 4, 11–12, 41, 75–6, 102–3; Sikh separatism 35–8, 43, 51–2, 57–60, 70, 75, 84–6, 92–4; and Sri Lanka 45–6, 48, 53–5, 68, 78–9, 91–2
indigenous peoples 4, 34–5, 48, 105–6
Inter-Services Intelligence Directorate (ISI) 80, 96
Iran 18, 31, 53, 79, 95
irredentism 6; and Kashmir 108
Islam 6, 19, 35, 37, 40–1, 49, 60, 69, 72–4, 76, 79, 82, 85–6, 95–6, 98–9, 101–2, 121

Jainism 42, 75
Jammu 66, 99
Jammu and Kashmir National Conference 35, 41, 86, 98–9

Kaptai Dam 46, 118
Karim, Prince 32
Karbi Anglong 50–1, 87
Kashmir 6, 30, 40–1, 54, 86, 89, 102, 117, 119; accession 35; development of separatism 52–3, 59–60, 72–3; electoral politics 97–9; human rights abuses 19, 60, 66, 69, 97; Pakistan 79, 82–3
Karuna, A. 83–4, 92
Khalistan *see* Sikh separatism
Khan, Nasir 31–2
Kumaratunga, Chandrika Bandaranaike 90

language 4, 36, 38–9, 41, 45–6, 49, 55–6, 75, 78, 86, 102
Larma, Manabendra 61
Liberation Tigers of Tamil Eelam (LTTE) 11, 20, 54–6, 67–9, 75, 78, 80, 82–5, 88, 90–2

Maoism 22, 54, 81, 104
Manipur 13, 33–5, 40, 76–7, 81, 87, 99–100, 104

Meghalaya 33, 76–7, 81, 100
migration 43, 48–9, 66, 77, 110
Mizo Accord 76
Mizo National Front (MNF) 77, 87
Mizoram 33, 40, 46, 71, 76–7, 81, 87, 100
Mountbatten, Lord 33
Muslims *see* Islam
Muslim United Front (MUF) 59, 86, 98
Myanmar (Burma) 81–2, 87, 91, 103–6

Nagaland 33–4, 40, 50–3, 72, 76, 81, 87, 100–4
national identity: decolonization 1, 32; mutable character of 50–1; relation to separatism 2, 16–19, 25–7, 29, 34, 36, 39–42, 45, 48, 50–1, 56–8, 68–9, 74–5, 79–80, 90, 92, 95–6, 99, 102, 114, 117–19; source of unity 1, 61
nationalism *see* national identity
Naxalite 22, 93, 109, 121
Nepal 22, 32–3, 48, 54, 81, 102

Pakistan 1–2, 22, 36, 41, 74, 119–21, 1971 partition of 48, 53, 61, 78, 89; Balochistan 32, 39, 41, 44–5, 79, 91, 95–7, 109, 118; Chittagong Hill Tract 32–3, 52, 61; foreign policy of 19, 53–5, 79–82, 91; Kashmir 41, 54–5, 60, 72, 79–80, 85–6, 97–9, 108; Sikh separatism 37, 41, 60, 93
Parbatya Chattagram Jana Samhati Samiti (PCJSS) 61, 105–6
Patel, S. 33
partition of India 32, 34, 37, 48–9, 58, 74, 78
Prabhakaran, Velupillai 20, 83

Rahman, Sheikh Mujibur 61, 81
Rajapaksa, Mahindra 90–1, 121
rational agent theory 8–10, 13–16; and self interest 19, 25, 70
Russia 14, 31, 53, 79

Saideman, S. 10–12, 14, 16, 117
secularism 6, 19, 25, 37, 40–2, 50, 60, 70, 74–5, 79, 85, 92, 96, 98, 102
separatism: antecedents of 38–9, 47; definition of 4–5; difficulties of explaining 1–3, 7–18, 20–3; history of 6; multiple causes of 18–23; violence 19–20
Sikh separatism: electoral politics 49–50, 57–8, 70, 86–7, 94–5; history of 35–8, 41–2, 49, 89, 119; human rights abuses

59, 66, 69–71; internal discord 84–7, 92–3; language 49–50; Nirankaris 57–8
Sikkim 33, 102
Singapore 5, 8, 10
social contract theory 25–9, 112; and legal-rational legitimacy 3, 25–7, 29, 34, 60, 64, 68, 73–5, 77, 87, 119
social product 25, 28, 111, 117–18
sovereignty: and British colonialism 2, 30–1, 116–17; justification of 26–8, 111–18; non-binary nature of 25, 28–9, 30–1, 108–24; and states 25–6; twin elements of 24–8, 39, 47, 51, 60–1, 63, 68, 77, 88, 111–16; Western origins of 25, 29–30, 111–12
Sri Lanka 7; history of conflict 38, 40, 45–8, 53, 55–6, 83–4, 89; human rights abuses 66–9; Indian intervention 54, 74–5, 78–9, 91
state of nature 65–73, 113
Swabasha 45, 55
Switzerland 115

Taliban 28, 96–7, 109
Tamil United Liberation Front (TULF) 46, 56
territory 10–11, 110–11
Tripura 33, 40, 46, 53, 76–7, 81, 87, 99–100, 104–5
Two Nation theory 33, 79

United Liberation Front of Assam (ULFA) 34, 49, 53–4, 66, 71, 81–2, 101–2
United Nations 6, 27–8, 115, 122
United States 53–4, 78–80